FOLKTALE
MAORI

FOLKTALES OF THE MAORI

Alfred Grace

Folktales of the Maori

First published in 1907 by Gordon & Gotch
Proprietary Ltd, Wellington, New Zealand

This edition published in 1998 by Senate,
an imprint of Senate Press Limited,
133 High Street, Teddington,
Middlesex TW11 8HH, United Kingdom

3 5 7 9 10 8 6 4 2

ISBN 1 85958 533 7

Printed and bound in Guernsey by
The Guernsey Press Co Ltd

TO

ANDREW LANG, M.A., LL.D.,

FOLKLORIST AND MYTHOLOGIST,

Who has done more than any other living writer to foster in the British race a love of such tales as are here collected,

This Book is Dedicated;

And it is placed in his hands with the hope that he will accept it as a genuine, if humble, contribution to the vast store of mythological lore which he has so lovingly accumulated, and of which no one appreciates so well as he the importance to posterity.

A.A.G.

NELSON, N.Z.,

November, 1907.

ON THE PRONUNCIATION OF MAORI WORDS.

IN pronouncing Maori words, single vowels are given their full value. Thus, the name *Hone* possesses two syllables; *Onetea*, four syllables—O-ne-te-a; *herehere*, four—he-re-he-re. There is no such thing as a true dipthong. Where two vowels come together, each is distinctly heard, though more or less coalescing. Thus, in the word *Maori* it is not correct to convert the 'ao' into 'ou,' as in the English word *house*, the 'a' possessing a broad sound, the 'o' being distinctly heard.

'A' may generally be said to be pronounced as in the English exclamation 'ah!' though there are important exceptions: 'e' is pronounced somewhat after the fashion of the final 'e' in the French word *félicité;* 'i' sometimes as our 'ee' in *proceed*, at others as in the English word *pin;* 'o' as in the English verb *owe;* 'u' as 'oo' in *cuckoo.*

As for accent, in dissyllables the emphasis is usually divided, in trisyllables the antepenultimate is usually accented; in words of four syllables, the first and third are usually emphasized; but in regard to such dreadful polysyllabic words, as *kurumatarerehu* or *whakapungenengene*, no grammarian can help the unfortunate Pakeha.

PREFACE.

IT has been a pleasant task to preserve from forgetfulness tales which, while they illumine for us the mental workings of a primitive people, at the same time prove indubitably that the sturdy Maori, who tattooed his body with grotesque patterns, was possessed of a soul, sensitive beyond belief to romantic and sentimental impressions, and that in his musings his barbaric mind frequently leaped to a mental altitude as high as that attained by the great mythologists of the ancients. Indeed, what will perhaps be regarded as the most remarkable feature of these tales is the similarity which some of them bear to certain Greek myths. In "The Moon Girl" there is a distinct likeness to the story of Orpheus and Eurydice; "The Courting of Kirika" will probably recall the tale of Hercules and Deianeira; "The Tame Taniwha" will suggest the stories of Arion, of Neptune and Amphitrite, and the great Apollo myth. Other resemblances to Aryan mythology will be found in them, but nevertheless they all are tales whose authors had never so much as heard of Homer, Hesiod, or Herodotus, and to whom Greek mythology was a sealed book.

All but four of the tales treat of the Maori in his aboriginal state, and have been handed down by word of mouth from generation to generation; three belong to the period when contact with the white man was beginning; and one is included for the purpose of showing that even at the time of writing, when an imperfectly assimilated civilization has done so much to ruin a fine race, there exist members of it whose minds are still as primitive and simple as were those of their ancestors.

Karepa Te Whetu, who gave me most valuable assistance in the work of compilation, was a member of the Ngati-Koata tribe, a man of acute and artistic mind, a lover of tales for their own sake, and a humourist of no mean order. When I told him of my wish to make a collection of the folk-tales of his race, he entered into my project with enthusiasm. Persistently he sounded the depths of his memory, untiringly he collected during his peregrinations, extending over seven years, the best and most representative tales told by his people in their wharepuni, or sleeping-houses, at night. Many of these I had heard before, not a few I found unsuitable to my purpose, and others I had read in the pages of such writers as Grey and White, but those, which besides being new to me were most characteristic of the race, or appeared to be most perfect in form or whimsical in detail, I have re-told in my own way, but without embellishment; my object being to preserve in the telling as much as possible of the atmosphere and colour of the originals. The entire collection first appeared under the title of "Tales of a Stone-Age People" in the pages of *The Weekly Press*, Christchurch, N.Z., to whose editor I owe a debt of gratitude for the interest he took in the work.

Four tales there are—"The Maero," "The Ngarara," "Big Piha and Little Piha," and "The Poriro"—which, included in my "Tales of a Dying Race," may be read in conjunction with this book, for they gave me the notion of collecting in one volume the folk-tales which Te Whetu might tell me.

Though a man of no very great mana, he nevertheless was the chief rangatira of his hapu and the eldest son of one of the notorious Te Rauparaha's lieutenants. Imbued with his father's warlike instinct, he fought on the Queen's side in the Taranaki war, throughout which he served as colour-sergeant in Major Brown's Native Regiment, and for his services obtained the New Zealand medal. When past seventy years of age he went to live at Croiselles, in Tasman Bay, and it was during his frequent visits to Nelson that I learnt to know and respect him. In May, 1905, he died, and it is my hope that this book, in the writing of which he took so great an interest, will perpetuate his memory and at the same time preserve something of the sentiment and humour of the race to which he belonged.

A.A.G.

Nelson, November, 1907.

CONTENTS.

PUTA AND HER DOG KUIKUI.

KUIKUI had been caught when a wild puppy in the mountains, and had been given to Puta by her playfellow, Haumia.

Nurtured in her arms, Kuikui had become the pet and constant companion of his mistress. As he grew out of puppyhood, Puta grew out of girlhood and became a pretty wahine: and the intimacy between Puta and Haumia, which had commenced with the present of a pup, ended in an exchange of hearts. The courting had been the most natural thing in the world. Under the trees of the forest, in the cool shades of fern-clad gullies, in the plantation where the women grew taro and kumara the two made love.

And then came the Ngati-Toa tribe.

They came suddenly out of the forest, with which the pa of Hawera was surrounded, and overwhelmed the place before a defence could be made. The fierce warriors rushed into the huts and slew all who had not effected an escape through the back of the pa into the "bush."

In the midst of the panic, Haumia begged Puta to flee with him, but she tarried to look for her dog, and so fell into the hands of a brutal warrior who dragged her to the ground by the hair of her head. But her beauty stayed the captor's uplifted arm, and instead of his victim she became his bride.

That night the Ngati-Toa men held a fearful orgie, of which Puta was an unwilling spectator, and next day she was dragged off through the forest towards Kawhia, whence the marauders had come. Before starting she asked one favour of her captor. He went with her into the open ground outside the pa, and there she called her dog. Kuikui,* who was hiding in the fringe of the "bush," heard his mistress's voice and came out, wagging his tail. So Puta and her dog were united in captivity.

The journey from Hawera to Kawhia was made by the roughest track in Maoriland, and long before she reached her destination Puta was worn out and footsore with carrying over uneven paths the burden of spoil and food, which her ferocious husband had laid upon her. But Kuikui trotted beside her, and in his canine way bestowed on her an affection for which she looked in vain to her new lord, Hakuai.

At Kawhia her lot was hard. She was merely a slave-wife, though at first she had a hut to herself. But Hakuai, whose fame had become great through his war-like deeds at Hawera, took as his chief wife, Tipari, a woman of his own tribe ; and Puta, instead of being the slave of one, became the slave of two.

* * * *

Tipari's baby lay sleeping in the hut, and Kuikui, imbued with a feeling of comradeship for the brown morsel of humanity, stood watching it Puta, who was in charge of the infant, had fallen asleep too, weary with its wailing. But the quiet of the hut soon palled on Kuikui, and he sought for some diversion. At first, he stretched himself on the mud floor with a grunt of dissatisfaction ; then he got up and indulged in an exciting chase after his tail ; next he made his toilet with his tongue ; then he thought of the baby. First, he walked gently towards it, and suddenly scuttled back to his mistress's side, as though afraid ; next he bounded boldly forward, and stood, growling with mimic rage, over the small brown particle of humanity ; then he rushed round the hut as if the taipo, or the devil himself, were after him. For a few moments he stood in the middle of the floor, with his

---

* Pronounced "Cooee-cooee,"

head on one side, expecting that his little playmate would stir. Then he began to bark.

The infant moved an arm, and gave a little cry. Kuikui was standing over him, and growling in simulated anger. The child opened his eyes, and screamed with dread at the white teeth and fierce barking. In a moment, Puta was awake, but Tipari, whose motherly ear had heard her brat's first faint squeal, was before her. With a cry the enraged woman rushed at Kuikui, seized him by he scruff of his neck, and belaboured him with the first thing that came to her hand—a tomahawk. In a few brief moments Kuikui would have breathed his last, but Puta sprang to his rescue, dragged Tipari to the ground, and held her by the throat.

By this time, the noise of Kuikui's howling, of the baby's screams, and of the general scuffle, had attracted an audience whose heads filled the door of the hut.

"The slave-wife is killing Tipari!"

"Pull her off!—she is choking the wahine-nui*!"

"Hakuai! Hakuai! your wives are quarrelling. Tipari is being killed!"

Hakuai, the brave warrior, the slayer of little children, was not slow to act. He dragged Puta from the hut, and in the open air, where his arm could have free play, he beat her till she swooned. Then, when the girl was passed all power of resistance, Tipari came out of the hut, and finished the punishment with a deliberation which left nothing undone.

That Kuikui escaped with his life was owing to his fleetness of foot. For the second time in his life he had "taken to the bush."

* * * *

Puta lay out in the dew and the dark. The people had gone to bed, and had as much care for the slave-girl as if she were a bit of firewood. With returning consciousness came back her pain, but no recollection of where she was. As she lay groaning on the ground,

---

* Literally "the great woman," the chief wife.

she was aware of something licking her face. There was a whimper and the smell of a dog's hot breath. Kuikui had come from his hiding-place to take care of his mistress. He licked her face, her hands, her neck, and exhibited all the signs of canine affection. For an hour or more she lay, gently patting her dog, smoothing his coat with a weak hand, and trying to collect her scattered senses.

Bit by bit the truth of her condition dawned on her, and then her determination was quickly made. Staggering to her feet she walked with stumbling steps to the whata, or store-house, where the choicest food of the tribe was kept: larded pigeons, "kakas," and "tuis," preserved in their own fat. With these and dried fish she filled the biggest basket she could find.

But she was naked—her mat had dropped from her shoulders in the scuffle with Tipari. Quietly she walked across the marae, or open ground in the centre of the pa, to the hut where Hakuai and Tipari lay sleeping. On tiptoe, her bare feet making no sound, she stole into the hut and picked up her korowai cloak and a rough pureke cape. But for all her stealthiness the picaninny woke and began to cry. Puta crouched in the farthest corner of the hut.

"Keep the child quiet," growled Hakuai.

"I can't—he screams with fear of your slave-wife," answered Tipari.

"Puta is dead. She will give no more trouble."

"Don't talk—the child has gone to sleep again."

For half-an-hour Puta lived in dread that Kuikui would follow her into the hut, and by his very faithfulness discover her. But the dog was too clever: she heard him snuffiing outside, and twice he whimpered his anxiety.

When Tipari breathed heavily and Hakuai snored, the girl crept out of the hut.

Every Maori fears the dark, for it is at night that the taipo and his kindred spirits roam the earth. But

* Literally "the great woman," the chief wife.

Puta's fear of the taipo was as nothing to her dread of her husband, and she plunged into the black forest, with Kuikui at her heels.

* * * *

"Where is Putahanga? She lay on this spot last evening."

"She is dead. Tipari finished her off after Hakuai had done with her. She tried to kill Tipari's baby."

"'Serve her right, miserable low-bred girl of Taranaki. But who buried her?"

"Here! Hakuai. Who buried your slave-wife?"

"No one. She isn't buried."

"Then, where is the body?"

"I don't know. I expect we shall find it in the shed over there, or in the scrub. She must have crawled away and died."

"We have searched every hut and the bushes about the pa, but can find her nowhere."

"Moreover, the dog has gone too."

"They have run away."

"I tell you, she is dead," said Hakuai. "Tipari hit her over the head with a board. Twice, before I fell asleep, I went to see her, and she was cold and almost stiff."

Some suspected that the taipo had claimed her corpse, others suggested that the dog had dragged the dead body into the "bush," but no one blamed Hakuai for Puta's death. Such a killing was no murder, for a man might do what he pleased with his slave-wife.

* * * *

"Kuikui, I can go no further. We have lost our way. I am dead-tired. Good dog, go on alone—leave me to die. Look at my arms, once so plump and strong, now so thin and weak. I have no strength. I will die here. Without me you would have reached home long ago. If you stay we shall both die."

Kuikui barked, and pulled at his mistress's cloak; but Puta, unable to move another step, laid herself down at the foot of a mighty totara tree.

Kuikui perceived the seriousness of the situation—he had not tasted food for two days. He went into the "bush," and his mistress fell asleep through sheer exhaustion. But when she was awakened by Kuikui's barking, she saw that the dog had laid a dead wood-hen at her feet. He had but followed his instinct, and wood-hens are stupid ground-birds, plentiful in the Maoriland "bush."

A Maori track is tortuous, rough, frequently overgrown, intersected by other tracks, and confusing to the traveller. Puta had journeyed for weeks and, carefully avoiding the few villages she had passed, she was now lost in the vast uninhabited forest which lies south of the Mokau river and west of Lake Taupo.

Kuikui supplied her with wood-hens, and she ate besides the berries of the fuchsia, of the tawa, and of other trees of the "bush." By night she would shelter herself in some hollow rata tree, or if this were lacking and there were near a bush of flax, she would tie together the tops of the six-foot leaves which grow straight out of the earth, and crawling inside her verdant bower she would find protection from the wet and cold. But, nevertheless, she was lost. She simply followed Kuikui, in the hope that he would guide her homewards. She had lost count of time; she had ceased to reckon distance. The track had so many twists and turns, the foliage was so thick overhead, that Puta was quite unable to say whether she was travelling north, south, east, or west. She blindly followed the dog, who supported her in her loneliness, procured her food, and guided her steps. When they came to a dividing of the way, he would unhesitatingly choose his path, and stedfastly refuse to be lured from his course. The girl had been courageous, for weeks she had hoped to reach some spot which she could recognise as belonging to her native plains. What her eyes most longed for, was the sight of the tall summit of Taranaki, the great conical mountain which is visible for a hundred miles around. But with seldom a glimpse of the sun between the dense foliage of the tree-tops, Puta had given up all hope of seeing the mountain peak she knew so well.

* * * *

Hungry and worn, the lost girl had risen from a damp bed of leaves to face another weary day. Kuikui went on before, now pausing to examine some tangled thicket, now coursing along the track at full speed, now trotting companionably by his mistress's side. When she rested by the way, the dog hunted; when Puta rose, Kuikui, her guide and protector, would trot ahead joyfully. Never did a dog enjoy responsibility more thoroughly, or acquit himself more sagaciously.

The girl's steps dragged wearily over the ground, as she stumbled through supple-jack thickets or over thick carpets of ferns. Now she splashed through a rippling stream, now she clambered up some rough acclivity where the "bush lawyer" hung thorny tendrils to catch her at every step.

Thicket, underscrub, and thorns; the forest giant and the lean sapling; black-trunked tree-ferns and the spreading palm; damp, dripping banks covered with tender fronds, the noisy stream, the dark and dewy night: was there to be no end to these things?

The girl had the fortune to snare a kaka parrot in a trap which she had set for its cousin the kakapo, the ground-parrot which comes out at night. Avoiding the bird's sharp and cruel beak, Puta tied the screaming captive by its legs to the bough of a tree and, armed with a heavy stick, she stood by to await results. The screeching parrot attracted hundreds of its fellows inhabiting the tree-tops. Down they came in flocks, to know what ailed their comrade; like a cloud they filled the air, and as they thronged inquisitively about the maimed bird Puta beat them to the ground by scores.

And now the wanderer might rest. Close at hand there was a hollow rata tree—a mass of red flowers over-head, a dry and comfortable house below—and in it the girl made her home. Fire she made by a laborious process of friction—with the kaureure, or lower board, and the kauati, or rubbing-stick—and for food, she and Kuikui ate "kakas" till they could eat no more. Not far from her sylvan abode she found a rippling, crystal stream, containing shoals of eels. First she broke down a long birch sapling and tied a line of knotted flax to its tapering end. Next she called the dog, and with voice and gesture encouraged him to catch a wood-hen for her. With a piece of the oily bird she baited her line and, in the evening, with a fire-stick in one hand and her fishing-rod in the other, she went down to the water's edge. Here she made a bright fire and, sitting on the bank, she cast her line into the flame-lit river. Before long her bait was swallowed at a gulp, and the end of the rod dipped into the water; but in a moment the girl had whipped the tackle over her head, and a six-pound eel lay on the bank behind her.

In this manner she was able to procure an almost inexhaustible supply of food; and what with that and shelter and warmth, Puta determined to live where she was in the forest till some party of travellers, chancing to come by, should tell her whither she should go in search of her own people. At night, she and Kuikui would creep into the hollow tree, where was piled a thick bed of dry leaves, and with a bright fire burning in the doorway they were as comfortable as in any pa. For the Maoriland "bush" is a harmless place: it harbours no beast but the deer, the wild pig, and the goat, which in Puta's days had not yet been brought to the islands: it shelters no snake or venomous reptile, no creature inimical to human life. But the Maori girl dreaded the loneliness of the great forest; her mind was troubled by the supernatural terrors which each night brought without fail. She pined for her home, for the much-loved faces, for the well-known scenes which surrounded the conical mountain; she longed to know which of her loved ones had escaped death on the awful morning when the ruthless Ngati-Toa broke into their pa; her heart yearned for her mother and father, and not least for Haumia, her lost lover.

Thinking sweet thoughts of those she loved, she fell asleep in the hollow tree. Sleeping, she dreamed. She was in the pa; her brother and Haumia were beside her; the women were cooking at the fires; the children were playing among the huts; above the tree-tops of the surrounding forest stood the tall peak of Taranaki, snow-clad, symmetrical, immovable, eternal. In her dream she gazed at the great white cone, and gazing, said, "I have looked for the top of Taranaki for days, for seasons, I know not how long. At every turn of the track I looked for it, from every bit of rising ground, and yet I could never see it: and there it is!" and speaking, she wept; and weeping, she woke to find herself crouching with Kuikui in the hollow tree, and the embers of the fire all but dead.

Next day she sat listlessly in front of her door, with no spirit left in her. She had tasted fellowship, comradeship and love in a dream, and had awakened to the desolation of the "bush."

But regardless of his mistress's sorrow, Kuikui had gone a-hunting; he had disappeared along the unexplored track.

Until then, Puta had not gone more than a hundred yards from her camp in the direction pursued by the dog; she dreaded almost the time when she should have to arise and, with hope ever disappointed, explore turning after turning of the endless track. But when Kuikui returned, he was excited and covered with dirt: he barked at his mistress; he barked at the fire; he barked at the smoke-dried eels which hung over the fire. Barking, he ran along the track, and came back to seize the cloak on which Puta lay, and drag it away with him. At length, the girl, divining the meaning of the dog, followed him. Kuikui dropped the cloak, and bounded on before. Round a bend of the track, across a rippling rivulet, under a great totara tree which had fallen across the gully down which the path ran, over a slight rise, and the girl was in a forest "clearing!"

Now she saw why Kuikui was covered with dirt. In the ground were numbers of self-sown kumara plants, which were growing wild. Puta went to the hole, which Kuikui had dug, and quickly saw why the "clearing" had been abandoned and why the dog had scratched in the earth. A human thigh-bone was protruding from the ground and a skull lay at the bottom of the hole!

"The place is tapu. Away! away!" cried the terror-stricken girl as she ran further along the track in fear and dread. But what a sight appeared before her and brought her to a standstill!

There, as though a few miles distant, stood the mountain she knew so well, the white peak of Taranaki, lifted high above the level country, standing above the flat top of the forest which stretched below her, and over which it seemed she might walk till she reached the mountain's foot.

She was in her own country, at home at last. On she ran, on she pressed, down into the low-lying lands, towards the smoke of a fire which floated above tops of the trees.

"Run! Kuikui. Good dog, run! You have brought me within sight of Taranaki, you have guided me back to my own country! Now I shall find my home, now I shall meet my tribe. Good Kuikui, clever dog, brave companion of my wanderings."

* * * *

"Make the ditch deep, make the wall high, men of Hawera, men of Taranaki; for Ngati-Toa and the men Waikato come to burn and slay."

Old Tokopa the priest was haranguing the people as they lashed the palisades, and fortified their pa. Men and women, boys and girls, were working with tremendous energy; for they were determined that their fortress should not be demolished a second time.

"Now is the time when the crops are ripe," continued the old priest; "the kumara and the taro are ready for digging. Now is the time when thieving tribes make war. Therefore make deep the ditch, make thick the wall, and store your food within your stronghold. Ngati-Toa came, and where now are Toro and Tiki, where Reta and Hene, where the girl Puta who took away her dog? They are in Kawhia: they are in Te Regina—in Hell. But the day will come when they shall be avenged."

The old tohunga had worked himself into such a state of eloquence that the people forgot their work in listening.

A strong young fellow, his muscles swelling under the strain, was heaving up a great post for the strengthening of the palisade which was being built on the top of the earthen wall. He had lifted the post as high as his shoulder, when he suddenly dropped it, and, pointing towards the "bush," he cried out, "The dog Kuikui! the dog Kuikui!" In a moment he had jumped from the earth-work, and was patting the coat of the dog he had caught as a pup.

"But where is his mistress?"

"It is the dog—I remember his markings. But where is the girl?"

"Ah! where is Putahanga?"

"It is Kuikui, I am sure. Good dog, good dog."

Presently, out of the "bush" there came a woman. Her hair hung knotted and tangled over her shoulders and breast, her arms were outstretched, her eyes were wild, and she called and called as she ran forward, "Haumia! Haumia! my people! my tribe! my loved ones! I have found you, I have found you—all that I hold so dear!"

A strong arm was placed round her, loving eyes peered into hers, but when the tumult of the greeting was over and the tears of joy were dried, and the people seemed to overlook the companion of her wanderings, Puta called Kuikui to her, and with his head between her hands, she told them the story I have been telling you.

TITO AND PIRITA.

"PIRITA, the way to accomplish our end is simple. Return with me to my pa, and I will recognise you as my wife before all my tribe."

"Tito, that would be the happiest thing in the world, but think how angry my father would be. He would make war on you and your people immediately he found out what had happened."

"What would that matter?—we should fight him."

"But I don't want men to be killed on my account. No, Tito, we must wait till our tribes are friendly: then perhaps, my father will consent."

The young brave drew the girl towards him, gave her a long, last embrace, accompanied her to the edge of the scrub wherein the lovers' meeting had taken place, and watched her to the gate of her pa, which stood but half-a-mile off. When she had disappeared inside the hostile fortress, he heaved a deep sigh, and threaded his way through the thick manuka bushes towards his home.

Ngati-Pou, his tribe, were an evil people. Being notorious thieves, they were rightfully regarded with suspicion by the neighbouring Ngati-Tipa tribe, to which Pirita belonged, but which feared them because of the number of their relations, Ngati-Tahinga, Tainui, and Ngati-Koata, who lived not far off.

The season had been very bad, and Ngati-Pou had planted too little, and too late in the year. But they purposed to fall back on fish, for the prowess of their ancestors had preserved for them valuable fishing rights and the sole use of a sandy beach, situated but three miles from their pa and convenient as a landing-place.

But Ngati-Pou were a lazy tribe. One day, having caught little, they neglected to pull their canoes high and dry upon the sand, before they returned for the night to their pa.

About midnight, a terrific gale struck the coast, and when in the morning Ngati-Pou went to the landing-place, they found their canoes smashed to pieces, and the wreckage strewn along the shore.

Now, a canoe was not built in a day. First, the mighty monarch of the forest had to be laid low, and that merely with the aid of fire and of stone axes. Next, the great trunk had to be rough-hewn, when it would be left to dry till such time as it could be hollowed out by burning, after which the stone axes slowly completed their work. Often the undertaking was delayed by bad omens, and the tohunga would spend much time in incantations and in waiting for propitious signs of the time when each part of the work should be effected. So Ngati-Pou knew that it would be a matter of years before their fleet could be rebuilt; and in the meanwhile winter and starvation stared them in the face.

But their neighbours of the powerful Ngati-Tipa tribe had laid in large quantities of dried fish, and the store-houses in their great plantation were full of food. The men of Ngati-Pou, being of a thievish disposition, wasted no time in making up their minds as to how they should act.

Topographically, the position favoured them. The coast ran north and south. In the south lay Ngati-Koata; north of them lay the Tainui, beside a stream which ran swiftly down to the sea; on the north bank of the stream lay the pa of Ngati-Tahinga; and north of these famous fighting-men lay the thievish Ngati-Pou. But theirs was a strategical position: between it and the nearest Ngati-Tipa pa lay a flat piece of country, covered with manuka scrub through which inroads could be made with equal effect upon the landing-place or upon the plantations of Ngati-Tipa.

Dividing their forces into two bands, Ngati-Pou suddenly swept down on each of these unguarded points, and returned to their pa over-burdened with dried fish and succulent kumara and taro, sufficient to last them till the spring.

The Ngati-Tipa people lay in five strong fortresses, and without giving Ngati-Pou time to seek their allies' assistance, swept down on them, slew ninety per cent. of their warriors, and recovered the stolen food. But among the few who escaped the wholesale slaughter, was young Tito, who owed more to his fleetness of foot than to the strength of his arm.

Perhaps the pakeha mind might judge that there the matter should have ended, but that was not the opinion of the chiefs of Ngati-Koata, Tainui, and Ngati-Tahinga, relatives of the massacred tribe. They determined to make reprisals. It was of no consequence to them that their dead relations had been thieves: it was a pleasure, as well as a duty, to avenge Ngati-Pou.

Kawharu, the chief of Ngati-Koata, was the man for the occasion.

"Ngati-Tipa is a great tribe," he said, "Their five pa are so strong and well-guarded, that we cannot hope to take them by assault. But I have devised a plan which promises success. I want one-hundred-and-fifty men, so brave that they fear nothing, and so strong that not even an onrushing flood of Ngati-Tipa warriors can overwhelm them."

Immediately three-hundred volunteers sprang forward, and amongst them Tito, anxious to do something to prove his bravery, to avenge his relatives, and perhaps to win the wahine of his choice.

"That is good," said Kawharu. "That is as it ought to be; but half the number will be enough. We will now go down to the river of the Tainui, where we will make a whakapuni, and put your bravery to the test."

Now, a whakapuni is a dam, and all his hearers wondered what Kawharu could mean by saying that he would test the men's bravery by means of a dam.

However, all those present, except the three-hundred volunteers, set to work with stones and baskets of earth to make the whakapuni across the stream.

"How are you to test the bravery of men with a whakapuni?" people asked Kawharu.

"Never you mind," replied he. "The quicker you get the whakapuni finished the sooner you will see." So everybody being inquisitive to know what the chief would do, the dam was soon constructed.

When sufficient water had collected to form a lake above the whakapuni, Kawharu ordered the volunteers into the dry river-bed below.

"You say you are all brave men," said he. "You say you fear nothing. Very good: we shall see. You say you can withstand the charge of any number of Ngati-Tipa warriors. We shall see whether you speak truth. It is big mana, great honour, that I offer you, and the names of those who stand this trial will never be forgotten. It will be a thing to boast of. Are you all ready?"

He was answered by a mighty shout from the men in the river-bed.

"Good," said Kawharu. "Link arms along your lines, place your feet firmly on the ground, draw a deep breath, bend your heads, and stand firm."

The people of the three allied tribes lined either bank, and gazed with astonishment.

Kawharu ordered fifty men of the crowd to go to the middle of the dam. "When I have counted ten," he said, "destroy the centre part of the wall, so that the water may rush through. Then run to the banks as fast as you can: the water will do the rest."

All was ready.

"One! two! three! four! five! six! seven! eight! You men in the river-bed, are you ready?—the water is coming. Nine! ten!"

The men on the dam worked furiously, and soon the water broke over the lip of the gap they made in the wall.

"Run!" cried Kawharu, and the men on the dam ran swiftly to either bank.

At first the water came down like a small waterfall, but gradually the breach grew deep and wide, and the volume of onrushing water increased.

The volunteers stood in a solid mass, line behind line, their arms linked, their heads bowed, their left feet forward, their deep voices joining in a stirring war-song.

The muddy water was rushing between their feet; now it was up to their ankles; now it was past their knees; now the great weight of imprisoned water completely burst its barrier. Down came mud and stones and bags of earth in a vast discoloured flood. The men in the river-bed ceased their song, and disappeared beneath the overwhelming torrent. For a space the spectators held their breath; thinking that the dauntless warriors had been swept away amid the debris of the dam, which lay strewn for quarter-of-a-mile down stream.

But now the water was clearer, and in the river-bed could be dimly seen beneath the rushing flood the solid mass of men.

Soon the pent-up water had escaped and spent all its strength, and the stream assumed its usual shallow depth. In the midst of it, with the water up to their waists, stood what were left of the volunteers; their lines broken here and there, their mass rent through in places, but their formation more or less intact.

A shout rose from the onlookers, and a responding cry broke from the volunteers who came ashore in detached groups, panting, but beaming with pride and joy. Of their three-hundred one third had disappeared, but those who had stood the test were fit for the great purpose which Kawharu had in view.

"Never mind the missing men," said he: "some of them will find their way ashore. I have enough left."

Among the warriors tried by water stood Tito, the sole survivor of his hapu.

* * * *

They moved out of the pa in two companies of unequal size. With the larger body was a conspicuous and curious standard, consisting of long streamers of flax covered with the blue feathers of the swamp-bird. With this remarkable ensign some five-hundred warriors marched towards the level country which lay between the ruined village of Ngati-Pou and the Ngati-Tipa strongholds. The intervening country was covered with manuka scrub, tall enough to hide the advancing men, but short enough to allow the tall standard to be seen for miles around.

After the taua* with the flag followed the two-hundred men who had stood the trial by water at the whakapuni, and at their head Tito, who was well suited to act as guide through the scrub which he knew so well, and where he had kept many a tryst with Pirita.

Taking care to keep the standard always in sight, he bore away to the right, while the big taua bore to the left, till the two bodies were fully half-a-mile apart, when they marched towards the chief Ngati-Tipa pa—where Pirita lived—in two parallel columns.

Now, the men of Ngati-Tipa expected that reprisals would be made upon them for the massacre of the Ngati-Pou people, therefore they had mustered a great force at their strongest pa.

When Tapa', their chief, Pirita's father, from the rampart first caught sight of the blue standard, conspicuous above the scrub, he said, "Our foes are brave: they intend to make no surprise. They say, , We are here. Come, and fight us.'"

As has been said already, the scrub stretched to within half-a-mile of the pa. "We will let them come into the open," said Tapa', "and there we will fight them."

So the Ngati-Tipa men poured out of their stronghold, formed themselves in battle-array, and threw out scouts.

But there was an air of mystery about the blue flag: it seemed to wobble as it advanced. First it

* War-party.

pointed one way, then it pointed another. But when the first men of the enemy appeared in the open, Tapa' thought his foes were about to disclose their strength. Instead, however, a disorderly mass of men stretched along the fringe of the scrub, and the flag was halted some two-hundred yards in the rear.

Tapa' was puzzled. His scouts could not approach the main body with the flag except by first passing through the enemy's skirmishers, and his main body did not dare to enter the scrub till the number of the enemy was known. So the Ngati-Tipa men were irresolute. First they advanced boldly, then they retired. Next their scouts fell back and joined the main body, and the whole advanced to a position on some high ground in front of the flag.

Now Tito, the leader of the little taua, was in complete ignorance of what was happening in his front. His duty was to keep his eye on the blue flag and be guided by its motions. When Ngati-Tipa advanced, it pointed this way; when they retreated towards their pa, it pointed that. Knowing by its motions where the enemy was, Tito advanced till he was directly opposite the pa. Cautiously he reconnoitred the country in front of him. All was clear. On the walls of the pa were a few armed men and numbers of women and children, eager to watch the approaching fight between the two big "tauas."

From where he stood Tito could not see the Ngati-Tipa force, but the flag was plainly visible, lolling like a broken bulrush towards the enemy.

Quietly he reformed the somewhat broken ranks of his little taua, and then he watched the standard till it fell. That was the signal for him to advance. Out into the open he sprang, and after him his men.

The people on the walls of the pa sent up a weird and wailing cry of fear, which could be heard in the still atmosphere by friends and foes alike. Tito lost no time. He knew it was a race for victory. With a rush he started on his wild career, and behind him charged his body of tested warriors.

Hearing the cry from the pa, Tapa' and his men were at a loss to know how to act. If they ran back to the pa, the big taua with the flag would pursue them; if they remained stationary, some unknown danger might overwhelm their stronghold.

In hestitating they lost all. Tito had got halfway across the open ground before he was perceived by them; and when his enemies turned to save their pa, the taua with the flag left the scrub and chased them.

The scene which followed was typical of Maori warfare. Tito rushed into the pa, his men slaying all before them.

But amid the tumult and shouting, above the shrieks and groans of the dying, the shrill voice of a woman could be heard calling, "E Tito! E Tito! E hoa!" and, huddled among a group of screaming women and children, the young warrior found Pirita struggling in the grasp of a brave who had spared her for her good looks.

"My wahine," cried Tito. "Let her go."

"Mine," said the warrior.

"She was mine before you got her."

"If she is yours, take her if you can. Fight me for her."

There was a fierce struggle, a tangle of writhing limbs in a cloud of dust, and then one of the rivals rose.

It was Tito: his antagonist lay prone. The victor took the shuddering Pirita by the hand, and led her lovingly away.

Tapa' and his men, caught between the forces of their foes, were well-nigh exterminated; and then the plundering of the plantations began. But in these subsequent proceedings Tito took no part, for he was engaged in comforting the bride he had won.

THE GIRL WHO WAS COURTED WITH EELS.

RUKU' was a pretty maiden who loved eels, and Tupou was a young warrior who loved Ruku'; but whereas she often gratified her appetite, he was left desiring, for Ruku' had no thoughts of marriage. Beside which, Tupou lived with his tribe on one side of the river, and Ruku' lived with her tribe on the other side; and between the two tribes there was a little friction and heat, owing, strangely enough, to an eeling difficulty. It was what in European politics would be called a fishery dispute—both tribes claimed the sole right to the eels in the river, and as has been stated, Ruku's love of eels was her prevailing passion. Moreover, she was the chieftainess of her tribe, and if there was a firm and lasting plank in her political platform it was resistance to her neighbours' pretensions to an eeling monopoly. Tupou might as well have courted the moon.

But fortunately he had a friend named Hikaka, a man of resource and imagination, a great schemer, who stood by him like a friend and a brother.

Hikaka saw the solution of the problem at a glance. "It is of no use to send Ruku' love-messages through her walking-about friend," said he. "You should send her eels."

"First catch your eels," answered Tupou. "You know that if we fished in the river, Ngati-Maru"—that was the name of Ruku's tribe—"would probably declare war, though Ruku' might eat our eels."

"Well, then," retorted Hikaka, "let Ngati-Maru catch the eels—we shall make the present to Ruku' just the same."

"I don't understand," said Tupou. "I think you're mad to talk such nonsense."

"When Ngati-Maru next go a-fishing," said Hikaka, "send your sister across to their village to visit Hinekino, Ruku's walking-about friend, and leave the rest to me."

"Had we not better get ready our eel-pots and lines and bait?"

"Do nothing of the sort. All you have to do is to cut down some nikau palms and tree-ferns. We shall get all the eels we want. Leave everything to me."

"I never heard of catching eels with fern-fronds and palm-branches."

"Perhaps not, but I will show you how it's done." And the deep schemer Hikaka laughed.

Now, Tupou's sister was known by the beautiful name of The Heavenly Mansion. The very day after the above conversation was held, she went across the river to Te Hau, the Ngati-Maru village, and had a long talk with Hinekino—The Bad Girl—Ruku's walking-about friend, whom she found busily making an eel-basket. Indeed, the village seemed full of eel-baskets, and all the talk was of eels, fricasseed, "hangi'd," stewed, boiled, baked, and sun-dried.

"Surely, you are going on an eeling expedition," said The Heavenly Mansion.

"We're going to catch all the eels in the river," pertly replied The Bad Girl, "so that there will be none for you wicked Ngati-Paoa people, if you ever dare to poach on our preserves."

"We should never think of doing that."

"Your best plan," said The Bad Girl, "is to come over here when we have a feast, and you may then carry away all you can eat. That would be quite tika, good Maori custom."

"Thank you; I shall certainly tell my tribe," said The Heavenly Mansion. "I'll bring over all the biggest eaters."

"You see," continued The Bad Girl, "our chieftainess has a perfect passion for eels. She has determined to dry all that we can't eat fresh, for she has a saying that a dried eel is better than a live eel to be caught by Ngati-Paoa."

"Well, tell her," said The Heavenly Mansion, "that my tribe is not going to fish in the river this summer, though next year we shall resume our rights. Tell her not to trouble to dry the eels—they will be quite safe in the river."

"No, no; we know your tribe." The Bad Girl laughed as she spoke. "We wouldn't trust you while a single two-inch tuna* remained in the river. We mean to catch them all, and dry them. Then we shall know what we have got."

"You are a very suspicious people,"—The Heavenly Mansion's face wore an expression that was anything but beatific—"and I think you are all most disagreeable. There is no living with you amicably. I shall go back to my village, and tell my brother."

Tupou and Hikaka were anxiously awaiting her on the further bank of the river.

"Ah! here you are at last," said her brother.

"I hope you have got all the information I want," said Hikaka.

"I don't know about information," said The Heavenly Mansion, "but I'm only too glad to get back. But you look very miserable, Tupou. What's the matter?"

"Look at the tuna in the river," said Hikaka.

"And we mustn't catch one," said her brother, "for fear lest Ngati-Maru should fall upon us. It's enough to make a man wish he had never been born."

"Ngati-Maru fish to-morrow night," said the girl. "They have made hundreds of eel-pots, and intend to catch every tuna in the river. That's the way they intend to settle the dispute between the two tribes. We can fish when they have caught all the eels."

"That's all right," said Hikaka. "I hope they will make a good haul. Have you got the palm-branches and the ten-foot fern-fronds, Tupou?"

"They are in the pa," replied the chief, "but why you want them is a mystery to me."

---

* Maori for "eel."

"Are they long ones?"

"As long as any in the forest."

"The longer the better," said Hikaka. "Now let us go home and tell the tribe of the projected fishing-expedition of Ngati-Maru."

* * * *

The night was clear and still; the sky was cloudless, but there was no moon. Dark figures, dotted at regular intervals along the river, were fishing. The face of the water was still, but for the splash of a baited line as a fisher made his cast.

Amid deep silence, the work of catching the succulent eel proceeded with great success. Piles of eels began to rise beside the fishers, and Ruku', as she walked from group to group of her loyal and industrious people, felt happy beyond telling.

This wahine rangatira was a fine girl, if rather on the plump side—but what can you expect in a girl who feasts on eels?—with a face which was wreathed in smiles as she contemplated the piles of fish.

"It is a wonderful catch," she said, speaking softly to The Bad Girl, who walked with her from group to group. "We shall have enough dried eels for the next six months; and Ngati-Paoa will have to eat their sweet potatoes dry and without a relish."

"They will fish, and fish," said The Bad Girl, "and then they will send over to us for just one kit of eels, and we will send back word that we always thought Ngati-Paoa were great fishermen who could catch eels for themselves."

The two girls had paused beside a fire at which some of the women were broiling a few of the delicious fish, that their chieftainess might taste and approve.

"Ah!" exclaimed Ruku', as she took a dainty morsel between her finger and thumb, "you have done well here; you deserve great praise—these are delicious. I shall stay to watch you—I think you are the best fishers in Ngati-Maru." But of course the real reason of her stopping was that she might eat as many eels as she wanted.

The men cast their lines skilfully, and the women tied the bait to the lines quickly and firmly—there is no need for a hook in fishing for eels: all that is needed is a manuka rod, eight or ten feet long, and a flax line with a piece of wood-hen tied to the end of it—and soon every line was taut, and with a steady pull, ending with a sudden jerk, the eels were swung over the heads of the fishers, and landed on the top of the grassy bank.

"This is famous," said Ruku'. "There is good fishing to-night, for the others are as successful as you are here. I think I'll take a line myself, and see if I can catch eels too."

She took a rod and line from the man nearest her, and made a cast. The bait sank, and slowly she drew it towards her and made another cast further up the stream. Quickly there was a sharp jerk at the end of the line, which was suddenly drawn tight. "Hine', I have caught one! I have got him fast!"

"Haul him in gently, and then fling him over your head," said The Bad Girl.

"I can't," replied Ruku'; "he won't come." The rod was bent double, and threatened to break.

"He's coming, he's coming," said Ruku', who longed to scream with excitement, but was deterred by the injunction which she herself had placed upon her people, that there should be no noise, lest all the eels should be frightened and flee away.

Her rod rose, and with it rose from the water something dark and pointed and dripping, something which by the flickering light of the fire looked jagged and full of teeth. Up it came, long after Ruku' had dropped the rod and stood trembling on the bank, three feet, four feet, five feet—would it never end?—six feet, seven feet. All eyes were riveted on the awful object which rose slowly out of the river.

"The taniwha*!" screamed The Bad Girl.

"Run! run!" cried Ruku', "I have caught the taniwha!" and she ran for dear life towards the village.

---

*A mythical monster.

As she ran, there were cries up and down the river, on either bank, "The taniwha! Flee, the taniwha is after us!" Then followed piercing screams, as people who fished for eels hauled to the surface monsters with ten-foot jaws which bristled with teeth.

The fishing of Ngati-Maru was over for the night. Regardless of the eels they had caught, the fishers, amid a pandemonium of shrieks and shouting, fled from the river towards their village, where, huddled in frightened groups within their huts, with trembling lips they told each other their awful experiences.

"The river is tapu; it is too sacred to be fished."

"Its waters belong to some priest who controls all the taniwha in all Maoriland."

"We have offended the gods: we shall never be safe till we have gained the assistance of some great priest who can charm these monsters, or who with more powerful monsters of his own can drive them away."

"The eels in that river belong to some man who deals with the spirit-world. We have been stealing his food, and great it his resentment. I shall never eat another eel as long as I live."

"I shall eat kumara* and fern-root—I shall be frightened to eat a fish of any sort, lest it too should be the property of this tohunga who owns the eels."

"The taniwha that I saw was forty feet long. He opened his jaws, and I saw hundreds of teeth."

"The taniwha that tried to catch me came silently out of the river as if he hoped to surprise me, but his head was so long that twenty feet of it stuck out of the water. What his body must have looked like I do not know, for I ran before it appeared. I think he must have been a hundred feet long."

"Anyhow, there is no more fishing for us in that river. It is not our river—it belongs to these innumerable and terrible monsters."

And so the talk went on; no one in the village daring to sleep, that night. But all the discussions

* The sweet potato.

ended in the same manner: there was no more fishing for Ngati-Maru in the river which they had claimed as their private preserve.

* * * *

Slowly in the middle of the night one taniwha rose out of the water, and picked up the eels which lay on the river-bank. All the fishers had fled. Slowly another taniwha came ashore, and joined the first that had appeared. One by one, what seemed to be all the "taniwhas" in the world collected on the bank.

"Build up the fire," said the chief taniwha: "we want to see how many eels we have got." As he spoke, he unbound the flax thongs which were about his waist, and there dropped to the ground a long palm-branch which had projected far above his head. "Take off all your taniwha teeth," he said, "they have bitten the men of Ngati-Maru deep. You have no more need of them."

There was a great unstrapping, and to the ground fell giant fern-fronds and mighty palm-branches, and there stood Hikaka, Tupou, and two dozen men of their tribe.

"We are the great and terrible taniwha of Hauraki," said one. "We own all the eels in this river."

"We hold dominion over the waters and everything therein," said another.

"But now we give our friends of Ngati-Maru the right to fish in this river, if they care to do so."

Then they all laughed till they rolled on the ground in the exuberance of their mirth.

At last, when they were weak with their merriment, Tupou said, "Fling all these ferns and palms into the fire, and go along the banks and collect all the eels caught by Ngati-Maru, and I will return to our pa and send the people to carry them home."

* * * *

Ruku' was disconsolate—she had to exist on fern-root and sweet potatoes, for there was not an eel in her village. A cloud of misery lay heavy on the people of her tribe; their minds filled with a superstitious dread, and their stomachs filled merely with the coarsest food.

"But why do you take this misfortune so sadly?" asked The Bad Girl of her mistress. "Ngati-Paoa are no better off than we, and I'll be bound they are happy enough."

"They have not incurred the anger of the spirit-world," replied Ruku'. "They have not been visited by all the monstrous taniwha that are alive. We might have fought with men, but who shall stand against a taniwha army?"

"We must get a priest possessed of strong incantations to fight them for us," said The Bad Girl.

"I have heard of a priest defeating one taniwha, but it would need an army of priests to overthrow all the monsters that abound in that river."

"Then we must make the best of it, and be content with kumara and taro and fern-root."

"We must be content," said Ruku', and she sobbed as she spoke.

Just then a man came running to them, and said, "There is a party of people coming across the River of the Taniwha"—that was the name by which Ngati-Maru now knew the waters of their former preserve—"and they are carrying heavy loads on their backs."

"Who are they?" asked Ruku'.

"I don't know," replied the messenger. "They come from the other side of the river. I think they are Ngati-Paoa people."

"Receive them," said Ruku', "but tell our folk to say nothing about the trouble we are in with the taniwha."

Slowly the visitors approached the pa, which stood on an eminence, heavily stockaded, and dropped their burdens outside the gate.

When they were admitted, they filed in decorously, and said they wished so see the ruler of the place.

Ruku' received them on the marae,* with all her people around her.

* The open space in the middle of the village.

"Where do you come from?" she asked.

"We are of Ngati-Paoa," they replied.

"Are all your people well? Is Topou well, and his sister?"

"They are well. We hope that Ngati-Maru are well also."

"Everything is well," said Ruku'.

"We have come from our chief," said the spokesman of the party, "with a present. It is probable that he will give himself the pleasure of visiting you in a few days."

"We shall be very glad to see him. In fact we shall be delighted," said Ruku'. "Our tribes are at peace—there exists the warmest feeling betwixt them. What is the present he has sent?"

The men returned to the gate, and brought forward their bundles. These were placed before Ruku', who ordered her women to open them quickly.

"They are eels!" exclaimed Ruku'. "It is a present of dried eels! Where could you have got them? Delightful! There is nothing I so much appreciate as eels."

The Ngati-Maru people looked at each other in astonishment.

"We have some great fishers in our tribe," said the spokesman of Ngati-Paoa. "They have been most successful of late. I expect you have a good supply of the fish, for we heard that you made a great eeling expedition recently."

Again Ruku's people exchanged glances, wondering how much Ngati-Paoa knew.

"When you return to your pa," said Ruku, "tell Tupou we shall be glad to receive him and his tribe, and that we shall give him the best hospitality we can afford. But tell him that I think the eels he caught are bigger than any I have ever seen; I should be delighted if he would bring a few more when he comes."

So the men were dismissed, and Ruku' and her walking-about friend were left alone.

"Don't you think you were rather unwise to invite

them to come at the present time?" said The Bad Girl. "We should have asked them to come later on, when we have really good food to give them—they will despise us when they see we have nothing but fern-root and sweet potatoes."

"I am hopeful that Tupou will bring some more eels," replied Ruku'. "If we wait, his supply will be finished. My idea is that when we have entertained him here, we shall visit his pa, and stay there till we have eaten all the eels he has got."

"I don't much fancy crossing that taniwha-infested river." The Bad Girl's conscience was no better than her name would indicate.

"But we will go over in the daytime," said Ruku', in whom the love of eels dwarfed her fear of the supernatural, "and we will make such a great splashing that the taniwha will be frightened away. Go, and tell the people to lose no time in getting together a few pigeons, parrots, and other birds. We must have some sort of meat to give Ngati-Paoa."

* * * *

Tupou arrived in great state. First came a party bearing a special present for Ruku'. Then followed the main body of the tribe, all the warriors, with weapons in their hands, rich cloaks on their backs, and feathers in their hair; and lastly came the women of the tribe and low-caste men, bearing burdens.

There was a great greeting, and then Ngati-Paoa filed into the pa, and lined up on the marae; and the speeches began. These were of a very formal character and consisted chiefly of fulsome compliments.

Then came the feasting. The piles of food were taken quickly from the steaming ovens, but what was the disgust of Ngati-Paoa when there was set before them nothing but sweet potatoes and a few pigeons and wood-hens!

Etiquette forbade any open expression of feeling, but some of the visitors remarked covertly, "Ngati-Maru evidently value us very lightly if they think this food good enough for us." Others said, "No, this is all they have got—they are eating it themselves. The fact is they are a poor people."

When Tupou grasped the situation, he sent his slaves down to the place where his baggage had been left, and presented Ruku' with another present of eels, larger than the first.

"Ngati-Poa must be a very rich tribe," said Ruku', delighted almost beyond expression at the gift. "How do you manage to catch such quantities of eels?"

"I would have brought more if I had known you were so fond of them," said Tupou with infinite art. "I thought Ngati-Maru had a big eel-catching awhile ago, and that your storehouses would be full of eels."

"We had bad luck," said Ruku', "the—ah—eels wouldn't bite. We caught none at all."

"They bite for Ngati-Paoa fast enough. Where were you fishing?"

"In the River of the Taniwha," said Ruku', quite forgetting herself.

"The River of the Taniwha? Where is that?"

"The river that you have just crossed—that is what we call it."

"Indeed, it is very strange," said Tupou, "for that is where we fished. We had excellent results."

On hearing of this distinct flouting of her fishing rights, Ruku' felt inclined to burst into a paroxysm of rage, but on second thoughts she said to herself, "It is not Ngati-Paoa that has usurped my rights, but the taniwha." Aloud she said bluntly, "I do not believe you are speaking the truth; no one on earth will ever catch eels in that river."

"What!" exclaimed Tupou, "Never catch eels in the River of the Taniwha? Why not? Does Ngati-Maru still claim all the fish in that river?"

"Ngati-Maru has given up the river, but not to Ngati-Paoa. The river would be of no use to either tribe."

"Why? Who then will eat the eels in it?"

"The taniwha."

"Not my tribe, or your tribe?"

"No, the taniwha."

"The taniwha! I don't understand."

Then Ruku' told him the story of her night's fishing, and how her people were scared by the supernatural monsters which rose out of the water.

"Well, well," said Tupou, when she had finished, "I am astonished. But these taniwha are enemies of your tribe only: they don't interfere with my tribe."

"We shall see," said Ruku'. "They will serve you as they served us. One night they will eat you all, unless you can run as fast as Ngati-Maru."

"And in the meanwhile I will undertake to supply you with eels. I have, as you know, a deep regard for you. I shall be glad to send you half of the eels I catch in the River of the Taniwha."

"You are very kind indeed." replied Ruku'. "I shall be delighted to accept them, for I don't see any prospect of getting eels from elsewhere. I'm very fond of eels."

"So I have heard," said Tupou. "I have some more baskets of them down at the gate of the pa. Let me make you a present of them."

"You are really too kind," replied Ruku' with pretended bashfulness, "but as I hardly think you will catch any more, and being convinced that my own tribe will not, I will accept them."

So Tupou sent down all his slaves and women-folk, and they brought up hundreds of baskets full of eels.

Ruku's eyes grew larger and larger with astonishment, as she saw the pile of dainty food grow bigger and bigger.

"Ah, you are a great chief," she exclaimed to Tupou, who stood beside her and ordered the arrangement of the victuals, "you have plenty of food. You are a rich people." She examined sample baskets, and found them full of delicious eels. "I believe, now," she said. "I see with my own eyes. I believe the taniwha in the river are on your side."

"Come and see us fish to-morrow night," said Tupou, "and see us catch the few eels that may be left in the river."

"I'll come gladly," replied Ruku', her heart quite melted by the gastronomic possibilities of the heap of food before her. "I will gladly go anywhere you wish."

Tupou turned, and looked lovingly at her. "Come to my village," he said, "I'll catch the eels, and you'll eat them. Come and stay as long as you please."

"I will stop for a month, two months, three months, so long as you catch the fish I most enjoy."

"Very good," said Tupou, "we'll start to-morrow. You will never wish to return."

There is but little difference between fishing for eels and fishing for love. The man who catches the one may catch the other. In either branch of the art Tupou was equally successful, and when Ruku' learnt the true nature of the bait with which she had been caught, all she said was, "Now we can go and fish together. I hope we shall catch twice as many eels."

THE DEMON-SLAYERS.

KARIRI possessed a famous bone fish-hook, a fish-hook so famous that it had a name, Te Rama (The Torch) by which its maker had been known, a hundred years and more before. Indeed, Te Rama the fish-hook was regarded as an actual part of Te Rama the man; possessing not only the same name, but the same tapu and mana, which are the Maori equivalents of sanctity and power. It was such a marvellous hook that whoever owned it always caught plenty of fish. Not only was it sacred and magical, but it was an heirloom which itself inferred the continual protection of Te Rama, the hook's maker and Kariri's own sacred ancestor. There be relics which are worshipped in churches, but Te Rama the hook was reverenced by an entire race, and into the bargain possessed the power of catching any fish which came within a mile of it

And this sacred hook Kaumariki stole. Imagine a thief stealing the tooth of Buddha, and the enormity of the offence in a Maori's eyes may be comprehended.

With two companions, Tawhai and Kupe, accessories before and after the fact, the thief fled in a canoe, and after four days reached an island, around whose shores there swam multitudes of fish.

The guilty party of pilferers landed on the sandy beach of a land-locked bay, pulled their canoe high-and-dry above high-water mark, and imagined themselves safe from pursuit.

So were they, from Kariri; but not from his witchcrafts. It was not necessary for him to pursue—all he did was to pray, and curse, and cast his spells. The patupaiarehe did the rest. You will hear what they are presently.

The three thieves were forced to sleep on the sand; and as it was winter-time the night was very cold. So Tawhai and Kupe dug above high-water mark holes in the sand, in which they lay down, after covering themselves with their flax cloaks, upon which they piled quantities of dry sand.

"No," said Kaumariki, the arch-thief, as he surveyed his companions in their peculiar beds, "I think you look too much like men buried in the earth. I shall sleep by the fire."

Collecting an immense quantity of bone-dry driftwood, he placed it in a stack, and about this collection of combustible material he made a circle of fires which warmed him on every side.

Then he went to sleep.

Of course his rest was broken by the necessity of occasionally replenishing his fires, but such interruptions to repose were as nothing compared with what occurred at midnight.

Kaumariki was suddenly awakened by the wild shrieks of his companions, and from his circle of fires he saw such a sight as froze his very blood in spite of the flames which cast their lurid glare upon the scene.

About Tawhai and Kupe were grouped half-a-dozen of the strangest creatures. Shaped like men, their skins were white and their hair was red, and with long talons they busied themselves in tearing the vitals of their victims.

Kaumariki at once recognised these monsters as the dreaded patupaiarehe,* man-eating demons from the nether regions. Piling large quantities of wood upon his fires he watched the devils' gruesome feast, and when that was finished the patupaiarehe gathered round him in a circle outside his fires, which barrier they did not dare to pass, since in Te Reinga† they had possibly,

---

*Te Whetu informed me that the first white men who visited New Zealand were believed by the Maoris to be patupaiarehe. This would account for the reception that Tasman received at Massacre Bay. But my informant said that so soon as the Maoris examined the bodies of their victims, they knew that they had killed men of another race. Hence Cook's kindly welcome.

†The Maori name for Hades.

like the burnt child, learnt to dread the fire. But they mouthed at the shuddering Maori, and stretched their white arms threateningly towards him; whereat he piled more wood on his fires till the flames almost roasted him, and the patupaiarehe, dazed by the brightness of the glare, went away groping into the darkness, and left him to himself.

His experience had been awful, but by it Kaumariki had learned two things: first, that it would be the height of wisdom to return the famous hook to its rightful owner, and, secondly, that the devils of the underworld were afraid of fire.

* * * *

How Kaumariki navigated his canoe single-handed and reached his home in safety, was a deed worthy of Crusoe. His plea of peccavi, or Maori words to the same effect, and the restoration of the magic hook to its lawful owner, at once won him forgiveness and likewise the good feeling of everyone in the pa.

"But," said Kaumariki, after he had related the thrilling story of his adventures to a breathless audience, "I am going to take utu from the demons of the island, I am going to make them pay for the deaths of Tawhai and Kupe. First, I shall want a hundred brave followers, the best canoes of the tribe, and food; next, I shall want all the women to collect great quantities of bulrush leaves and manuka boughs, with which to build the house in which I shall entertain the demons; thirdly, I shall need from fifty to a hundred wooden images, representing men, and dressed in flax cloaks; and, lastly, I shall need four oil lamps—but I will make those myself."

The man who had repulsed devils might be trusted to do anything. Kaumariki's proposed expedition became the talk of the tribe, and in a few days everything was ready for starting.

It required six canoes to carry the war-party and all Kaumariki's strange paraphernalia, but after a calm passage the little fleet put into the land-locked bay of

Devils' Island. It was early morning when the disembarkation was effected, and before noon the house for the entertainment of the demons was erected. Then the wooden images, dressed luxuriously in feather-cloaks, were brought from the canoes and were carefully laid in rows inside the house, feet to feet, with their heads against the walls, so that they looked just like sleeping men. In the four corners of the house were erected as many raised platforms, on which were placed the four lamps which Kaumariki had made. They consisted of cup-shaped gourds in which was placed a species of dried fungus, soaked in shark-liver oil. Each lamp was provided with a cylindrical cover, to which was attached a cord which was passed over a beam in the roof; so that the light could be obscured or revealed at pleasure by simply pulling a string.

The working of the lamps having been explained carefully, a staunch and trustworthy man was placed in charge of each, and all the rest of the party were told off to collect firewood.

As night approached, the hearts of the devil-hunters beat anxiously. They had built a circle of fires, at some little distance from the house where the images lay, and as the flames shot towards heaven there was cast over the scene a glare which would plainly reveal the approach of the dreaded patupaiarehe.

Kaumariki, anxious that his scheme should not miscarry, hovered perpetually between the four fearless fellows in charge of the lamps and the men grouped within the circle of protecting fires.

At last, about midnight, a great black object was seen to be moving over the sands. As it approached it gradually resolved itself into a multitude of devils walking in Indian file and preceded by four scouts. As these last advanced they looked this way and that, and finding all was silent and still, they ejaculated, "Kei te moe! kei te moe!" meaning that all the men were asleep.

Avoiding the fires, the guides led the way straight to the house, into which they peered cautiously.

"Kei te moe!" Word was passed from demon to demon down the whole length of the line.

The leader of the infernal band approached—a big white devil with a long red beard—and looked into the house. "Kei te moe!" said he, seeing the images, and thinking them sleeping men.

Then he went inside.

Silently all the patupaiarehe followed their leader, and soon the house was full of devils.

As soon as the men in charge of the lamps perceived in the gloom that all the evil beings had entered, they simultaneously removed the shades of their lamps, and the interior of the house was flooded with light.

Immediately the demons were seized with blindness and groped about with outstretched claws for the door. But the four men, dropping from their perches, threaded their way through the dazed demoniacal throng, and escaped.

Then Kaumariki shut the door, and fixed it firmly. All the patupaiarehe were prisoners in the house.

Fetching burning brands from the fire the men thrust them into the dry walls of the house, and in a few minutes the inflammable structure was ablaze.

Thus were the demons burnt, and Tawhai and Kupe amply revenged.

DREAM-FOWLS.

HIKOIA was a heathen who followed the teaching of the prophet Te Whiti, and believed in witchcraft and spells and all the devilments appertaining to heathenism. Physically he was a big-limbed youth, with a healthy appetite, and of immense strength.

This last endowment was the reason of Tuarangi's anxiety to acquire the young man's help in felling "bush."

Tuarangi was a convert to the Christian karakia,* a proselyte who had got the founder of the faith, Ihu Karaiti, as a firm ally and defender against all the terrors of the spirit-world which hold the Maori mind in thrall.

Tuarangi's piece of "bush" lay about six miles from the kainga,† and comprised some two-hundred acres which he had persuaded the Judge of the Native Land Court to vest in him, for services rendered to the Government in years gone by, and as his share of the tribal lands.

It was in the bond that Tuarangi should find the necessary tools and provisions for one week, and that Hikoia should swing his axe with all his might for something like two shillings per diem and the prospective right of acquiring as his wahine Tuarangi's pretty daughter, Kiritea.

Tuarangi's notion concerning food was simple: he took fowls, plucked and dressed by Kiritea, and half a sack of potatoes. The fowls were packed in a couple of tin "billies," and the men took it in turn to carry the sack of potatoes.

They spent the first day in reaching the ground and in building a whare‡ to sleep in; and the latter

* Religion. † Village. ‡ A hut.

was the minor task, for the hut consisted merely of walls of scrub twisted between sticks which were driven into the ground, and a roof of bulrushes.

That day two fowls were eaten.

On the second day the men began to fell the "bush;" big totara trees which had stood hundreds of years were ruthlessly brought to the ground; mighty 'rimus," stretching their magnificent boles above the surrounding forest, came to earth with the sound of thunder; the sombre and sturdy black-birch, with its mighty outstretched boughs and feathery foliage, lay prone beside the lowly ferns which carpeted the ground.

"Ah-ah!" exclaimed Tuarangi, as the giants of the forest tumbled one by one, "you are good with the axe, Hikoia."

"I learned from the white man," answered the big youth, "the way to chop bush, but I leave his karakia to you."

"By and by we'll make a good burn," said the father of Kiritea, taking no notice of the sneer at his religion, "and then we'll sow the grass and feed the sheep. Do you know how to look after sheep?"

"Yes, I know that," said Hikoia. "The white man taught me to shear."

"Very good. When we get the sheep you shall look after them and marry Kiritea, and we shall have plenty of good food and shall be looked up to by all the people in our kainga."

Of an evening, when the "bush" was growing dark with the shades of falling night, they would light a big fire in front of their whare, and sit in the face of the glowing flames, and smoke their pipes.

"I like the fire," said Hikoia, "it frightens away all the taipo* and evil spirits in this forest."

---

* This is not a genuine Maori word. It seems to be the corruption of some English word which has crept into colloquial Maori speech. Its true Maori synonym was *kehua* or *atua*. In this relation *atua* was generally used to describe a white ghost or spirit or demon, whereas a *kehua* was red or of a fiery complexion, not unlike the *patupaiarehe* of the previous story, which appears to be the familiar spirit of the *wairua*, or demi-god; while the *taipo* seems to be the spiritual attendant of the *tohunga*, or wizard of to-day.

"I have no fear," replied Tuarangi. "When I get Ihu Karaiti on my side, the taipo can't touch me. The spell of the bad tohunga falls from me like water poured on my head. I am all right. I am the man with the new karakia."

That night saw two more fowls disappear.

"I don't think you bring enough food with you," remarked Hikoia. "Felling bush makes me hungry. I eat one fowl, and chop, and chop, and I soon get empty again. We each eat one fowl a day, and still I am hungry. I think I'll have another."

"No, no," ejaculated Tuarangi, hastily shutting the "billy," into which the greedy eyes of the ravenous youth were peering. "If we eat all the food now, we shall have to return to the kainga before we have felled any bush at all. No, no. One fowl each day and plenty of potatoes, that's enough for any man."

"All right," replied Hikoia, "I'll cook potatoes, and fill my belly that way," and he placed a dozen immense tubers on the glowing embers of the fire.

No white man can gauge the appetite of a healthy Maori, for the native is well-mannered in Pakeha* company and reserves the full display of his gastronomic powers for the delectation of his own folk. Hikoia could easily have eaten a leg of mutton at a sitting: he might even have consumed a sucking-pig without help. What to him was one fowl? Potatoes might have a distending effect, but they stayed his hunger for a short time only.

When he had half-finished his meal of baked "riwais," Tua' was snoring in the whare. Hikoia could not resist the temptation: he took another look at the fowls in the "billy." How good they smelt. He took one out, and held it lovingly in his hands. The birds had been stewed, and the thick jelly lay, fragrant, at the bottom of the tin pot. He could not forbear: he took a handful as a relish for what remained of his potatoes.

But he went to sleep that night feeling very

* Maori for a stranger, a white man.

virtuous, in that he had resisted the strong temptation to consume at least two of those succulent roosters.

* * * *

The last day of their sojourn in the "bush" had closed—the last because their food, but for two fowls and a few potatoes, had come to an end. The two men sat in their whare, and talked.

"I think we'll make a good burn by and by with this 'bush,'" said Tuarangi.

"Yes," said Hikoia, "I shall get the tohunga* to give me the proper karakia† to make it a good burn."

"No, no, I will have no Maori karakia said over my 'bush.' I shall get Ihu Karaiti to give me the right prayer: that will make a good burn for me."

"All right. You try Ihu Karaiti: I will try the Maori karakia, the good old kind that your father and grandfather used. I think that a very good way."

"I don't want to have any Maori prayers in my 'bush.' I have the new religion. That is enough."

There was a pause, and then Hikoia said, "Why belong to this karakia? I think it very good for the white man. It makes him strong; it gives him plenty of food and lots of picaninnies;‡ it makes him live a long time. But it is no good to the Maori. The Maori is getting weak. Before he gave up the old karakia of his grandfathers he was strong and his picaninnies grew up. Now they die—they have got no good incantation with which to kill the spell of their enemy, and they die. They say the karakia of your man Ihu Karaiti, and it does no good. They die."

"Oh, no," said Tuarangi. "That's wrong. That's the bad talk of the tohunga, who tells you things like that to keep you to his religion. That's the way he gets plenty of taonga from you, bread, potatoes, meat; and money which will buy wai piro, beer, spirits, rum. I know the tohunga—he's a bad man."

---

* A priest. † In this case, an incantation; sometimes a religion.

‡ Though "picaninny" is a North American word, it is a strange fact that the Maori has adopted it colloquially.

"You give money to the white priest," retorted Hikoia. "He makes you give just as much as I give to the tohunga."

"No," said Tuarangi, "I don't give. I tell him I'm too poor—I've got nothing. Then he goes to the white people, and tells them the Maori is too poor to pay for the karakia, and the white man says, 'All right, we'll pay for Tuarangi and the Maoris.' I get my karakia for nothing. That's good, I think."

"You get nothing for nothing," answered Hikoia. "If you give a good price, you get a good karakia; if you give a little, you get a little karakia; if you give nothing, you get nothing—only a lot of words which have no power. I know. I have seen the white man, in New Plymouth. I have seen him pray—oh, fifty, a hundred, two-hundred white men—I see them pray to make Queen Wikitoria live. But she died all the same. The white man's karakia is very good to make the sheep breed, to make the picaninny come, but it is no good to make the sick man get well or to make Wikitoria live after old Hatana has come to fetch her."

There was a distinct pause, and then Tuarangi said, "Now then, make a finish; say everything, and then I'll talk."

"I've done," said Hikoia.

"All right, then I'll begin," said Tuarangi. "You know the taipo that comes in the night and frightens you, the fellow with the big body, big eyes and big hands? He comes to you, and catches hold of you, and pulls you about. 'You very frightened?"

"I know him. What about him?"

"You know the makutu, the spell that the old tohunga puts on you? You eat good food, pigeons, eels, and kumara; but he puts the makutu on you and makes you sick. You have the wahine, a very good girl, fine, fat, and strong: all of a sudden the tohunga puts the spell on her, and she gets ill and dies. What do you do?"

"I go to another tohunga, a man with more power, stronger in his karakia, and with a greater name. I get him to give me the proper prayer to drive that kind of makutu away."

"All right. You get the proper karakia and you drive it away. But your tohunga says, 'I want that horse of yours, that pig, five pounds, ten pounds,'—anything he thinks you've got. Then he goes to the other tohunga and tells him to make another makutu for your wife, and she gets ill again. You pay five pounds more, and get another incantation to make her well. Oh, yes; he gives you the proper incantation to make her well quick. He knows. He goes to the other tohunga and asks him what sort of makutu he has sent, and then he knows the proper incantation to drive that makutu away. But by and by you have got no more money, no horse, pigs, or sheep, no more taonga.* Then you get no more karakia, and your wife dies. That's it."

"Yes, that's true talk," said Hikoia. "The tohunga is a very hard man."

"Now you know," said Tua'. "That's good talk—the old religion is bad, the new religion is good. In the morning we'll eat the kai,† fowls, potatoes, and then we'll go back to the kainga."

The old man lay down, pulled his blankets over him, and soon was snoring. But Hikoia could not sleep. There was an aching void in his inside which drove away all idea of repose. He thought of the two fowls left in the tin "billy" beside the fire.

At first he tried to stave off the pangs of hunger by smoking, but it was to little purpose.

"This won't do," he said, getting up and putting some wood on the fire. In doing this he knocked his foot against the "billy."

"Dear me, this is too much." He took the lid off the pot, and regaled his olfactory nerves with the fragrant smell of stewed fowls. Then with a watering mouth he went and lay down.

How soundly the old man slept. He was beyond the pangs of hunger and bitter temptation. How loudly

* Goods, property. † Food.

he was snoring. Surely it would be safe to look at the fowls again.

Hikoia rose from his uneasy couch, and once more lifted the lid of the "billy."

The birds were more tempting than ever. Yes, there were two, one for Tuarangi, and one for himself. Why should he not eat his now? If he were hungry in the morning, he would make all the greater haste to the kainga.

Out came one bird, juicy, tender, soaked in thick gravy, delightful to his palate.

In five minutes it was eaten. And yet Hikoia felt hungry. He counted the potatoes, and found there were seven. He would bake four, and leave three for Tuarangi's breakfast.

As the potatoes baked, the insatiable youth sat beside the fire, listened to the old man's snoring, and thought of the one remaining fowl.

At last the potatoes were cooked.

They had a filling effect, but were very dry. Hikoia then remembered that he had not taken his fair share of the gravy. Gravy and potatoes are good.

And now he had eaten all his food. He would have nothing more till he reached the kainga. What a terribly long time that would be, fully twelve hours. He felt afraid that he would not be able to exist for that length of time without food. Perhaps Tuarangi would give him half of his fowl in the morning. Tuarangi was a kind man and had not a great appetite—when he saw how hungry Hikoia was he would have pity.

The big-boned youth took the remaining fowl out of the "billy." He had made a mistake: this was the larger fowl of the two. He should have left the other and have eaten this. Tuarangi was going to get the best of the bargain. This bird was certainly the more tender too. What a mistake to make! Things would be even if he were to take one leg.

The old man moved in his blankets, gave a sigh of sweet contentment, and again began to snore.

Yes, the remaining fowl was by far the better of

the two. Hikoia held the picked drum-stick between his fingers, and sadly contemplated the fire. Of course Tuarangi would give him a share of his fowl in the morning. There was no doubt of that. He would see if the white flesh of the breast was as good as the dark flesh of the leg foreshadowed. Oh! it was better.

There were three potatoes. He would take one—Tuarangi would not begrudge him a potato.

As it baked he contemplated the mangled remains of the bird. Tuarangi might be angry when he saw his breakfast was half-devoured: he might say that Hikoia had taken the best part and left him only the gravy and bones. Perhaps it would look better to eat all up, and clean the pot. He could then say a wood-hen had come in the night and had turned the "billy" over and that the Maori rats had devoured the entire contents of the pot. Anyhow that would be a better story than the confession of having eaten half of Tuarangi's bird. The potato was baked. Now was the time.

The ways of transgression are subtle. Before long all the food was gone, and Hikoia sat beside the cheerful blaze, and felt that he had dined.

Now he could sleep contented.

When the embers of the fire burnt low, he crawled quietly into the hut and lay himself down beside the victim of his gluttony, pulled his blankets over himself, and in a few minutes was snoring as loudly as his companion.

As quiet settled down upon the hut, a wood-hen emerged from the undergrowth of the forest and explored the camp; a ruru owl raised his plaintive voice from a tree near by; a coterie of bats came out to see the night. But with the first streak of dawn the dismal cries of the night-fowl gave place to the notes of the bell-bird, resounding with metallic clearness from the tall tops of the giant trees. The light stole softly into the Maoris' whare, and Tuarangi awoke, and stretched himself.

"Get up, Hikoia. To-day we go back to the kainga."

THE REMARKABLE EXPERIENCES OF PUTAWAI.

PUTAWAI was young and beautiful, and she disappeared: and though the frivolous Pakeha may perceive in her tale a subject for mirth, yet to all sober-minded Maoris the thing is perfectly credible, even if it lacked the corroborative evidence of Wetenga, the girl's lover, who of all men might most reasonably have doubted her story.

Be it known that Wetenga with three companions went pig-hunting in the thick "bush" which stretched illimitably on all sides of the pa. The sport was good and the hunters slew three tuskers,* which they placed upon their backs, and so started for home; but in the mazes of the forest Wetenga became separated from his companions. However, there was nothing alarming in this, for when he called "Oooee" he heard a responding cry, and so he trudged on hopefully in the direction of the sound. But when he repeated his cry, the answer was appreciably fainter; but following fast upon the guiding call, he very soon found himself lost. The answers to his cries led him he knew not where, but presently they became louder, and, just as he expected to reach his comrades, he came upon a huge man who smiled malignantly at him from behind the trunk of a great tree.

"Who are you?" asked the monster.

"Wetenga is my name. I have lost my way in the forest."

*Seeing that Captain Cook introduced pigs to the islands, this story would seem to date back no further than some hundred years, but it is my opinion that the incident of the boar is extraneous, and that the story is in reality very old.—A.A.G.

"That need not trouble you," said the huge stranger. "Follow me: I will show you the way."

But when Wetenga acted upon this advice his enormous guide merely ran round the tree, first one way and then the other. But all at once the Maori felt himself forced against the trunk, with his face towards the bark. A long, sinuous creeper encircled the bole, and, pulling the plant up by the roots, though leaving it fastened above, the monstrous being was binding Wetenga to the tree by the simple process of running round the trunk with the root of the creeper in his hand. Soon the poor Maori was tied hand and foot, and could not move; his struggles were futile and his cries unheeded: with the pig on his back he was lashed so tightly to the tree that he could not hope to get free.

"Let me go" he cried to his captor, "and you shall have my pig."

"Do you know who I am?" the monster asked, laughing. "I am Hiritoro, the wairua, the great spirit —I do not eat pigs. But I am very partial to the flesh of girls. You are the bait that will decoy them, and I hope to catch plenty. Yes, the thigh of a girl, about seventeen years old, that is good. I expect you possess such a girl, and possibly she will come to look for you. If so, I shall catch her."

Wetenga shivered with horror at the fate intended for his sweetheart, Putawai, but he said not a word to the wairua, who peered into his face and said, with a laugh, "I will now go to watch for her as she comes from the pa."* And with a malignant chuckle he left Wetenga bound to the tree, and disappeared into the thick jungle.

When Wetenga's three companions arrived at the pa, Putawai at once inquired after her lover.

"Oh, he'll come along by and by," said they. "You see, we got separated from him in the forest, but he'll find his way all right."

However, two days went by and Wetenga did not appear. Then the people grew anxious for his safety,

* Fortified village.

and the men of the pa formed themselves into search-parties and scoured the forest. Putawai, her heart full of love and fear, accompanied the searchers; but, like her lover, she became separated from her friends, and lost her way. Tired with wandering fruitlessly through the forest, she stopped to drink from a rippling stream when, hearing a laugh behind her, she turned to find Hiritoro, the huge wairua, standing over her.

In a moment he had seized her, and in spite of her cries, which reached no sympathetic ear, he dragged her, struggling, into the underscrub.

Quickly binding her with the trailing tendrils of a creeping plant, he swung her on to his back, and after the manner of a wairua, who traverses the air without the aid of wings, he sped with her over the tall tree-tops, over intervening forest-clad hills, and dropped into a deep valley where all was dark and still. Here he discovered in the thick bushes a deep, black hole, into which he disappeared with his burden.

Putawai came to her frightened senses in the light of the underworld. Around her stood a score and more of white-skinned beings, shaped like men, with ruddy complexions and red hair, whom she knew to be patupaiarehe, fearsome devils of the Maori Hell, all eager to taste a morsel of her flesh.

But as they pinched her body and descanted on her plumpness, one saying he would have a piece of the arm, and another declaring that he preferred a piece of the leg, there stood by another wairua, as big and powerful as Hiritoro himself, but less ferocious in appearance, who silently gazed at the girl as she lay quivering with fear like a pigeon in the hand of the fowler.

"Well," said Hiritoro, "I have had a successful day's hunting. We shall have a good meal. I will now go, and prepare the oven."

He disappeared, but the patupaiarehe lingered to gaze on their victim.

The other wairua then spoke for the first time. "The fire will need fuel," he said. "What are you devils doing, standing by idle? Go, and collect firewood!"

In a moment, frightened into activity by his threatening attitude, they all disappeared.

Then this new wairua approached the girl, and untied her thongs.

"I am Manoa," he said, "I am a greater spirit than Hiritoro. He is fond of eating the flesh of men and women, and he thinks he is to have the pleasure of cooking you; but I have other notions. I have long desired just such a woman as yourself—I like your looks; I think you will make me a most excellent wife. Get up."

Putawai rose stiffly to her feet.

"Put your arms round my neck," said Manoa. "Get on my back."

The girl did as she was told.

"Now hang on tight," said Manoa, and without any effort to obtain volitation the two sped through the air of the underworld. When Hiritoro and his satellites returned—their oven being made ready for the cooking—they found the bird flown, their dinner gone.

The first place at which Manoa and Putawai alighted was the pa of the ngerengere folk. These poor people, having died of the dread disease, were doomed to be leprous in the nether regions. They gathered round the new-comers, with strange cries of greeting; some without hands or arms, some without feet, hobbling on sticks, some a mass of festering sores, but all doomed to live for ever in their misery.

But Manoa and Putawai had not long been in this dreadful place when Hiritoro arrived in pursuit of his victim. The ngerengere, all subject to the will of Manoa, tried to bar the passage of the new wairua, but by reason of their sickness their efforts were futile; so Manoa, taking his bride upon his back once more, sped through the air.

He next alighted at the pa of the blind people, who had lost their sight in the world of men never to regain it. But they all knew the voice of Manoa, and greeted him with expressions of gladness, for he was a great spirit. However, when Hiritoro arrived in quest of his victim, like the lepers they failed to impede him, because, being blind, he easily eluded them when they strove to catch him.

So, for the third time, Manoa was forced to fly with his bride upon his back.

He next alighted at his own pa, which was full of patupaiarehe, red-and-white devils, who were assembled in thousands.

Obedient to their lord, they disposed themselves so as to thwart Hiritoro, who, coming at immense speed into their midst, found himself immediately seized and thrown outside. Again and again he tried to reach his victim, but always to be beaten back, unsuccessful.

At length he abandoned his purpose, and returned to his own place.

"Now," said Manoa to his bride, "we shall live in peace and happiness. I told you that I was too strong for Hiritoro, and you have seen how I have worsted him. I am the greatest wairua in Te Reinga." *

So Putawai abode in the spirit-world, and became the wife of Manoa.

* * * *

When Wetenga's friends had searched unsuccessfully for three days, they returned to their pa to cry. What was their consternation upon finding that Putawai was also missing?

Back they went to seach the forest once more, and this time they took with them Wetenga's dog, which had returned without its master to the pa. Again they scoured the forest, and about mid-day the dog, sniffing at the breeze, guided them to where Wetenga was tied to the tree.

His state was pitiable. The flies had attacked the dead pig upon his back, and the whole carcase was a crawling mass of corruption which had already begun to attack his living flesh. Tenderly they unbound him

---

* The place of departed spirits.

and, loosening his dreadful burden from off him, they carried him on a litter to the pa.

It took much care and skill to restore him to health and strength, but in time he recovered, only to find, however, that this bride had vanished.

"I know," he said, "that the wairua has got her—he tied me to the tree that she might be decoyed to look for me. He caught her as a fowler catches a bird in his snare. It is no use looking for Putawai; by this time Hiritoro has eaten her."

So the whole pa "tangied"* for the lost girl as though she were dead.

Then the everyday work of the people was resumed: the men went out to fish, the women to work in the plantations, and the boys to trap birds. And soon the tragedy of Putawai was forgotten.

A year or more went by, and Wetenga, recovered from his dreadful experience, was throwing aside his grief for his lost bride, when, one evening as he returned to the pa from the beach, he saw a woman waiting for him in the path.

"Tena koe,"† he said. "You are a stranger here. What is your name?"

"Putawai," replied the woman.

"Putawai? No, no: she died more than a year ago."

"She did not die. Hiritoro, the wairua, took her away."

"What? You know that, do you?"

"Of course: I am she."

"You Putawai?—the wairua ate her."

"No, he did not. Another wairua, named Manoa, took me away, and saved me."

"You cannot be Putawai!—but yet you are not unlike her."

"And I know you. You are Wetenga. I was going to marry you when I was taken away to Te Reinga. Look at my face—it is Putawai's. Look at my hands. Do you remember the scar on my

* "Cried." † Form of Maori greeting.

shoulder where a burning stick struck me when I was a small girl?"

"Yes," said Wetenga, "yes, I see."

"Look at the tattoo on my chin. Look at it close: you will recognise it."

"Yes," said Wetenga, "it is Putawai's tattoo. Well, well; it is hard to believe, but it seems true. But how do I know that you are not some being sent from the spirit-world to deceive me?"

Putawai put her arms round him. "Feel me," she said. "My touch is as warm as ever it was. I am not a wairua, but flesh and blood like yourself. I am the same girl that ever I was."

Then as from a dream Wetenga awoke. He caressed her, and they wept together for joy. He knew she was Putawai come back again.

But when they were married and were in the privacy of their hut, Wetenga asked his wife to tell him what had happened to her in the underworld, and she related the story of her escape from Hiritoro to the towns where the lepers and the blind people lived, and explained how it was owing to the red-and-white devils subject to Manoa that her pursuer had been kept at bay. But, womanlike, she refrained from divulging the secret of her marriage with the wairua.

However, truth will out, with Maoris as with white men. In the middle of the night, Wetenga was awakened by a strange noise, a noise he had not expected to hear so soon, the crying of an infant small and puny before the strength of its lungs had fully come.

"What is that?" he asked. "There must be a baby in the hut!"

Putting out his hand, he found the cause of his awakening being nursed by his wife.

"What does this mean?" he demanded.

"It is my baby," said Putawai, "the baby I bore in the underworld."

"The baby you bore in the underworld! What do you mean? Who is its father?"

"Manoa. He has brought it to me that I may nurse it. You wouldn't have it starve, surely."

"But I don't want a 'wairua's' child," said Wetenga.

"It will be no trouble," answered his wife, "for each night, before dawn, when you are fast asleep, its father will come to take it way."

"H'm," said Wetenga, "that is a very strange arrangement. I think you are the 'wairua's' wife still."

"You need not worry about that," replied Putawai. "Manoa brought me back because he was tired of me. But he wants his child to be reared: that is why he takes the trouble to come up from Te Reinga every night to bring it to me."

"I think he had better stop there," said Wetenga. "I don't want to share my wife with anyone." And he tried to keep awake to see the wairua. He lay with his taiaha* in his hand, intending to kill Manoa when he came, but just before dawn a remarkable drowsiness seized him and he fell asleep; and while he slumbered the wairua came to fetch his child. Then, when Wetenga awoke, and spoke to his wife of the matter, she said, "You must have been dreaming: there is no child here. Being tied up by Hiritoro has made you dream of 'wairuas.' Turn over, and go to sleep again." And her husband believed her.

So it happened every night till the spirit-child was weaned, and after that the strange dreams of Wetenga ceased, and he settled down to the even tenor of married life and became the father of a large family, each member of which, however, caused him more broken rest than did the babe from the spirit-world.

---

* A flat, two-edged weapon of hard wood, about 5 ft. long.

THE KIRITEA GIRL.

THIS tale would be clear and plain from the beginning, if I could explain exactly what a taipo is in nature and substance: but as I have not so much as seen one, I can but describe that fell spirit at second hand. The taipo is some sort of a devil; but devils are so many, that when I say that this particular offspring of the nether world is a Maori devil, I convey no distinct mental impression either to your mind, dear reader, or even to my own. One thing is certain: there are no horns or cloven hoofs about your taipo. Apparently, he takes different shapes at different times, and is sometimes monstrous, sometimes diminutive, always terrible. At one time he will be invisible to all save those who have an insight into the back of the beyond, at another time he will appear in all his gruesomeness and terror to a dozen men simultaneously.

In the second place, it must be understood that the Maori wizard commands not merely companies of men but also battalions of the air; and it is a recognised sequence that if he loses the subservience of his familiar spirits, he loses also the obedience of his people.

Paawa, the wizard chief of Rangitoto, was happy in possessing the allegiance of both spirits and men. He had but to say the word, and his pa was filled with stalwart warriors, eager to shed their blood in defence of their great chief and high-priest in devilry, whose fame in matters material and spiritual stretched from end to end of Maoriland. He had but to repeat his incantations, and immediately the air was filled with protecting demons, invisible, ubiquitous, invulnerable, alert to defend their lord and master against all comers. And since the hatred of Paawa and his witchcrafts was as great as his reputation was evil, his enemies were ever on the watch to molest him, and his body-guard of devils was never off duty.

Seldom venturing from his stronghold to pay those social courtesies so dear to the heart of the Maori, the wizard had small opportunity of acquainting himself with his neighbours, and this was the more distasteful to him as he was bent upon marriage. True, he was somewhat aged, and his face bore many wrinkles beside the deep furrows of its elaborate tattooing, but in other respects his occult art kept him young. His step was light, his eye bright, his body vigorous, his appetites insatiable. Therefore, summoning his head taipo, the chief of his evil spirits, he commanded him to search out the prettiest girl among the neighbouring tribes, that he might have a wife suited to his taste and worthy of perpetuating his malignant seed.

* * * *

Who shall say what a devil's taste in beauty may be? In the opinion of Hakawau of Kawhia, however, there was no doubt that Rona was the loveliest of girls. She was what is known as a kiritea: her skin was several shades lighter than the ordinary Maori's. This made her conspicuous, but her pretty face, with its merry expression, and her little but perfectly-moulded figure made her resistless. Her lovers were many, but so far no ardent aspirant had succeded in claiming her for his own.

Hakawau lived miles away from her, but distance makes the heart grow fonder, with Maori as with Pakeha, and his constant dream was of bringing the kiritea as a bride to his pa. Of the five-and-forty suitors who surrounded her more immediately, there was not one whom Rona had not known from childhood, and while she felt flattered by their unremitting attentions, her thoughts were with the distant chief who had carried her heart to Kawhia.

In order to avoid addresses which were distasteful to her, Rona would sometimes accompany her brother on his fishing excursions, when, taking canoe, he would drift down the river to the sea. Upon other occasions, she would spend much time in wandering outside her pa, amid the glades of the adjacent forest, or beside the pleasant banks of the broad Waikato, everflowing to the sea. On these excursions she was usually accompanied by her walking-about friend, a bouncing, laughing girl whose admiration for the kiritea was but one degree removed from that of the warmest of her amorous suitors.

* * * *

A demon in search of a bride makes a striking figure in story; and, while it is interesting to speculate on the taste of Paawa's familiar, it is not a thing to be wondered at if his methods of selection were peculiar. Invisible, no match-maker was more competent than he to report upon the charms of the coy and modest fair; possessed of vast supernatural power, no go-between was better able to enforce compliance. Armed with a roving commission, his secret investigations may have extended from end to end of both islands of Maoriland; obedient to his malign master, he certainly performed his task as conscientiously as any devil could; but naturally, as Rona's village was so near to Rangitoto, it was impossible for her to escape his demoniacal scrutiny.

* * * *

The day was perfect: in the azure sky not a cloud was to be seen; not a breath stirred the tall, pointed leaves of the luxuriant flax-bushes growing beside the murmuring river, in which the kiritea and her companion, Koko, were bathing.

The girls swam to the further bank, and from a convenient ledge they dived into the deep, pellucid water, where, splashing, laughing, and shouting with merriment, they gambolled like true daughters of their mother, Nature. Finally, tired of their sport, they landed at the spot where they had left their feather cloaks, and there continued their games, chasing one another over the green sward till they were dry.

Then it was that the strange abduction was effected. The light-skinned girl was suddenly seized by invisible hands, and was forcibly dragged away from her frightened companion. Her piercing screams fell merely on the ears of the helpless Koko, and her struggles to escape from her unseen captor availed nothing. Slowly, relentlessly she was carried away; her faithful friend following till she saw the fair-skinned Rona drawn captive into the pa of Rangitoto. Then the weeping Koko turned her steps sorrowfully homeward.

* * * *

Now, the brother of the kiritea loved her no less than did the most devoted of her suitors. Calling her lovers together, Korokia—for that was the brother's name—assembled as ardent a body of braves as ever owed fealty to a fair maid. Koko's tale of the supernatural abduction was the common talk of the pa, and Korokia had no need to repeat the harrowing details to his hearers.

"You all knew my sister, the kiritea," he said. "You all wished to marry her. Is not that so?"

There was silence, till a lithe young warrior, speaking for the rest, said, "That was so."

"Very good," said Korokia, "you were all in love with her, and no one with taste could be surprised at that; but she has been carried off by the wizard Paawa, so if you still would like to marry her you must help me to rescue her from her captor."

"We will kill Paawa, and end his witchcrafts for ever," said one of the lovers.

"You must all have noticed," remarked another, "that being in love with the same girl caused considerable jealousy between us. Tiki would not speak to Toroa, and Riki entertained thoughts of killing Heke. Indeed, I believe there was not a man of us who would not gladly have shed blood to gain the love of the kiritea. Let us then join in shedding the blood of this villain Paawa, and free the kiritea from his dreadful bondage. Then she shall choose which of us she will marry."

The suggestion was received with acclamations of approval, and Rona's five-and-forty lovers rose, and swore to release her or die. Arraying themselves in the accoutrements of battle, they danced a furious war-dance, in which they defied their enemies and heaped scorn upon the heads of Paawa and all his tribe. Then they dispersed, in order that they might prepare for their warlike expedition.

When they reassembled next day, each lover had brought with him one or two friends, willing to take part in the tribe's quarrel; so that the war-party mustered fully one-hundred-and-fifty men, ready to shed their blood in a mighty endeavour to rescue the kiritea girl from the clutches of the fell wizard who commanded malignant spirits of the underworld.

They went up stealthily, hoping to surprise the great pa of Rangitoto. Forsaking the customary tracks used by travellers, they traversed devious and unfrequented ways. Making use of the cover afforded by scrub and undergrowth, availing themselves of the folding ground of hills and of desolate valleys, at length they came within a mile of their destination.

Hiding their clothes and baskets of food in the thick bushes, they debouched in warlike array upon the open plain in front of the pa. They marched valiantly in perfect order, rank behind rank, every man pressing forward with eagerness, and watching attentively for their leader to give them the command to rush and take the unguarded pa.

What then was the surprise of Korokia, who at his chief's order remained in charge of the baggage, to see his comrades seized with a sudden dementia which quickly changed their precise order in chaos. Some ran this way and some that, without apparent purpose and regardless of any concerted plan. Some ran forward, some back; some danced a maniacal and absurd dance in defiance of nobody visible; some set to work fighting fiercely among themselves; some fell upon the ground and writhed their limbs into knots; some, foaming at the mouth, staggered aimlessly about, and died in fits; some leaped into the river and, struggling insanely for a while, disappeared beneath the water and were drowned; none reached the enemy's pa; none returned to the baggage. Sole survivor of the force which had set out confidently to subdue Paawa and rescue the kiritea girl, Korokia fled incontinently from the strange battle-field, and never halted till he reached his own pa.

"All the men were stricken with madness," said he, when he told his remarkable story, "some fell victims to the weapons of their comrades, some died in their frenzy, of all who set out I only am left."

"Our warriors were killed not by men, but by demons," said the old priest of the tribe, "by malignant taipo commanded by Paawa, who fell upon them suddenly and slew them. Now, Korokia, go to Hakawau, the chief of Kawhia and our near relation. He will tell us what to do."

So Korokia departed.

When Hakawau, who was a great and notable warrior, heard the tale, he said, "I am at a loss to know how to act. I can fight men, but how can I fight with devils who are invisible or who take the shape of invulnerable men?—I am a fighting-man, not a priest who deals in witchcraft.

But Hakawau's father, a veteran who in his day had done great deeds, was standing by, listening.

"This man Paawa," he said, "is a priest deeply versed in spells and devilments. It is of no use to fight him with ordinary weapons such as the mere, the taiaha, and the spear. He must be fought with his own weapons, the karakia, the incantation, the makutu, the spell, and the taipo. Now, I have a brother in the Urewera country who is without doubt the greatest tohunga in these islands. Go to him, my son: he will give you the strong karakia with which to settle our business with this Paawa."

The suggestion received Hakawau's immediate approval. Following the Waikato river towards its source, he crossed lake Taupo and passed on into the wild country which lies towards the East Cape, whence after many months he returned.

"Well, have you seen my brother?" asked his father.

"Yes," said Hakawau.

"Did he give you the karakia?"

"He did. I have got it."

"The karakia to overthrow Paawa's devils?"

"Yes, that's what I have got."

"Very good. When are you going to use it?"

"Soon," said Hakawau. "I want fifty good men to go with me, twenty from Kawhia, and thirty from Waikato,"

"What! you will take only fifty men?"

"Only fifty—the incantations of my uncle the tohunga will do the rest."

Hakawau called for volunteers, and taking twenty picked men he set out for the Waikato. There he easily recruited his company to its required strength, and amid the farewells and applause of the people the little taua dropped down the river in a single canoe.

Hakawau disembarked his force some way from Rangitoto, and, without any attempt at concealment, marched his men in a compact body towards the hostile pa. Halting them in the shade of some tall scrub, he went forward to reconnoitre.

In front of him the ground stretched, bare and level, to the very walls of the pa. At the edge of this little plain Hakawau paused, and repeated his karakia, the potent spell which the great wizard of Urewera had given him.

Presently he saw the familiar spirits of the wicked Paawa assemble on the flat ground where they had slain the Waikato men some six months before. They looked for all the world like warriors, stripped ready for battle and armed with innumerable weapons. He said another karakia, and his own demons appeared. These, greater in number and more ferocious than Paawa's devils, advanced to meet their demoniacal foes. A fierce battle followed, but Hakawau's fiends, more powerful and more skilful than Paawa's, overwhelmed their adversaries of the nether world, and killed every one.

When Hakawau saw that his spirits had conquered, he went back to his men, who had been anxiously and intently straining their eyes for a sight of their enemies, but had observed nothing save the figure of their chief, as he stood repeating his prayers in a conspicuous position between them and the pa.

"Well," said Hakawau, "it is all over."

"What is over?" asked his men.

"The fight of the taipo, the battle of unseen spirits. We may now advance on Rangitoto without fear."

"What fight is over? We saw no taipo."

"No, you could not see them, but my taipo have fought those of Paawa, and have conquered them. My spells are the stronger, my spirits have triumphed. All the devils of Paawa are dead."

The warriors had seen nothing of this combat between Apollyon and Beelzebub, but great was their faith in Hakawau. They knew he would not lie, and they were convinced that he was not the man to journey all the way to Urewera for a spell, and to come back without it. So that when he ordered them to advance upon Rangitoto, they all stepped out gladly, confident of victory.

But Paawa had also seen the battle of the taipo, and had now retired into the darkest corner of his sleeping-house in order that he might hide his diminished head. So that when Hakawau arrived at the gate of the pa, all he had to do was to walk straight in; for when Paawa's warriors went to bestir their chief, they were told not to fight.

"It is of no use," whined Paawa. "The mana of Rangitoto is gone. My spirits have been overthrown by spirits stronger than themselves. My spells have been conquered by mightier spells, my reputation as a wizard has vanished, and nothing is left me but to die."

When Hakawau perceived the state of affairs, he boldly called for the necromancing chief.

"Where is Paawa?" he demanded. "Tell him I

must speak with him."

"He is in his hut," replied the men of Rangitoto. "He is pouri."*

"Fetch him before me," ordered Hakawau. "I have something to tell him."

So they brought the trembling wizard before his conqueror.

"Are you the tohunga who slew men through the agency of devils?"

"Once I slew a few of your relatives by the hands of my taipo."

"One hundred and fifty men," said Hakawau.

"Perhaps, but I should not have thought there were so many. However, I never counted."

"Did you not?" Hakawau took his greenstone mere from beneath his cloak. "For their death I will take your life." He seized Paawa by the hair of his head and then, instead of dashing out his brains, he merely passed the edge of his weapon across the old priest's forehead. Next, he plucked the feathers out of Paawa's hair, pulled the piece of carved greenstone from his neck, threw his costly kiwi cloak† upon the ground, and said, "I won't kill you. I have done worse than that. I have broken your sanctity, I have destroyed your reputation: henceforth you are a man scorned, despised, destitute of all that prestige which has now passed to me. That is all. I will kill none of your tribe. The quarrel has been the quarrel of priest with priest, of devils with devils: your devils are destroyed, and I have turned you into one of the lowest of the people, a mean tutua,‡ whose hair I have plucked, and whom I have insulted before the men of Rangitoto, Waikato, and Kawhia."

After suffering these indignities Paawa was like Lucifer, son of the morning, fallen from heaven. But Hakawau had not finished with him.

"Where is the kiritea?" he asked.

---

* Ill, sad, distressed, obfuscated generally. † A cloak of flax covered thickly with the feathers of the apteryx. ‡ A nobody.

"The kiritea?" said the crafty Paawa, as though he knew not who was meant.

"The girl Rona? Where is she?"

Now, the old priest could lose his reputation for devilments, and survive; but to part with his beautiful young wahine was to lose the prop of his declining years.

"You have taken my mana from me," he whined; "you have destroyed my power; you have desecrated my tapu, and my sacredness is gone; you have disgraced me before all my people and have made me as the lowest-born slave in my tribe: surely you will not rob me of the one solace that remains. There are many beautiful women among your captives who would gladly follow so great a conqueror to Kawhia, but spare me my wife."

"Where did you get her?"

"Where did I get her? From Waikato."

"Who gave her to you?

"Ah——I——That is to say——The truth is I won her."

"That is so. You won her by theft."

"No. Believe me, you are mistaken. I never so much as laid hands on her."

"But your evil spirits did."

Paawa smiled. "You are too big a tohunga to be deceived," he said. "She is a good girl, and much beloved by me. I treat her excellently."

"That is as it may be," responded Hakawau. "Please, bring her here."

The old wizard demurred, but his conqueror was obdurate, and presently a girl led Rona into the middle of the assembly. She had been well cared for; she was plump, and beaming with delight.

Hakawau contemplated her unique beauty for a few brief moments, and then he gently approached her. Resting his hands upon her shoulders, he drew her face close to his, and they "hongi'd" after the fashion of their race; calling each other by every endearing name, shedding tears of joy, and expressing in tones of weird shrillness the happiness of their reunion.

Yet that was but their formal greeting, dictated by etiquette. Separating himself from Rona, Hakawau quickly regained his composure.

"You were brought here against your will," he said, standing over against her that all might see and hear, "by the evil spirits of the priest whom I have degraded this day. Tell me now, Rona, will you stay with him, or will you accompany your relatives who have delivered you?"

"That lame, old swamp-bird," said the fair-skinned girl, pointing derisively at her lord and master, "is not worthy to be the husband of the lowest slave-girl of our tribes. He is already half-way on the road to Hell, and before many years are gone he will be forgotten. My husband should be young and brave, strong and active like myself. I will come with you. I leave Rangitoto gladly: I belong to my own people. I cleave to my own tribe."

Running to Hakawau she placed her arms about his neck, and before all he took her as his wahine.

When the conquered had feasted the conquerers, Hakawau departed with his wife and followers to spread the news of Paawa's discomfiture through all the tribes. That malignant old man became a tohunga who was no tohunga, a worker of miracles whose miracles were of no avail, the master of demons whose demons were dead. And the kiritea girl, freed from his horrible affection, and happy in the love of a brave and powerful husband, lived in happiness and peace ever afterwards.

THE MARRIAGE OF THE NGARARA.

THE Arawa people lived near their friends of the Waikato tribe, but the Ngarara lived between.

That monster was black, with big bat-like wings which stretched twelve feet from tip to tip; his great head, set on a long supple neck, ended in a sharp snout; his jaws were full of teeth, and the talons on his feet and shoulders were as sharp as scythes. Moreover, his favourite food was human flesh.

Therefore it is not to be wondered at, that when the Waikato people visited Te Arawa they had to take a circuitous route through the tangled forest, in order to avoid the rua, or den, of the ferocious Ngarara. It was a journey over steep rocks and along winding forest-tracks which seemed interminable. But Kahu-ki-te-Rangi, the Waikato chief, often traversed it, because—well, there could be but one reason: he was in love. He had seen the daughter of old Pouwhenua, the priest of Te Arawa, and having once seen her he must see her again and again.

Now, Kahu' had an organizing genius: he had a mind full of schemes and plans. So it is not remarkable that on one occasion, when he visited Te Arawa, he should say to the old priest, "You want a new road here, along the flat. Why don't you make it?"

"Look at the labour," replied Pouwhenua, who was a lazy man, except with prayers and incantations. "And then there's the Ngarara."

"There need be no fear of him," said Kaku'. "I will settle with him myself, and you can help by casting a spell upon him. As for the road, I will make it, if——"

"If what, Kahu'?"

"If you will give me your daughter."

The old tohunga pondered. He thought of the love he had for the Waikato tribe, of the kindness they had shown to his people when the kumara crop failed three years before, of the warlike strength of the united tribes. He said, "Very good, you may have Koka. I hope the new road and the marriage will increase the love of our people."

* * * *

The Ngarara's home was among the hills, where the forest was thick and impenetrable. Now, Kahu' knew all about the Ngarara, for his father, who was a great slayer of such creatures and knew their language, had schooled him perfectly in all knowledge of the reptiles.

So, unafraid, he went to see the fearsome monster, which lived half-way between the friendly tribes.

The Ngarara was sunning himself in front of his den when Kahu' arrived.

"Hullo! Ngarara. Were you asleep?" cried the Maori. "You're bigger than I thought you were. What fine eyes you've got, what magnificent teeth! And your skin is beautifully black."

The Ngarara, scarce awake, snapped his great jaws, for here was human flesh; but the voice, speaking in his own reptilian tongue, arrested his bloodthirsty intention.

The winged monster lay still as a rock lies on a mountain, with his neck extended and his chin on the ground. Like all creatures of the bat-like kind, he was tormented with an intense itchiness, and as Kahu's fingers touched his rough skin he broke into a murmur of satisfaction, like the purring of a cat. From the head Kahu' worked his hand down the Ngarara's neck to the spot between the great pinions where the itchiness was greatest.

The creature grunted with pleasure, and said, "A little lower down, if you please; now under the left wing; now under the right; thank you; I haven't had such pleasure for twenty years; you must come to see me often—I'll always give you the warmest welcome. Thanks a thousand times; now on the chest—ah! how clever you are, you put your hand on the exact spot. Look out, look out—I can't help it—I'm going to roll."

The Ngarara began to heave in a manner dangerous to the Maori, who jumped behind a tree; and the monster rolled over on his back, and began to kick and fling up the dust with wings and feet and claws and tail. Then he scrambled on to his feet, shook himself well, sat on his haunches, and gave a sigh of satisfaction and contentment.

"Really, I can never repay you for this," he said. "That you should come so far to scratch my back, is a kindness almost beyond belief. How can I serve you? What can I do for you?"

"Well, Ngarara," said Kahu,' "the chief object of my visit is to make friends with you. My mother,* you must understand, was the widow of a Ngarara such as yourself, and her account of your race made me wish to know you. Besides, living as you do so isolated a life, I imagined that you would be glad of a visitor who could speak your language and oblige you in a reasonable manner as I have done."

"If you would come regularly and scratch my back, I should be unspeakably gratified."

"Certainly, Ngarara, I'll come gladly. But I have thought of even a better plan. You must feel very lonely here."

"Lonely is no word for it," said the reptile.

"It has occurred to me that you would be glad of a wife, who would scratch your back whenever you wished."

"A Ngarara wife?" asked the monster—"they are very scarce."

"No, a Maori wife. There are plenty—I could get you one."

"You could get me one! My dear friend, nothing would please me more. I should much prefer a Maori

* See "The Ngarara," (Tales of a Dying Race.)

wife to a Ngarara wife—she is so much softer, so much gentler, so much more useful, more obedient, without teeth or claws. See, I would fold her in my wings, so, and nurse her on my knee, so,—and look how snug she would be. The thought delights me."

"And you would then be related to us," said Kahu'. "But before I give you your wife, I shall require you to make me a promise."

"With the greatest of pleasure. What?"

"The Arawa tribe and mine are very friendly. If I gave you a wahine, I should expect you to confine your hunting to the other side of the mountains: that is to say, you would promise not to touch an Arawa or a Waikato."

"I give you my word gladly. I would not think of touching them."

"Man, woman, or child?"

"I would not take the smallest child, the weakest maiden, or the feeblest old man in your whole valley. I would hunt only on the other side of the mountains, where your enemies dwell."

"That is right. Hunt there as much as you please."

"And when will you bring my wife?"

"To-morrow, or the next day—as soon as I can get her."

* * * *

Now, near the Waikato pa there lived a woman named Pukaka, a burier of the dead, who in consequence was shunned by all her tribe. She was haggish, skinny, foul with vermin and dirt, frightful, almost less human in appearance than the Ngarara himself. Her Kahu' chose as the reptile's wife, and Pukaka, content to change her horrible mode of life to become a bride, was glad to barter the insults and scorn of her tribe for the endearments of even so awful a monster as the Ngarara.

"You may think him rather strange at first," said Kahu' to her, "but when you get used to him, you will find him gentle enough. But there are two things you must remember: see that he hunts only amongst the tribes on the further side of the mountains, and always scratch his back when he is angry. If you do these two things you will please both the Ngarara and myself."

So the two went up the mountain where the Ngarara lived, passed through the dense and tangled forest which covered every slope, and arrived at the door of the reptile's den.

The Ngarara was in his cave, busy making it a little bigger for the reception of his wife, and a mound of newly-dug earth blocked the entrance.

"Hullo!" Kahu' called, "are you in there, Ngarara? I've brought your wife."

There was a scuffling noise inside the cave, and presently the great head of the Ngarara appeared, then his shoulders, armed with their immense claws; and finally his huge body emerged from the earth.

Pukaka shrank back in horror. Used as she was to dreadful sights, the aspect of her future husband, however, filled her with terror. But Kahu' held her firmly by her skinny wrist, and stopped her from running away.

The Ngarara walked on his webbed feet into the middle of the cleared space in front of his door, where the bones of his victims lay strewn upon the ground; and sat down on his tail, like a vast featherless bird.

"So you have come," he said. "I'm glad to see you. And you've brought my wife." He spoke, of course, in his own language, which as yet Pukaka did not understand. "Isn't she a little thin?"

"Oh, no," replied Kahu'. "Besides she'll get fatter by and by."

"But isn't she rather old?"

"Dear me, no. What do you call old?"

"Well, I'm about eighty years old," said the Ngarara. "I would like my wife to be not more than sixty." He spoke of age as he knew it among the Ngarara tribe.

"She's not so old as that," said Kahu' with perfect truth. "And as to appearance, we haven't a woman like her in the pa."

"Kahu' stood Pukaka in front of the Ngarara, and turned her round and about that her husband might see all her beauties.

"I would prefer her to be a little plumper," said the Ngarara, "but I'll see if I can't fatten her up."

He held out his wings to welcome Pukaka, Kahu' led her forward and placed her on her husband's knee, the great wings enveloped her in their loving folds, and the monster's great chin rested on her shoulder.

"I take her," said the Ngarara, "I take her as my wife. My compact with her and with you shall be faithfully kept. I am now related to your tribe."

"The great creature scrambled to his feet and placed his bride on his back.

"Hold on tight to his neck," Kaku' cried to Pukaka, "he's going to take you for a short flight." The immense bat-like wings began to flap; up soared the Ngarara above the trees, above the mountains, into the blue sky. Pukaka was wedded to the Ngarara, and when a Ngarara is married the first thing is for him and his wife to go for a trip to the clouds.

Kahu' watched the bride and bridegroom till they were a mere speck no bigger than a hawk in the heavens, and then he went down the mountain.

* * * *

The new road between the two villages had been made, and Kahu' decided to go with a large body of his people to claim the lovely Koka as the reward of his toil.

The Arawa people welcomed him with a feast, after which there was a great korero, or conference.

"You all know," said Pouwhenua to the assembled people of both tribes, "why our Waikato friends have paid us this visit. We desired to have a shorter road between our two villages than the old roundabout track through the forest. But there was the Ngarara to be considered. He had made a practice of snapping up any of our people who used the lower and shorter route which skirts the raupo swamp where the country is clear of forest. Now, Kahu-ki-te-Rangi is the Ngarara's friend: he knows the reptile well: he talks the Ngarara's language. So he undertook to make an arrangement with the monster, that when the new road was open no Maori travelling between our two villages should be molested." Turning to the Waikato chief, he asked, "Now, Kahu', what have you done in the matter? You have made the road, but what about the Ngarara?"

"Well," said Kahu', rising to his feet, "my tribe has come safely by the new road—that ought to show you that there is no danger. As for the Ngarara, he wanted a wife; so I gave him our burying-woman, and he is quite contented. He promises not to eat a single man, woman, or child belonging to either of our tribes."

"But suppose he should not keep his word, what will you do then?" asked Pouwhenua.

"There are two ways of disposing of the Ngarara," replied the young chief. "Firstly, being a great priest you might makutu him with your witchcraft; secondly, I might lay a trap for him. At anyrate, I will hold myself responsible for the good conduct of the Ngarara."

"That's very satisfactory," said the old and cautious tohunga. "That's as it should be. Moreover, I understand that the Ngarara is to be employed in preying upon our enemies on the other side of the mountains."

"That is so," said Kahu'.

"Very good, then," said the priest, "we will consider the business finished. Here is my daughter—she is your wife."

Koka rose and, before the whole assembly, sat herself down beside Kahu'.

* * * *

The Ngarara had heard all about Kahu's marriage —an inquisitive weka, a bird that pokes his beak into everybody's business, had told him of the nuptials, and the great reptile determined to go down to the new road, and see the young chief's bride as she passed on her way to her new home. So putting Pukaka in his cave, the mouth of which he securely closed with a great rock, the monster waddled down the mountain by a track which he had made through the undergrowth of the forest. When he reached the valley, where there grew nothing larger than toe-toe bushes and bulrushes, he hid himself in the fringe of the forest, and awaited the arrival of the bridal party.

He had not long to wait, for soon he heard the sound of voices, and there appeared a company of women bearing babies and burdens on their backs, and talking as they walked, one behind the other in single file. After these came children, who laughed and shouted as they ran. The Ngarara looked with greedy eyes: the women, he thought, were stronger and larger than his wife, and the sight of the plump, brown children made his mouth water.

But he remembered his compact with Kahu', and allowed them to pass unmolested.

Presently Kahu' himself appeared, and, walking beside him, his wife, the beauteous Koka. She was a magnificent creature, who in the heat of the day had flung off her korowai cloak and wore only her piupiu which dangled from waist to knee; so that the Ngarara could plainly see what sort of wahine she was.

"Ah!" he said to himself, "that is Kahu's wife. Why, she is young and ten times more beautiful than the hag he gave me. Look at the roundness of her limbs! How high she holds her head! Observe the strength and life of her movements! I cannot see so much as the outline of a single bone. Kahu' has cheated me—he said that thin women were considered the most lovely, but he has taken good care not to choose such for himself. Now I know. Now my eyes are open. The rascal! the rogue! the taurekareka!"*

* A slave, a scoundrel: a term of the deepest reproach.

The last was a word his wife had taught him, but, as he spoke, Kahu' and Koko disappeared, and a band of pretty girls came in sight. They were laughing and talking merrily as they walked; each one wearing no more apparel than that which so became her mistress.

The Ngarara's eyes almost started out of his head. "Why," he said, "here are wives in abundance that he might have given me—strong, healthy girls who would be a credit to any Ngarara; but I am to be conciliated with a bag of bones. No, no, I will marry whom I please." With a great flapping of wings he rose in the air and swept down on the knot of girls, who scattered, screaming, at the apparition of so great a beast.

With one great claw the Ngarara seized the tender forms of two girls, and then he swept onward towards Kahu' and Koka.

"Run, Koka, run into the forest!" cried her husband. But before she could act on the advice, the Ngarara had swooped down and seized her, and she was borne away, screaming for help, to the monster's cave in the mountain.

* * * *

First of all Kahu' made a mighty rope, a great flax cable, fully five chains long; then he got together a band of one hundred dauntless men who feared neither man nor Ngarara.

The great cable they carried along the new road to that point where the Ngarara's private track entered the valley, and with its mighty coils they made a gigantic noose like a reef-knot, which they placed cunningly in the entrance of the track, and lashed it in position with strands of flax to the trunks and boughs of two great trees which stood on either side of the leafy aperture. One end of the cable stretched away on one side of the trap, and the other end on the side opposite. Fifty men were stationed at each rope.

"Now, are you all ready?" asked Kahu'.

"Yes, we are all ready," answered the men.

"Very good," said their leader. "I will now tell

you what you are to do. You, Kohere, will stand here beside the trap where all can see you; bearing in your hand this pole, with the tuft of flax on the top. I will go up the track alone, and when I have roused the Ngarara in his den I shall pukana* at him and insult him in the grossest manner possible. Then I shall run, and he will pursue me down the track. I shall pass through the noose, and he will follow me. Just as his head passes through the noose, you, Kohere, will drop your pole, and shout, 'Toia!' Then every man must pull with all his might, and the Ngarara will be caught."

Kahu' slowly ascended the track; carefully examining every inch of it, heaving aside stones, broken boughs, and various impediments which might trip him in his downward course. At length he emerged from the forest, and found himself in the 'clearing' immediately in front of the Ngarara's cave. A horrible sight met his gaze. On the bare ground, in front of him, lay bones of the brute's most recent victims; here lay a skull, there a limb, half-eaten and covered with dust; there a thigh-bone, and here a human foot.

"Hah! come out, you treacherous monster!" cried Kahu'. "Come out, you cowardly reptile, come out of your cave where you skulk out of sight!"

"There was a rustling sound, as though a man took a bundle of raupo† reeds and rattled them together, and the Ngarara's head protruded from the mouth of the cave.

"Oh, it's you, is it?" said the monster. "You've come to take my new wife, I suppose—you who thought to cheat me with the ugliest hag of your tribe. But I am the Ngarara: I must have as good a wife as you. You chose well for yourself, and badly for me. But I am even with you now—I have got your wife in my cave."

Kahu' advanced openly towards the reptile.

---

*Grimace. † Maoriland bulrush.

"I have come to fetch her," said he. "I have come to take her from you. First I will kill you and burn your rank body, and then I will take my wife back to my pa."

"You?" exclaimed the Ngarara, coming out of his cave. "I will break you in two with one snap of my jaws, and tear you limb from limb. After that I will eat every man, woman, and child of your tribe."

Stealthily the reptile crept forward, and then crouched for a mighty spring. But Kahu' stood his ground, and grimaced insultingly at the Ngarara, to show how little he feared.

The monster leaped. Kahu' sprang aside, and as the Ngarara reached the ground with wings and claws outstretched, the Maori fled down the track.

After him sped the reptile with great strides, his wings impeded by branches of trees which overhung the path. Down in the valley the men heard the breaking of boughs, as the Ngarara crashed through the forest, and his fierce, unhuman cries, as he pursued his prey.

Presently there was a shout, and Kohere, who was peering up the track, cried, "They are coming! Stand ready!" A naked runner shot like a spear from the forest into the open. Kohere's pole dropped, the ropes tightened with a terrific jerk, the mighty noose broke loose from the boughs to which it was tied, and the great, black Ngarara, caught round the neck, lay writhing and struggling upon the ground.

The ropes were passed round the boles of two big trees to prevent the captured monster from moving, the hundred men pulled with all their might, and before many minutes were passed the Ngarara lay stiff and dead.

Then Kahu' reascended the track. In the mouth of the cave sat Koka, crying. But as for Pukaka, nothing was ever seen of her again.

THE LITTLE ALBINO.

THE Dancer lived on a little island. He had been married to Broken Girdle some two years when he was presented with a son.

Next appeared on the scene an under-chief, named Land Breeze, who proposed a name for the boy. "You should call him The Albino," said he.

"But that is the name of our great chief," replied The Dancer. "If I call him that he will be bewitched, and my wife will be made barren."

"On the contrary," said his adviser, "the name will make your son great, and with it you will confer on him something of the mana* of his renowned namesake. As for his mother, she has nothing to do with the matter."

"Well," said The Dancer, "I will make a compromise. He shall be named The Little Albino."

We ourselves know how we resent the appropriation of our time-honoured names by poor relations. What therefore must have been the indignation of the wizard-chief who found that his semi-sacred name had been bestowed upon an underling?

But mark the working of witchcraft. First the child sickened and died; then The Dancer went a-fishing with eight companions, and his canoe was blown out to sea. It was in the early winter, and the weather was cold as well as rough. Two men were told off to bail, two were set to steer at the bow and two at the stern, and the rest plied their paddles. But that night the two bailers died of cold. In the morning their bodies were thrown overboard, and the canoe con-

---

* Prestige, greatness.

tinued to drive before the wind. Next day three men died, but as they were well-born their bodies were kept on board. The following night two more died, and The Dancer and a man named Miru alone were left alive.

The canoe was in sight of land, but the coast presented an unbroken line of breakers. However, the sharp eyes of The Dancer espied a rock, situated about half-a-mile from the shore, and to leeward of this protection he slowly worked the canoe, and dropped his stone anchor.

After a rest from his strenuous labours, The Dancer swam to the rock, up which he climbed, and from its summit scanned the shore.

The line of breakers seemed impenetrable except at one spot, where there appeared to be a gap in the white stretch of foam. Into this opening he determined to thrust the canoe.

Swimming back to Miru, he begged his disconsolate companion to eat some raw fish, the only food they possessed, but Miru demurred. However, The Dancer ate, and felt strengthened.

The anchor was hauled up, and the canoe was quickly swept into rough water. The two men exerted their full strength in guiding the craft, and eventually their efforts were rewarded by their arrival opposite a strip of sandy beach.

Upon this the canoe was quickly piled up, and dead bodies and live men were thrown into the water. But The Dancer and Miru swam ashore and were saved.

* * * *

At Motiti, as the little island was called, all was weeping and wailing. Broken Girdle would not be comforted. The women might bring her the choicest food—pigeons, fat and tender, were in season—but she would not eat. Indeed, she was in imminent danger of starving, when some boys, seeing a white parson-bird in a poporo tree which grew near the village, tried to kill it by throwing stones, but to their amazement it cried out, "How dare you try to kill The Little Albino? Go home to your mothers and tell them to whip you."

The children, filled with alarm at hearing a bird—a white bird which ought to be black—rail at them, ran helter-skelter to the kainga, where they breathlessly told their seniors of the white tui which talked. Some scoffed at the story, others laughed, and some went to the poporo tree to see for themselves, but when they reached it there was nothing to be seen except the tree with its branches and yellow berries, for the wonderful talking bird had flown.

That night, in the big wharepuni where forty or fifty people were sleeping, there was a noise which disturbed Broken Girdle, who could not sleep for thinking of her lost husband, and cried quietly to herself. The noise was as though someone were climbing upon the roof. Presently she heard a sound as though the thatch were being torn aside.

"Who's that up there?" she cried.

There was no answer.

"Who's that up there?" she repeated, and her voice awoke some of the sleepers.

"What's the matter?" asked one.

"There's somebody on the roof," replied Broken Girdle.

All lay still, and listened. But as the noise was not repeated, someone said, "There's no one there. It must have been a bird which had settled on the roof—an owl perhaps."

But the words were hardly spoken when a voice, coming from the rafters, said, "Who are you down there? What members of the tribe?"

All were silent and still, waiting to hear more. But as the voice was hushed, one asked, "Did you hear that?"

"It was among the rafters of the roof," said another.

"No, no, it was outside," said a third. "Someone thinks he is having fun in waking us up."

Then all was quiet again.

Presently the mysterious voice repeated its question, "Who are you people down there? What are your names?"

"Miro," answered one under her breath, hardly daring to reply.

"Toroa," said a man, loudly and boldly.

There was another silence.

"Is that all?" asked the voice.

"Kamokamo," said another.

"Broken Girdle," said a fourth, speaking for the wife of the lost chief.

"Indeed. And where is The Dancer?"

"We don't know. We think he is dead."

Everyone in the sleeping-house was now awake, and listened to the strange voice.

"The Dancer is not dead," it said. "His canoe was washed ashore at Hauraki. He and Miru were saved, but the seven men who were with them are dead."

"Who are you who know all this?" asked Land Breeze, who was really the originator of all the troubles of The Dancer and his wife. "Why don't you come in at the door instead of through the roof?"

"I am The Little Albino, son of The Dancer and Broken Girdle. I have come to watch over my father."

The people in the house held their breath, for the voice had swelled to a volume beyond the power of human lungs. It was the voice of a wairua, a voice from the spirit-world.

"The Dancer must be saved," it said in tones of thunder. "To-morrow you will man your largest canoe, and I will go before in the form of a white tui and guide you to where my father and Miru are cast ashore."

"The tui," whispered Toroa, "the white tui that talked to the children from the poporo tree!"

"Be quiet," said Land Breeze, "let us hear what more he has to say."

But the voice was silent. There was a rustling among the thatch of the roof, and then all was quiet."

"Are you up there?" asked Land Breeze.

"Korako-iti, Little Albino, spirit from the underworld, are you still up there?" asked Broken Girdle.

"Tell us something more of The Dancer. Tell us if he is sick, or if he is well."

But there was no reply.

"The spirit has gone," said Land Breeze. "He has gone to tell his father that we are coming."

As soon as it was evident that the ghostly visitor had departed, the sleeping-house was as full of disturbance as is a hive where the queen bee is dead. There was no more sleep that night.

Broken Girdle sat, and listened to the flood of talk; now hoping, now despairing, now thinking that the whole incident was a dream which would fade away with the approaching dawn.

* * * *

Although through the destruction of their canoe they were unable to leave the land in search of their far-off home, The Dancer and his companion had fared well. They had found some wild turnips, and had caught fish with a line of flax and a hook fashioned from a paua* shell. They had made fire after the Maori method, with a kauati and a kaureure split from bits of the wrecked canoe, and then they had journeyed along the beach in search of a village. But in that part of the country all habitations were far inland, and they found no signs of human beings on the coast, though they travelled fifty miles.

Half-dead with misery and cold, Miru could go no further. The two men had slept beneath a rough shelter of boughs, torn from the trees which fringed the shore, and in the morning they had gone down to the rocks to fish for their breakfast.

But the fish would not bite, and the two hungry men were almost in despair, when they heard a shout, and saw two figures coming towards them. These were soon followed by others, and running to meet them The Dancer and Miru were rejoiced to find themselves in the arms of Land Breeze and his companions.

After the ceremony of crying was over, The

---

* The mollusc haliotis.

Dancer asked, "How did you find us in this uninhabited country? Who guided you here?"

"Our guide was your son, The Little Albino. He brought us straight to you."

"My son? He is dead."

"The Little Albino is dead, that is true. But he became a great spirit, and has power over all the birds. As a white tui he made himself known to us, and guided us here. In the night-time he becomes a man and speaks with a voice like thunder; his companions are the rulers of the spirit-world, and his favour rests on us and on our pa. We have lost seven men, it is true; but we have gained the help of a turehu who is stronger than a hundred men. Our turehu is your son, The Little Albino. Through you we have procured an ambassador with the gods. Great is your fame, greater still is the power of your son."

When The Dancer returned home there was held a tangi as for one returned from the dead. Every member of the tribe was present except The Albino, whose spells had been so potent, but who was now as nothing compared with his namesake. Absent through fear, he lived in dread of The Little Albino, who in the spirit-world thwarted all his malevolence, and brought fame, greatness, and prosperity to The Dancer and Broken Girdle, who eventually died, full of years and honour, and were mourned by a large family and a devoted tribe.

THE TAME TANIWHA.

RAKA, the wizard-chief of Hawaiki—that mythical country which cradled the Maori race—had every reason to call himself happy. He had vanquished his enemies, who, in consequence of defeat, were emigrating to a land which had been discovered to the southward of the island of their birth; his stores of food were ample; and his new wife, The Heavenly Girl, was the most beautiful wahine in Hawaiki. And yet Raka's mind was in a state of perturbation.

It was not that he felt old age creeping over him, for, thanks to his occult influences, in spite of his seventy-six years his muscles retained their elasticity and his eyes their clearness of sight; it was not that his enemies threatened to break the compact they had made with him, for their preparations for departure were well advanced; it was because The Heavenly Girl was cold. Raka's greatness, both temporal and spiritual, did not appeal to her; whereas the youth, symmetry, and strength of The Steersman, a chief of the departing tribe, exercised an irresistible charm over her romantic mind: and with his sorceries Raka had divined his lovely wife's infatuation, though to discover the cause was quite beyond his power. Thus, therefore, may a woman's subtlety defeat the diabolical machinations of the black art. Deprived of the pleasures of revenge, the old wizard was miserable. To his uucouth endearments The Heavenly Girl made only negative responses; his outbursts of jealousy she met, woman-like, by exercising her powers of deception, his paroxysms of uncontrollable anger she assauged with exhibitions of helpless beauty, or with floods of pitiful tears which melted even the wicked heart of the cruel old sorcerer.

Married by force, The Heavenly Girl purposed from her very wedding-day to rid herself of her unbearable yoke; and she now fancied that she might attain her object. Her tribe, subdued by Raka, was about to be banished to that far southern land, of whose existence daring navigators had brought word. A great double-canoe, built for the voyage, lay moored in the landlocked bay, and out to it the emigrants were lightering in small canoes the cargo of food which was to sustain them during their venturesome voyage. The captain was a chief named Full Moon, whose ambitions, curbed as they were by Raka in the too constricted island of Hawaiki, would probably reach their fulfilment in a new country; and the pilot who by his knowledge of the stars was to guide the great canoe, named appropriately Tainui, or The Great Sea, was The Steersman, beloved of The Beautiful Girl.

At length the omens were propitious, and it was decided that the vessel should sail. Fully manned, deeply laden with a full cargo, and with all her bailers, paddlers, passengers, priests, and chiefs on board, The Great Sea cast off her moorings, hoisted her sail, and, viewed by a large concourse of people on shore, passed out of the harbour, over the horizon, out of sight—and with her went The Heavenly Girl.

But the erring wife's going was not altogether of her own choosing, for The Steersman, finding her between decks as the vessel was on the point of starting, forcibly detained her in the womb of the ship, and so carried her off to New Zealand. But it was wonderful with what ease she adapted herself to the circumstances of her abduction.

* * * *

The great canoe had left port three days when The Heavenly Girl's wizard husband, ever jealous of his beautiful young wife, instituted enquiries for her among the neighbouring villages. But eliciting no news, he had search made through the whole island; and then, finding all his investigations were in vain, he did what he should have done at first, namely, by repeating the necessary incantation he summoned his taipo, or familiar spirit.

Obedient to his master's call the taipo immediately appeared, and said, "I am here, oh great Raka. What is it you wish me to do?"

"I want my wife," said the wizard.

"Which wife?" asked the taipo—"you have seven."

"Fool!" exclaimed the wizard, "are not six of them old and ugly? What would I care if they could not be found? It is The Heavenly Girl, the most beautiful creature in the whole island, who is missing."

"It is exceedingly serious," said the taipo, as deferentially as a devil may. "But if in your wisdom you had thought of instructing me to keep a close watch upon her, I might have prevented her from running away."

"Tut, tut!" exclaimed the priest of priests, growing testy. "Don't stand there talking of what might have been. Go, and find her!"

In a moment the taipo had vanished.

For three days Raka sat in his hut and refused to speak to his remaining six wives, but on the fourth day his familiar spirit returned as suddenly as he had gone, and said, "I am here, oh wizard of wizards."

"But where is my wife?" asked Raka.

"I have found her," said the taipo.

"Then, why haven't you brought her?"

"Because I was unable to do so, great priest. The Heavenly Girl is deep in the hold of Tainui, and I could not get her. Besides, how was I to bring her back across the water?"

"I will say an incantation, and swamp the vessel," cried the furious sorcerer.

"No, no," said the taipo, "you would then kill the object of your affection. She is not to blame so much as is The Steersman, who stole her.

"The Steersman!" exclaimed the wizard. "He shall die!"

"If you will come with me I will show you where Tainui is," said the evil spirit, "and you will find your enemy, and rescue your beautiful wife."

But Raka was no sailor: he hated the sea. He loved his comfortable quarters on land, his well-cooked and delicious meals, and the indulgent life of a priestly potentate. And to his familiar's suggestion he said, "No."

"Then," said the evil spirit, "nothing can be done. The Steersman must keep The Heavenly Girl."

At the thought of such a possibility the old priest rose up and cursed the kidnapper of his wife and all the men on Tainui. But he sat down soon, and in impotent rage began to bite his fingers, for he knew that the ship was too far off to be affected by his imprecations.

Then the familiar spirit made a happy suggestion. "Why not summon your taniwha," he said.

"A capital idea," exclaimed the chief. "Why didn't you think of that before? My mind was running on canoes: I quite forgot my taniwha. Go, taipo; fetch him."

The wizard's familiar spirit vanished like a shooting star; for it was night now, and by the moon's pale light the wicked old chief walked to the sea-shore.

Before many minutes were passed a dark object appeared floating on the water, and presently the taniwha backed his enormous tail upon the coral order for full speed ahead, and the taipo, assuming strand. Raka stepped aboard of him, gave the the shape of an albatross, took wing and attended his malignant master.

* * * *

When Full Moon had with The Steersman's aid safely brought his canoe to New Zealand, he worked her up the east coast to the portage at Otahuhu, where there is a narrow neck of land, upon which the flourishing town of Auckland and its wide-spreading suburbs now stand. Here the daring mariner thought to drag his vessel overland to Manukau harbour. So his men were employed in cutting down trees, out of which rollers were made, and the women made two huge hawsers of the leaves of the ti palm. These were made fast to the great canoe, and one half of the crew manned one rope, and the rest of them the other; and the good vessel Tainui lay with her stem ashore and her stern floating in the sea.

The men started to sing a chantey such as all sailors love, and with a mighty strain on the hawsers they sought to haul Tainui out of the water; but she budged not an inch. Then the men sang louder and pulled harder, but the vessel remained fast: nothing could move her. Full Moon, standing between the two lines of men, next sang a famous song which had many a time put heart into his crew, but for all they might pull they could not move Tainui an inch upon the land.

Like all great chiefs, Full Moon dabbled in sorcery; so he now repeated an incantation for the assistance of his men, but it made no difference: Tainui stuck fast, with her bow ashore and her stern floating in the sea.

"Somebody present must have tampered with my sacredness by touching my food," exclaimed Full Moon, "or by one of the hundred ways whereby a great chief's tapu may be broken. We have a bad man among us. I think it is you," he said, pointing to The Steersman.

"Me?" exclaimed that astonished navigator. "Why, I have hauled with the best of them. But I have an incantation too, perhaps a more potent one than yours. I will go into the canoe and repeat it, and if after that the vessel does not move, you may say that it is my fault."

So The Steersman went aboard Tainui, and said a karakia to cause the sea to lift her out of the water. In the meanwhile Full Moon had ordered all the women to take hold of the ropes, and then, men and women, stirred by an uproarious song, and aided by The Steersman's potent spell, pulled all together. But still Tainui would not move so much as an inch.

Then The Steersman looked over one side of the ship, and then over the other, to see if anything impeded Tainui from being pulled ashore. Then he looked over the stern, and the people heard him utter a cry of astonishment.

"Who are you down there?" they heard him shout to somebody in the water. "What are you doing there?"

The sea began to move, and to the surface came first the head, then the body of a taniwha—and there was old Raka, whom everybody could recognise, sitting on the back of the marine monster.

When The Steersman saw the mouth of the taniwha, full of jagged teeth, he ran to the bow of the vessel, leaped upon the land, and hid himself in the bushes which fringed the shore.

But Full Moon, secure in the possession of a clear conscience, had no fear. He boarded the vessel, and, going to the stern, he said to the man on the taniwha, "Hullo! I once knew somebody very like you, but not in this country. What is your name? What do you want?"

Carefully suppressing his anger, as is proper when one priest speaks to another, Raka replied, "I want my wife, The Heavenly Girl. I am told that you have her on board your canoe, and I have come to fetch her."

"Then you are Raka!" exclaimed the flabbergasted Full Moon.

"That is my name," said the old wizard. "The Steersman stole my wife—you see, I am well acquainted with the facts of the case—and I shall not let you pull your canoe out of the water until you have obeyed my commands. First you must surrender me The Heavenly Girl, and next you must hand over The Steersman to my tender mercies—the one I shall keep for myself, and with the other I shall take the edge off the appetite of my taniwha, after his long and fatiguing swim."

So Full Moon, perceiving the wisdom of bowing to superior force, led the runaway wife to the stern of the canoe.

"Oh, my husband," she cried, "have mercy. You are the greatest wizard in the whole world: there is nothing that you cannot do. I give myself up to you; but, I pray you, spare The Steersman."

"I shall make no rash promises," replied the sorcerer. "Most certainly I shall not be satisfied till your abductor is delivered up to me. Come along."

"What! Do you expect me to get on to that horrid monster?"

"I came all the way from Hawaiki on it, and I find no inconvenience," answered her husband. "Come at once, or a worse thing will happen to you."

The taniwha put his great nose on the stern of Tainui, and The Heavenly Girl, not daring to dally longer, walked along the monster's vast back, and greeted her lawful husband in the approved Maori style by rubbing noses.

When that important ceremony was finished, Raka said, "Very good. Now I want The Steersman."

But that guilty navigator would not deliver himself up to his enemy. He ran up and down among the people, shouting, "Pull! men of Tainui! The villain Raka will steal your ship. Pull! and prove that in this new country he has no mana."

The men and women hauled on the hawsers with all their might, but Tainui moved not a fraction of an inch, for Raka's monster had fast hold of the vessel's stern. Again and again they tried, and every time they failed.

"It is of no use," said Full Moon, "we can do nothing against the strength that the taniwha has in his teeth."

"Nothing whatever," said his men.

So they dragged The Steersman on to the canoe, and cast him over the stern. Catching him in his open mouth the taniwha swallowed him at a gulp, and he disappeared for ever.

"That is quite satisfactory," said Raka. "I am appeased. You may now pull your vessel ashore."

Tailing on to the ropes the men hauled, the taniwha gave the canoe a mighty shove, and Tainui went up the beach as if she had been as light as a dinghy. Before long and with no great labour Full Moon launched his craft on the waters of Manukau harbour.

Then Raka came ashore, and placed The Heavenly Girl aboard the canoe, which set sail for Kawhia on the west coast. But the wizard tarried at Manukau in order that he might rest himself after his unique voyage, and sending his taniwha round the North Cape, as the Governor might send his yacht to-day, he journeyed down the coast in the manner in which he had come from Hawaiki.

Arriving at Kawhia the doating sorcerer rejoined The Heavenly Girl, and finding that the new land was better than the one he had left, and that her extraordinary experiences had quite domesticated his beautiful wife, Raka decided to remain in New Zealand, where he became the progenitor of a mighty tribe, the remnants of which are with us at the present day.

THE BEAUTIFUL BAD GIRL AND THE SHADOW.

THE Beautiful Bad Girl lived at the village of A Hundred Huts, but lest her name should prove misleading it is but right to state that in the opinion of her friends and relations she was more beautiful than bad. The Shadow, a handsome young chief of a powerful neighbouring tribe, was the first to fall in love with her—which was quite a natural and pleasing thing for a man to do—and yet the courting was suddenly broken off through The Beautiful Bad Girl running away to a pa named Rocky Shore, fifty miles away, where she threw herself into the arms of Eight Freckles, a chief who also had made proposals of marriage to her.

No one would expect much of a man with such a name, but whatever her expectations were The Beautiful Bad Girl was woefully disappointed, for Eight Freckles turned out to be an eater of the dearest of her relations. It happened thus: After a fight in which his taua was victorious, Eight Freckles instituted a cannibal orgie; and in his ferocity he slew and dragged to the ovens his wife's younger brother, who had ill-advisedly taken up arms against his brother-in-law and had been made prisoner. It was natural that after this the heart of The Beautiful Bad Girl should revolt from so horrible a husband.

She had been the wife of Eight Freckles a full year and had borne a son whom she had named Te Naue, when, having thus lost her conjugal happiness, her thoughts turned again to The Shadow.

This dark, mysterious person was a tohunga as

well as a chief; that is to say, he was as deeply versed in spells and devilments as he was in diplomacy and war. Whether he divined her change of heart, or whether The Beautiful Bad Girl, in keeping with her name, gave him his cue, will never be explained; but to the pa of Rocky Shore The Shadow came, and brought all his witchcrafts with him.

Etiquette demanded an elaborate reception, and this Eight Freckles gave. A great feast was prepared in The Shadow's honour, and in the korero which followed he was given the freedom of Rocky Shore, to which were attached privileges unspecified but well understood, and beside which those bestowed with the freedom of the City of London would seem insipid.

The Shadow enjoyed himself to the full. Everything that a Maori could wish was his for the asking, and, to crown all, his reputation for witchcraft and devilment reached an unparalleled height. To win that sort of fame was the Maori's deepest joy, and yet in The Shadow's cup there was room for more delight. He coveted the wife of his friend Eight Freckles.

When the Pakeha breaks the Tenth Commandment he follow methods which appear tame beside those of a tohunga. The Shadow pursued a course peculiar to himself. It was quite original.

First he went in for what priests of another cult call a "retreat." He had a hut built outside the pa, and there, speaking to no one, not even to the wahine who brought him his food, he lived a solitary, celibate life for a fortnight. Next he returned to the pa and lived in complete communion with Eight Freckles. The two chiefs talked together by the hour, as Maoris love to do.

The avowed object of The Shadow's mission to Rocky Shore was to effect an offensive and defensive alliance, and with many words the chiefs thrashed out the terms of the treaty, prior to submitting it to their respective tribes. There were fishing-rights and land-rights involved, old feuds to settle, bygone reprisals to explain away, half-forgotten genealogies to be unravelled, and imaginary intertribal marriages to be invented. This necessitated days of talk. The people, getting wind of the great business which was going forward, became acutely interested in the chiefs' discussions, and developed an inquisitiveness which soon proved inconvenient to the two great men; for the walls of a wharepuni afford eavesdroppers a golden opportunity to gratify their ruling passion. So Eight Freckles and The Shadow took to sitting under a magnificent pohutukawa tree, which spread its blossoming branches in the centre of the village. But there they were open to constant disturbance from romping children, and were put out of countenance by the groups of silent, serious people who constantly sat over against them, watching, listening, almost threatening.

"Let us go down to the beach," said The Shadow, "where we can talk in peace and without being overheard."

So to the shore the arbiters of the tribal fates adjourned, and, sitting beneath the rocky cliff, they deliberated without further interruption.

The sands ran down towards ridges of furrowed rocks, behind which the beating, incoming tides of many years had piled them; beyond the rocks the water deepened suddenly, and the ocean stretched unbroken to the horizon. Along the shore, in the immediate front of the pa, was a gap in the reefs, through which the tribe's canoes could put to sea without danger, in almost any weather.

"We shall be a strong tribe when we are united," said Eight Freckles. "First we will fight Ngati-Toa and then Ngati-Raukawa, and our fame will spread through the whole country. Nothing will be able to withstand us. You and I will be the greatest fighting-men in the three islands!"

"Ngati-Toa have fine fishing-grounds. Those will be ours," said The Shadow. "Ngati-Raukawa possess rich plantations and forests full of fruit trees, on which in summer thousands of pigeons feed. All those will be ours: we shall be able to grow tons of sweet potatoes and have potted pigeons all the year round."

"Of our prisoners we will make slaves who will do all our work for us," said Eight Freckles; "and all the tribes, hearing of our great supplies of food, will visit us, and we shall increase in numbers as well as in riches."

"We shall be the greatest of great chiefs," said The Shadow. But just at this point of the conversation his head began to itch, and he scratched his scalp violently. "I think," said he, "that I have got too many kutu. Relieve me of them, my dear Eight Freckles."

Eight Freckles took the priest's head between his hands, and acted the part of a friend and a brother. "I think I have the kutu too," he said, when he had performed his kind offices.

"Let me assist you in the same way then," suggested The Shadow.

So Eight Freckles put his head on the priest's knee, and the work of brotherly love continued.

"I think you have them badly," said The Shadow. "I'm afraid it will take a long time. There's one." And as Eight Freckles' face was hid, he could not see the priest's lips as they muttered a fell incantation. "There's another," said The Shadow, as he pulled one of Eight Freckles's ears. "I have got that." The ear became long like a dog's. He pulled out the other ear, and said, "That makes two." Both ears were now like those of a dog. Next, the tohunga passed his hand over Eight Freckles's face and pulled out his nose, and behold! his head was a dog's head. "That's nearly all," said The Shadow, "I have almost finished." Lastly, he passed his hand over his friend's body, and Eight Freckles rose up a dog, and wagged his tail.

"It is a most excellent transformation," said The Shadow. "What a great tribe we shall be. The people from far and near will come to visit us, when they hear what my enchantments have done. Eight Freckles! Oooee! Oooee!"—the dog was racing after some seagulls along the beach. "Here, you come back. Have you so soon forgotten your master? Have you forgotten your wife and son? Isn't it time you let them see that you are the rangatira of the kuri Maori, the chief of all the dogs?"

So The Shadow and Eight Freckles walked up the beach together, the one full of the importance and dignity attaching to heathen men of occult influences, and the other panting and lolling out his tongue as he ran behind.

The Shadow approached the pa by an unfrequented path which led through some thick scrub. Here he paused, and the dog looked up into his master's face, and wagged his tail. But picking up a stone the tohunga threw it at Eight Freckles, and the dog ran, yelping, out of sight. Then The Shadow entered the pa.

"So you have come back at last," said The Beautiful Bad Girl.

"Yes," replied The Shadow.

"But where is my husband? Did he not go with you to talk upon the beach?"

"I think he must have come back before me."

"No, he hasn't come yet."

"Then I don't know where he is. Perhaps he has gone for a walk. Go and call him."

The Beautiful Bad Girl went outside the pa, and called, "Eight Freckles, come here! Dinner's ready!"

But her husband did not appear.

"I think you had better call 'Oooee,' as if he were a dog," So The Beautiful Bad Girl called "Oooee," and whistled, and called again; and up ran Eight Freckles on four legs.

"Whose dog is this?" asked The Beautiful Bad Girl.

"I think he is yours," said The Shadow.

"Nonsense! I have no dog. He must be yours."

"Good dog, good dog," said The Shadow. Eight Freckles ran to the tohunga, and wagged his tail. "Now, call him by name," said the wicked sorcerer, "and see if he will answer."

"What name?"

"Call him Eight Freckles. That's what I call him."

The Beautiful Bad Girl laughed; she thought it a good joke. Holding out her hand, she called, "Freckles! Freckles! Good dog, come here. Eight Freckles! Eight Freckles!"

The dog ran up, placed his cold nose in her hand, looked up into her face, and barked.

"It is makutu!" exclaimed The Beautiful Bad Girl. "Some one has cast a spell over my husband. He is bewitched."

Without saying another word she went down to the beach, searched the sand, and followed the tracks of the two men's feet to the place where the chiefs had stopped to talk. From there she could trace but one man's footprints and a dog's. She could see that they had entered the scrub, where all further traces of them were lost. Then, I regret to say, The Beautiful Bad Girl stood with her hands on her hips, and laughed.

"I was right; it is makutu," she said. "Somebody has bewitched my husband. I know who. I know who." In a flash she had realised what had occurred, and I lament exceedingly to say that her opinion of the wicked wizard was immensely heightened, and her affection for him increased ten-fold through the prowess he had shown in devilment.

Of course, presently, The Beautiful Bad Girl married The Shadow. But I don't know what happened to the dog.

THE DEVIL THAT PLAYED CARDS.

WHARE-PONGA and the three brothers, Hongi, Mahu, and Potihi, had become inveterate gamblers, and played at euchre or poker every night.

Perhaps it may seem strange that Maoris should be fascinated by games of chance, but it will seem stranger still that a patupaiarehe from the nether regions should become a confirmed gamester.

The four Maoris used to meet in Whare-ponga's hut, which had a table in it, and as they had recently returned from Alexandra, where the brothers had received large sums through the Native Land Court, they had plenty of money to gamble with; and Nene, their sister, used to attend on them, bringing them supper and liquor, or whatever they wanted.

Hongi, Mahu, and Potihi started to play with one hundred and ten pounds, five shillings and five pence apiece, and Whare-ponga with twenty-five pounds, which he had lately received from the Government for services rendered; but it was soon evident that Whare-ponga had all the luck or was by far the most expert player, for he quickly doubled his "bank." But his companions never suspected him of sharp practice, for they had lived but little in Pakeha towns, and knew nothing of the arts of "bluffing" or of "stacking" cards. Indeed all they knew of poker and euchre was what they had learned from Whare-ponga himself, who had been a Government assessor, and had contracted all the vices of the Pakeha.

Now everyone knows that a Government assessor is a taurekareka, who serves the Pakeha with one hand—the hand in which the money is placed—and sells the interests of the Maori with the other.

But so great is the charm of a new thing to the Maori, that Hongi, Mahu, and Potihi forgot Whare-ponga's questionable conduct in the enthralling interest they took in poker and euchre; and having plenty of money, of which they did not know the full use, they played recklessly, and treated sovereigns as if they had been of no more value than pipi shells.

It will therefore be seen that Whare-ponga, "the sharper," had easy work in plucking the pigeons that had fallen into his snare. Gradually the funds of Hongi, Mahu, and Potihi grew less and less, and Whare-ponga's pile of money grew bigger and bigger, until it almost seemed that the gambling must cease through "the sharper" winning all the available cash.

The four players had sat down as usual, each with his money beside him.

"I think my pile is getting too small to play with," said Hongi. "Whare-ponga has got it nearly all."

"I've got even less," said Mahu, "but what does it matter; we can easily sell more land, and get more money. Let us begin to play."

"Very likely you will win it all back again," said Whare-ponga. "I've seen a Pakeha brought down to his last shilling, and then win in one night more than he had lost in seven," and he began to shuffle the pack, "stacking" the cards as he did so.

Of course he went on winning as usual, and this time he reduced the brothers to their last shilling.

"I'm afraid we can't go on playing," said Hongi, "we have no more money."

"Pakeha people play for other things than money," said Whare-ponga. "Of course you have not guessed it, but I am in want of a wife, and have taken a fancy to your sister. I will put down fifty pounds, and against that you will put your sister. If one of you should win you will divide my money between you, and if I win I get a wife—it is all fair and tika according to Pakeha custom."

"All right," said Hongi, after consulting with

Mahu and Potihi, though he never so much as asked the opinion of Nene, who watched the game with no anxiety, since, like her brothers, she had completely fallen under the spell of the masterful card-player.

So the game continued, and, as usual, went against the brothers.

"There," exclaimed Whare-ponga, as he took the last "trick," "your sister is mine; but I will not be greedy—I make you a present of the fifty pounds, so that we can go on playing to-morrow night," and he pushed the money across the table.

But though he could hoodwink inexperienced men, the card-sharper forgot that there were unseen spirits who, when they were on earth, had been the ancestors of Hongi, Mahu, and Potihi, and were cognisant of his evil-doing. Indeed, there was one ancestor of the brothers who had been an especially great chief, and subsequently a leading spirit in the underworld. His name was Kanokano, and, determined to protect his descendants, he despatched to Pirongia Mountain, that mysterious dwelling-place of the patupaiarehe, the demon Whaka-wiri with instructions to look after their interests.

Next night, when the gamblers had played three or four hands, a voice outside the door cried, "Let me in, let me in; I want to take part in the game."

"Come in, come in!" cried Whare-ponga: "the more players there are the better."

In answer, the door opened slowly, and a man appeared. By the light of the single candle which burned dimly in the whare, it could be seen that the new-comer was dressed in an old coat and waistcoat, and had wrapped his legs in a blanket which reached down to the ground, and as he looked round the circle of players they all noticed that he sqinted with his left eye.

"Where do you come from?" asked Whare-ponga.

"From Te Awamutu," said the new-comer. "I learnt to play cards from the Pakeha soldiers at the post there: that was where I won this coat and waistcoat and this money." As he spoke he took from one of his pockets a few coins, which he placed on the table, and sat down.

"That's not very much," said Whare-ponga.

"No?" replied the stranger. "But I started with less at Te Awamutu, and yet I won."

"We're playing poker," said Whare-ponga.

"I know the game," said the stranger. "It was playing poker that I won at Te Awamutu." And picking up the cards, he shuffled them like an experienced player, and dealt.

From the moment he began to play, the luck turned and went against Whare-ponga. Hongi, Mahu, and Potihi began to win back their money, and the assessor's heap of gold and silver grew visibly less. He tried every device he had learned from the unscrupulous Pakeha, but it was all to no purpose, for his success had vanished with the stranger's advent.

But by midnight all were tired, and Whare-ponga, as the losing player, called a halt.

"The Pakeha taught you to play well," he said to the stranger. "Did he teach you anything else?"

"Oh, yes," said the stranger; "he taught me to drink wai piro—and I found it quite easy, as you might have seen by what I have drunk to-night."

"Did he teach you to talk the Pakeha language?"

"Yes," said the stranger.

"Can you say, 'He kanohi tiwha' in English?" That means "a squint eye."

"I never learnt that," said the stranger. "That was one of the things they never taught me."

"Can you translate 'Na wai tenei haere a te po'?" ("Who ever travels in the night?")

"That's one of the things I have forgotten," said the stranger. "But I know how to say 'He tangata kino'* in the Pakeha tongue, and without waiting for a reply he gathered up his winnings, and shuffled towards the door. "Hei konei ra"† he said as he went out, and no sooner had he gained the outer darkness, than

* A bad man, a worthless fellow. † Farewell.

hwff! he disappeared like a puff of smoke.

"A very strange fellow," said Whare-ponga. "I don't know what to make of him. I think he tells lies about his having lived at Te Awamutu."

"Anyhow he can play cards," said Hongi.

"And certainly he has got some Pakeha clothes," said Mahu.

"There's no doubt at all about his cleverness," said Potihi.

"All that may be true," said Whare-ponga, "but it does not tell us who he is."

Next night the four sat down to gamble as usual.

"I wonder if the man from Te Awamutu will come," said Whare-ponga. "I'd like to have a chance to win back my money."

"It's rather strange that he did not tell us the name of his tribe," said Hongi.

"No one in the kainga knows where he spent the night," said Mahu.

"Perhaps he slept the 'bush,'" said Potihi.

"Perhaps he went back to Te Awamutu," said Whare-ponga with a laugh.

But he had scarcely spoken when a voice cried, "Let me come in! I have come to play cards. Let me come in!" and the stranger appeared.

He was dressed as on the previous night, and as he sat down he placed a pile of money on the table.

"I have come early, so as to have a good game," said the stranger. "There's my first stake," and he put a sovereign in the pool.

It didn't matter what methods Whare-ponga used, or what tricks he resorted to, the stranger always held the highest cards, and won every trick.

At last the unscrupulous assessor was beggared, and then the stranger ceased to play.

"That's enough for to-night," he said. "I think I have done very well."

"But you haven't told us where you live," said Whare-ponga.

"If you follow me you will see," said the stranger.

"Or what your name is," persisted the worsted gambler.

"My name is Whaka-wiri."

"And your tribe?"

"That is no one's business but my own," replied the stranger.

Gathering his winnings together, he tied them up in a piece of rag, placed them in his pocket, and rose to go.

"Hei konei ra," he said, as on the previous night, but, as he was nearing the door, Whare-ponga tripped him up with his foot, and he fell sprawling on the ground.

From beneath his blanket protruded a pair of cloven feet.

"A patupaiarehe!!!" cried Whare-ponga, and he seized the stranger's blanket. But the demon fled with marvellous alacrity, and hwff! he had disappeared on the wings of the wind.

"He is a devil from Pirongia Mountain," said Whare-ponga. "No wonder he won all my money."

* * * *

Nene and her brothers were frightened beyond expression by the turn which affairs had taken, but Whare-ponga, who had lived so much among Pakeha people that he had learned in a great measure to despise all visitants from the underworld, was determined to recover his money. He therefore set out for Pirongia Mountain, which, as everyone knows, is the home of the patupaiarehe when they are above ground, and is in the district of Hauraki.

Day after day and night after night, the bankrupt gambler lurked in the neighbourhood of the devils' haunt, till one evening a patupaiarehe appeared, carrying a fishing-line which was weighted with a heavy sinker. He followed him down to a river, where the demon began to fish.

When it was quite dark Whare-ponga took off his clothes, and placing his knife between his teeth, he silently slipped into the water.

He had entered the river at a point above the place where the devil was fishing, and so he merely had to float downstream till he came to the line, which he cut, and pulling up the sinker, hook, and bait, he quietly swam ashore.

"That will astonish and puzzle the patupaiarehe," he said, as he dressed himself. "He will wonder what has happened to his line." And the crafty Maori laughed silently as he stole away from the neighbourhood of the devil-infested mountain.

But a patupiarehe is not easily discomfited.

* * * *

In the morning Whare-ponga was astonished to find that the sinker consisted of melted coins, one of which, a sovereign still showed plainly the head of Wikitoria, the great Pakeha Queen.

"So this is what he wanted my money for," said Whare-ponga, "but as he won about twice as much he probably has another such sinker. I will watch for him to-night also."

The patupaiarehe came as before to fish in the river, and repeating his trick, the Maori stole the demon's remaining sinker, which proved like the first to be made of gold and silver.

It was true that the unmelted sovereign had disclosed to Whare-ponga the purpose to which the demon had put his winnings; but the patupaiarehe was able to discover quite as easily that it was the card-sharper who had stolen his sinkers, for the Maori had dropped beside the river the tobacco pipe which he had smoked all the time he had played cards, and the demon easily recognised it as belonging to the Government assessor.

But the devil Whaka-wiri had no intention of trying to win back his melted money. He had in store a far more terrible revenge for the thief. Disguising himself again, he hovered about the kainga, whither Whare-ponga had returned in triumph, and marked surreptitiously the movements of the gambler's girl-wife.

Nene was glad that the card-playing was over, and had persuaded her brothers and husband to set about planting seed for the late potato-crop, so that they might have plenty of food in the winter-time. So the men gave up dissipation and turned to labour, and worked industriously till one day as they were digging, and Nene was cooking their dinner at the edge of the field, Whare-ponga saw a man appear from the scrub and commence to talk to the girl.

"That's some fellow who wants to have kai with us," he thought. "It's a good thing there is plenty for all."

But to his astonishment he saw the stranger go up to Nene and hongi with her.

"He must be one of your relations," said Whare-ponga to the brothers, and he started to walk across the broken ground of the potato-field towards the cooking-place, to see who the man was who had rubbed noses with his wife.

But before he had gone ten yards, the strange man had put his arms round Nene, and hwff! he rose with her on the wings of the wind, and sped in the direction of Pirongia Mountain.

"Hold! Catch him! Stop him! The patupaiarehe is stealing my wife!" But call as Whare-ponga might, and though all three brothers ran to intervene, nothing could stop the demon, and the astonished husband saw his wife vanish through the air.

But who can sympathise with a Government assessor, who takes his pay with one hand, and with the other sells the interests of the Maori?

THE FLAME AND HER TWO HUSBANDS.

RANGI had fallen hopelessly in love with The Flame, who lived at Waitara, where a white man's town now stands.

But love-sick men are common and pretty girls are rare, especially pretty girls possessing that strange quality called mana, which is not exactly reputation, or position, or wealth, but a compound of these, blended with the power of managing the genus homo. The Flame, however, was not only renowned for her beauty among all the tribes about Mount Egmont, whose great cone stands sentinel beside the sea; but, in her own pa and among her own people, she was famed for the manner in which she managed her grim old father, Little Tu, the bloodthirsty chief of Waitara.

Now, Little Tu's principal fighting-man, Wind-in-the-Tree, was also hopelessly in love with The Flame, and he had the great advantage of being on the spot, whereas his rival, Rangi, lived fifty miles away, at Hawera. But, on the other hand, Wind-in-the-Tree laboured under the disadvantage of being detested by the object of his passion; so that the odds seemed even between the two warrior-suitors.

The Waitara man made the first move. He demanded of Little Tu that he should be requited for his services, and with an eloquence born of love he pleaded for possession of The Flame.

"Am I not your fighting-chief?" he asked of Little Tu. "Have I not been conqueror in five battles? If I am not good enough for your daughter, I will attach myself to some other tribe where I shall be better appreciated."

"No, no, don't do that," said Little Tu. "Don't

think of such a thing. We will see what can be done."

"I must have your daughter—nothing else will satisfy me."

"Yes, yes, I am quite agreeable. I should like you to have her. But she is so imperious that I no longer am able to control her."

"I will control her."

"You could, of course you could—you are so much more masterful than I. Let us call her, and see if you can persuade her."

So saying, Little Tu fetched The Flame from her hut, but neither her father nor her lover could divine from her pretty, oval face, or from her winsome, girlish manner the thoughts of her heart.

"We have been having a little talk about you, my dear," said Little Tu. "The fact is that we both think you should be married. And as for your husband, The Wind, here, thinks that he would make as good a husband as you could find, and I quite agree with him. Indeed, he has conceived quite a fancy for you, and nothing would make him happier than that you should return it, and I hope you will."

"But what if I don't?" asked The Flame.

"My dear," said her father, "that would be girlish foolishness; you would love him warmly enough after you were married to him."

"Though I may be fierce in war," said the fighting-chief, bridling ferociously, "I would show you how tender and affectionate I can be in love," and he smiled evilly.

"But haven't you got three wives already?" said the girl. "Isn't that enough?"

"They are low-born women," said the fighting-chief. "I want a well-bred girl for my principal wife. They are ugly. I want a beautiful wife who will give me beautiful children."

Little Tu smiled with delight—such a manner of courtship pleased him. But his daughter turned away in disgust.

As she walked towards her hut, her father called

her petulantly.

"Let me tell you," he said, "I have decided that you shall marry my friend The Wind, here. I consider it a most suitable match."

"But what if I don't agree with you?" asked the girl. "What if I won't consent?"

"I wouldn't answer for the consequences," replied her father.

"I would," said the fighting-chief. "I can tell you exactly what would happen. You have been given to me: I am very fond of you, and will treat you with every kindness. But if you don't consent willingly, I will take you by force. And in the circumstances, that would be good tikanga and perfectly correct."

"Perfectly correct," said Little Tu, "even if it were a thing to be regretted." He looked at his daughter; his daughter looked at the ground.

"Very good," said the girl; "but I want ten days in which to prepare myself. After that, if nothing occurs to change my mind, I will consent."

For six days the village talked of nothing but the match, but on the seventh Rangi arrived with five hundred men, and the subject of conversation was changed. The Flame had sent a messenger to warn the Hawera chief of her impending fate, and his response had been immediate and remarkable.

Of course Little Tu was obliged to treat his visitors with every hospitality, or a feud would certainly have ensued; and, moreover, it would have been contrary to etiquette for him to have asked them when they intended to leave. He had to stand by and see them eat him out of house and home, out of whare and kainga, if they so pleased; which was just what they proposed to do.

At first The Flame kept herself in the background, but before long Rangi pointedly asked her father, "Have you not a daughter, a beautiful girl whom I saw when last I was here? Where is she?"

"Yes, I have a daughter, but she would not be called beautiful," replied Little Tu.

"I would like very much to see her," said Rangi.

So Little Tu had to fetch his daughter, though, on the way, he instructed her to show nothing but the severest politeness to his visitor; and though the girl complied openly with her father's wish, she secretly informed Rangi through her hoa takapui—that peculiar Maori institution, the walking-about friend—that her coldness was merely assumed.

The merry go-between treated the strangers as familiarly as if they had been her brothers.

"What fine fellows you Hawera men are," said she to Rangi. "How many more such warriors have you got at home?"

"About three hundred," answered Rangi.

"You must be a big tribe."

"We are."

"You should have brought a bigger taua—my mistress wishes to see all your people."

"They are coming," said Rangi. "I expect another body of men to-morrow."

"It will be a great honour to entertain them. My mistress will be delighted. But have you no women and children?"

"Plenty."

"Then send for them."

"By and by," said Rangi.

When the whole of the Hawera forces had assembled, it dawned upon Little Tu that he was practically in Rangi's power.

"You have a great many men here," he said.

"Yes, a good number," said Rangi.

"I had no idea that you were a man of such power."

"No? There are many chiefs greater than I."

"Hawera and Waitara should be friends after this," said Little Tu.

"That is what I came to effect. You have a daughter. She and I have formed a great liking for each other. Of course you would not object to our marriage—it would unite our tribes."

"It would," said Little Tu, "but much as I admire my daughter, there are women here whom you might like better."

"I have seen them all. I prefer your daughter."

"That is unfortunate, because my fighting-chief has asked for her."

"Tell him that when he comes to Hawera I will give him the prettiest girl in the kainga."

The old chief was ominously silent. Evidently the proposal did not please him. Without another word he walked down to the water, where the men were getting ready to go on a fishing expedition.

The fighting-chief was on the river-bank directing the canoe-men.

"Rangi has asked for my daughter," said Little Tu, taking his tattooed friend aside.

"That is why he has collected his men here," said the fighting-chief. "But we will send to every hapu round the mountain and collect double his force."

"It is too late. He will act before our friends can come; and, further, we have no food for such a gathering—we cannot ask our friends to come here and starve. These Hawera men have eaten up everything."

"Are we not going out to catch fish?"

"We have no sweet potatoes to eat with them. But I have a plan. If you will be content to let Rangi have my daughter, in six weeks she shall be yours for ever."

"You are talking nonsense," said the fighting-chief. "You have given in to the wish of the girl through fear of the Hawera man."

"I am talking like a wise tohunga. Rangi is too strong for us now; but in six weeks my daughter will be free to marry you."

"If you intend to kill Rangi you must prepare for war."

"Kill Rangi? I shall not kill him; but in six weeks the girl will be your wife."

* * * *

The marriage had taken place, and the Hawera people were about to return home.

Rangi, who at the farewell gathering of the two tribes had made a speech on behalf of himself and his people, now addressed his own men.

"This has been a great occasion," he said. "This visit to Waitara will never be forgotten by us. As you return you must spread through all the tribes the fame of Little Tu and his people, renowned for their hospitality, their abundance of food, the bravery of their men, and the beauty of their women. All these things are evident. We have eaten their food—it is good: so great is their bravery that I am determined Waitara and Hawera shall be at peace: and as to their women—I have taken one for a wife.

"But my wife so loves her father and her father so loves me, that he has persuaded me to stay here a little while longer; therefore you will return home without me, but I will rejoin you before the summer is ended, when the time for digging the crops has come. Then, when we have plenty of food, I will bring my wife and all her hapu, and we will empty our storehouses that our guests may feast."

* * * *

Rangi had been wrapped in connubial bliss three weeks, when he went a-fishing. He said that as he had helped to empty the storehouses of Waitara it was but right that he should aid in replenishing them.

"You are a good man," said his father-in-law. "You are the sort of man we want in this tribe, a man who understands the wisdom of having plenty of dried fish."

"Won't you come too? We shall then catch plenty, for you have the spell which will enable us to catch fish."

"I am too old," said Little Tu. "But you shall have a picked crew, and I will stand on the cliff and say the karakia for catching the hapuku, the kahawai, and the big shark. I will stand and repeat my incantations, and you will sit in your canoe and catch the fish. I could not help you more if I were with you, miles out upon the sea."

At the river-side all was ready; the canoe was manned, and the food, bait, and fishing tackle were all aboard. Little Tu led his son-in-law to the water's edge, told him that he would be sure to catch plenty of fish, bade him adieu in his own heathenish, Maori way; and Rangi boarded the canoe, dropped down the river, crossed the bar, and made straight for the fishing-grounds.

On shore, the old necromancer smiled malignantly as he walked slowly towards the edge of the cliff, from which he could view the broad expanse of the North Taranaki Bight; in the canoe, Rangi was observing his motley crew. One man was blind in his left eye, another was lame, another had hakihaki and his body was full of sores, a fourth was a porangi who talked nothing but nonsense and waved his paddle in the air, a fifth was deaf, a sixth was hunchbacked—a strange crew with which to go a-fishing.

On the cliff, the crafty old tohunga chuckled to himself, "I will pray for fish, I will pray for wind; he shall catch fish, he shall catch the storm." On the sea, Rangi was saying to himself, "Why am I given such a crew as this? Little Tu knows—he wants to show the strength of his incantations. He has lent me the hook of his ancestor Tunui"—Great Tu—"a hook that never fails. I shall catch plenty of fish."

"He thinks he has the hook of Great Tu," said Little Tu, at the edge of the cliff. "Ho! ho! it is the hook which the Waikato people made from the thigh-bone of his own grandfather—for him an unlucky hook."

The old wizard watched the canoe till it was but a speck upon the waters, and then he began his karakia.

Now a karakia is to Pakeha minds a thing ridiculous, but to the Maori it is fraught with magic powers, benign or malignant, as the case may be.

The old priest, with arms extended and head

thrown back, first said the karakia for charming "the mountain wind," which blows suddenly from off the great peak of Mount Egmont and lashes the sea into foam—a most effective wind for swamping a canoe. Next, he repeated the karakia which should stir up the north-west wind, and render the Waitara bar impracticable to canoes and fill the river-mouth with breakers. Then he applied his secret formula to the south-west wind, which brings hissing, driving rain, and lashes the lower slopes of the great mountain with salt spray. He conjured all the winds of heaven to blow upon Rangi's canoe, and when he had finished he said with satisfaction, "There! Let the strongest wind prevail. I have not called one, I have not called two: I have called all. Each wind will come, and being angry at the presence of the others it will blow the harder. We shall have the sea turned into a whirlpool, and Rangi will go to the bottom. But I will tell his people that his death was accidental. If his body is washed ashore we will make a big tangi over it, and The Wind—ha! ha! 'The Wind:' it is peculiar—shall marry my daughter."

At first a gentle puff of wind, speeding from the hills, struck the soft bosom of the sea and ruffled its serenity. It was like the scout, active and light, who goes before an army. Soon there was a roar like thunder, as the "mountain wind" burst through the forest-land from the far top of Taranaki and churned the sea into foam.

As Little Tu watched the working of his witchcraft a smile of satisfaction overspread his brown and tattooed features. He saw the squall strike the canoe—and after that there was no canoe to see. But far out upon the ocean he marked that the north-west wind, responding to his call, had scattered the land squall, and was rushing towards the coast. The great breakers burst upon the shore and dashed their foam to the top of the cliff on which he stood.

"Ha! my spells are potent," he exclaimed, as the gale sported with his grey hairs, and almost blew his flax cloak from his body. "They are stronger than an army. I spoke—the winds came: they blew—and Rangi's canoe is no more. I am a great tohunga."

It was of no use for the old man to watch longer—the salt spray and the driving rain obscured his view. So, turning his face towards the kainga, Little Tu sought the warmth and comfort of his whare.

* * * *

Thus it was that The Flame was given to the fighting-chief, and lived in the hut which Rangi had left. At first the girl expostulated with her father, who answered, "Rangi was a good man, but he is dead; he was a brave man, but he is now in a fish's belly at the bottom of the sea. Think no more of him."

"But suppose he came back some day, what then?"

"Yes, when we take our next catch of blue shark," replied her father, with a horrible chuckle.

But Rangi was always in the girl's thoughts. She would pace the beach near the village, hoping to meet him. In the night she would wake with a start, and say, "I thought I heard some one call. Perhaps Rangi has come back." So that her new husband hated the phantom Rangi as deeply as he had abominated the real one, and knew that though he was now absolute master of The Flame, the girl still pined for her first love.

One night, as the fighting-chief lay asleep with his wife by his side, and the silence of the starlit heavens rested on the kainga, suddenly The Flame awoke, and cried, "Somebody put his hand on me. There is some one in the hut. It is Rangi! He is here; I felt his touch."

"Go to sleep," said her husband. "Rangi is inside some great shark at the bottom of the sea."

"He is here. He came into the hut and placed his hand on my body, on my face, to feel if I, his wife, were here."

"He was drowned by Little Tu's incantation. He is at the bottom of the sea. The fish have eaten every bit of him."

"He is alive. He returned here, but when I moved he left the hut. If you are not a coward, get up, and see if he is outside."

In desperate fear the fighting-chief arose. If a spirit from the underworld were troubling his wife, he would rush back into the hut before it caught him; if a man, he would kill him. Seizing his taiaha—a species of wooden sword—he crept outside. All was still and silent. First he examined one side of the hut: there was no one there. He examined the other side: no one was hiding there. He was about to search the back of the hut, when he came face to face with a man, who, quick as lightning, gripped him by the throat before he could so much as cry out.

"I am at the bottom of the sea? I am in the fish's belly? And you take my wife? Take that!" and the hard edge of a stone mere was plunged into the side of the fighting-chief's head, and his skull cracked like an eggshell.

Without even a groan he sank to the earth, but the hand at his throat relaxed only when the last throb of life had died out of his quivering frame.

Then Rangi entered the hut.

"I knew you would come!" said his wife, holding out her arms in the dark. "I knew you were safe!"

"The storm almost drowned me, but my incantation was strong: it made the wind my friend, and the canoe was blown into Hua-toki. When I returned here, I came to your hut, I felt your face, I said, 'This is my wife, but there is a man lying in the hut with her.' Full of grief, I went out. By and by that man came to kill me, but he is dead. Tell me, who is he? What is his name?"

"My father thought you were drowned, and forced me to marry his fighting-chief."

"Instead of that I have been to Hawera, and have returned alive. Come, I will take you to my people—

three hundred of them are waiting for me outside the pa."

Thus was The Flame restored to her first husband, come back as from the dead.

FISH-HOOKS.

RUSHING River, the owner of the hook Taka-tahi, did not begin the trouble. He was really a most innocent person, and his connection with the celebrated instrument for catching fish was merely that of a beneficiary. He had inherited it from his father, who had inherited it from his father, who had inherited it from his father, and so on ad infinitum.

The true cause of the vendetta was the selfishness and ambition of Rea, the principal chief of Wakatu, as the Maoris called the place where the white man's town of Nelson now stands. His pa was situated at the mouth of the harbour, where shipyards and wharves now line the shore, and his co-chief, The Earthquake, had built his pa on the little hill where a wooden cathedral now rears its shingled spire in the centre of Nelson City.

It was the custom of the two "hapus," or divisions of the tribe, to go share and share alike after the communistic fashion of Maoriland. Rea had collected a great store of dried eels, dried shark, potted pigeons and edible parrots; The Earthquake had grown quantities of sweet potatoes, and had prepared much fern-root. So that conjointly they had abundance.

When The Earthquake saw how full Rea's storehouses were, he said, "That's all right. That is very good. We shall have plenty of food for the winter."

"Yes," said Rea, "and when visitors come from Motueka, from Waikawa, or from Takaka, we shall be able to feast them sumptuously, and we shall get a great name for our hospitality."

"That's so," said The Earthquake. "My sweet potatoes will go well with your potted pigeons and dried fish."

"Very well indeed," said Rea.

Soon after this conversation occurred, the people of Motueka, which is on the other side of Blind Bay, visited The Earthquake's hapu. A messenger was immediately sent to Rea, to tell him that a big taua had arrived overland from Motueka, and to ask him to send twenty full loads of dried fish, eels, and pigeons.

When the messenger returned, The Earthquake said, "Well, is the food coming?"

"No," answered the messenger. "Rea says he will want his food when his own visitors come."

"But that will never do!" exclaimed the Earthquake. "I have only got vegetables to give these people."

"Rea says 'Fill them with plenty of sweet potatoes, and then they will soon go away.'"

Now, the soul of the Maori's social life is hospitality. It is a compliment to be eaten out of house and home by your visitors; it is the depth of dishonour to force a strictly vegetarian diet upon your friends. It will be understood, therefore, that The Earthquake's vexation was of the greatest: already he saw himself stripped of his prestige, a mean and contemptible fellow with whom no well-bred person would associate; and he cursed Rea from the bottom of his heart.

In two days the visitors had tired of their poor fare. "This man is no chief," they said. "He has no food; he gives us nothing but sweet potatoes. He is a poor fellow. It is time we moved on." On the third day they went down to Rea's pa beside the sea, where they received a great welcome.

They were served with piles of the choicest food—tender pigeons, delicious eels, dried fish, hapuku, rock-cod, garfish, butter-fish—and Rea was voted a good fellow, a great chief, a man who deserved to have many friends. But the adulation had no good effect upon the recipient. Taking himself and his co-chief at the estimation of the visitors, Rea made so bold as to send a party of people by night to The Earthquake's plantations, and carry off half his crop of sweet potatoes.

After that, relations were strained between the two "hapus."

We now come to the second stage of the story. Rea had a son named Long Girdle, a youth of sixteen. "It's time you got married," said the father to the son. "Make a tour of the neighbouring tribes, and see if you can suit yourself." So Long Girdle went to Takaka, ostensibly to enjoy the fishing, but really to look for a wife.

And this is where Rushing River, owner of the famous fish-hook Taka-tahi, is formally introduced to the reader. He was a benevolent, tattooed old gentleman, passionately fond of fishing, the father of a most beautiful daughter.

Out they sailed upon the glittering waters of Golden Bay—the young man, Rushing River, the girl, and a stalwart crew. When they reached the fishing-ground they let go the anchor, which was a heavy stone with a groove cut round it, and got out the lines. Long Girdle was in the stern of the canoe, with the girl beside him; Rushing River was amidships. All the lines were quickly set, and the fishers were waiting for the fish to bite.

Suddenly Rushing River's line drew taut. "Ha!" he cried, as he drew it in hand over hand, "I have caught the first fish. Hold him, Taka-tahi. Be strong, my good hook! Keep your hold on his jaw, Taka-tahi! Don't let him go!"

Rushing River landed his fish, a big hapuku, and called on all men to admire his skill. But there was a groaning in the stern of the canoe; Long Girdle had been taken ill suddenly. He was holding his hands to his stomach, and rolled from side to side in great agony.

"What's the matter?" asked the old chief.

"Oh! Ah! Oh!" groaned the youth. "I am ill. I feel bad inside. I am going to die."

"Haul up the anchor," ordered Rushing River; "our visitor is too ill to fish. We must get back to the pa and fetch the tohunga to charm away the evil. It would never do for the son of the great chief of Wakatu to die on our hands. Pull for the shore."

Long Girdle was in great pain when he landed; he was in greater pain still after the priest had pronounced incantations over him. He begged to be taken home.

"Launch your swiftest canoe," he said to Rushing River; "man it with your strongest crew, and take me back to Wakatu before I die."

As was to be expected, Rushing River showed the generous feeling of a true Maori: he himself brought the sick youth to Wakatu, and that without delay.

The entrance to the harbour is narrow, and the people lined the shore as the canoe, with the eight-miles-an-hour tide behind it, shot through the gut. They saw their chief's son lying in the stern; they saw him carried ashore to his father's house, and they wondered what sad mischance had happened.

Rea followed his son into the house, where crying women crowded round the couch of the invalid. When the youth saw his father appear, he said, "Send these women away—they make too much noise."

"Oh, my boy," cried the chief when he was alone with his son, "what evil has befallen you that you come back to me in this state? What malevolent priest has bewitched you? Our tohunga shall say charms over you, and I will tell him to drive away the wicked spirit that has taken hold of you. Oh, my son, do not die, do not die!"

"Die?" said Long Girdle, rising from his bed, and smiling. "Die? I am not even ill. I haven't the smallest pain. I am as well as you are. But I have reached home safely, and I have delivered the villain, Rushing River, and two dozen of his men into your hand."

"Eh? What?" exclaimed his father. "What does this mean? I don't understand. One moment you are groaning with pain, and the next you are laughing. How does this come about?"

"I was in the canoe, fishing," replied his son,

"and Rushing River hooked a big hapuku. 'Hold him fast, Taka-tahi,' he cried. 'You were a good warrior when you were alive: be a good hook now you are dead.' 'Taka-tahi?' I said to myself. 'Taka-tahi was my ancestor. Have his bones been made into fish-hooks by this vile fellow?' And I at once thought of a plan to avenge my forefather. I have brought Rushing River into your hands, and you can wreak your vengeance on him."

"Ah!" exclaimed the chief with deep feeling. "So that is it? He has made fish-hooks of my ancestor. Very good. I will make cinders of this man's flesh and fish-hooks of his bones. You are a good lad, a clever lad; you will become a chief with more fame than your father himself."

Then Rea went out, and welcomed Rushing River and his men with a great display of hospitality. He caused to be served up to them some of the much-coveted birds preserved in their own fat, dried eels, and large quantities of sharks and other fish. And when his guests were feasting, he walked up to the pa upon the little hill, and asked to see his brother-chief.

The Earthquake came sullenly, and when Rea had unfolded his design and had asked for help in executing it, the other said, "What! help you to kill two dozen men? Are you so weak that you are frightened of two dozen men? I thought you were a great chief."

Rea resorted to persuasion, but The Earthquake remained firm. "No," he said, "you refused me food for my guests. You sent men by night and robbed my plantations. Now you have grown fat on my root-crops; you have grown strong with all the eels and fish you have caught; take, then, your brave warriors, a hundred, or two hundred of them, and fight these twenty-four men of Takaka. If you overcome them it will be a great victory." And, so saying, The Earthquake left Rea in scorn and strode towards his hut.

But that night there was a savage tragedy performed in the pa beside the sea-shore. At midnight great bundles of toetoe—a plant not unlike pampas grass—were piled round the hut in which the Takaka men slept and ruthlessly set on fire. As the terrified victims fled from the burning whare, they were killed in cold blood by the Wakatu men who stood around.

Thus was payment exacted for the matter of the fish-hook. Rushing River, when he was alive, used to say, "Ah, Taka-tahi was a great man—look how the hook made from his thigh-bone catches me fish. My forefathers got all his fame, and I have got theirs. I also have the hook. I am greater than Taka-tahi ever was." So Rea took the dead chief's bones, and from them made full a dozen hooks, and said, "Now things are as they ought to be. Rushing River had my ancestor's mana as well as his own; now I have taken it all from him. I am the greatest chief in the three islands." So it will be perceived how the vendetta grew deeper and more deadly.

* * * *

It was a lovely winter day. All was peaceful in Wakatu. The serene atmosphere enwrapping the distant azure hills lay undisturbed by so much as a breath of air. The smoke from the cooking-fires rose gently towards the placid heavens; mountain and forest, shore and sea lay tranquil under the still repose of the midwinter calm.

A solitary messenger, traversing the Waimea plain, came over the low inland ridge of hills into The Earthquake's pa, and changed the prevailing quietude into mad unrest. "Watch," said he, "the calm, blue surface of the sea where it stretches across to Motueka. Look at the advancing canoes of my tribe."

To the seaward fringe of the encircling hills the local chief repaired, and saw six small dots far out upon the sea, and marked them develop into long, thin canoes which landed on the beach, two miles away. Along the sands stole men like ants, and so round concealing cliffs approached the avenging force.

Below, Rea's people were disporting in the waters of the harbour. Children ran along the shore; women stood round the cooking-fires; men lay recumbent on the sand, telling each other tales of daring deeds: when round the projecting cliff swept a compact column of vindictive warriors, fully armed. There was a rush, a complete surprise, the slaughter of men, the capture of women; and one solitary figure fled inland to The Earthquake's pa. It was that of Rea, the cause of all the bloodshed. He cast himself on the mercy of the man he had hated, he craved protection from him whom he had wronged.

What shall be done with Rea, who killed the guests of his tribe? Run, Rea, into the toetoe and flax which fill the swampy valley between the hills; flee to the uninhabited forest which covers the great mountains. But it is of no avail. He is caught while crossing the river where he so often caught the savoury eel, not far from the very plantations he had robbed.

Let the sequel be brief.

This is a story of fish-hooks. The prestige of Rea was bound up with the fish-hook fashioned from the bone of his ancestor. It is the fate of his family—into fish-hooks also shall his bones be made.

[illegible] without his aid or consent.

[illegible]

[illegible] if he [illegible]

THE ANGEL-WIFE.

ORNAMENTS was the handsomest man of his tribe, and his mind, as that of a young chief should be, was set on nothing but sport and warlike exercises. For the love of woman he cared nothing, to him girls were beings who did the cooking and made themselves useful about the kainga; that they were intended for higher things was an idea which had not intruded itself into his philosophy.

This indifference to the sex was extremely hard on Marino, the belle of the tribe, who had never lost an opportunity of showing her affection for Ornaments ever since they had played together as children. In those days he had shown some sort of regard for her, but now it was simply, "Marino, I am going to catch pigeons: pack me some food in a basket," or "I intend to fish to-morrow: get some girl to help you, Marino, and bail out my canoe—it is half full of water afte yesterday's rain—and see that my lines are in good order." On none of his expeditions did he ask her to accompany him.

When his mother perceived her son's ripening manhood she at once had set about finding him a wife. But when she would say to him, "Ornaments, I have seen the prettiest kotiro, and a big chief's daughter, too, Te Tuna, of Ngapuhi," he would say, "I hope, mother, you have seen that the food-baskets are ready—the war-party leaves in two days, and we must take plenty of food with us." If she said, "Ornaments, have you noticed Marino? how pretty she has grown? how fond she is of you?" he would answer, "I want you and her to make me a new kiwi cloak, a long one which will reach down to my feet—to-morrow I intend to go and hunt for the birds, and will fetch the feathers from which you can make it."

Food, fishing, hunting, fighting, these seemed the objects of his life: but a sudden change came over Ornaments. The men might go a-fishing, but he stayed in his whare and slept. A fighting-party might prepare to wage war against the tribe's enemies, but he paid not the slightest attention to the drilling of the men.

His father, Great Heaven, the old and grizzled chief of the tribe, expostulated with him for such lethargy, but all the youth said was, "I have an inclination to sleep; leave me alone. I will fish when the spirit moves me, I will fight when the proper time comes; but for the present I will sleep." And he kept his word. He slept day after day, never stirring from his hut where his patient mother and the devoted Marino brought him his meals.

"Maro," said Great Heaven to his wife, "our boy has got the makutu—some wizard has bewitched him."

"No," replied the mother, "he is in communion with the spirit-world. He will surprise us all some day. Mark my words. He speaks to no one, not even to Marino and myself."

The people said, "We thought to see this boy stand beside his father and become a great chief, a skilful leader in war, but he is a lazy fellow who does nothing but sleep." And as for Marino, she thought he was sick, pouri, as she called it, and she redoubled her attention to his welfare.

* * * *

The pa was as still as the night, not a sound was to be heard save for the gentle sighing of the wind. Ornaments lay wrapped in the deepest sleep within his hut. Suddenly there came a knocking at the panel of his door. At first it was gentle, but grew louder and louder, till at last the sleepy youth awoke, sat up in bed, and cried, "What do you want? Who's there? What is all this noise about?"

But there was no answer.

Ornaments arose, pushed back the sliding panel of the door, and looked out. He saw no one.

Then he lay down again, after putting the peg in the door, that he might not be disturbed.

But no sooner was he asleep again than there came a rapping at the panel of his window, and, awakened a second time, he cried angrily, "Go away, and leave me alone. What do you want to wake me for?"

The panel of the window was pushed aside by an unseen hand, but Ornaments could discover nothing in the gloom. He ran to the door and put his head and shoulders out of the hut, but all he saw were the dim outlines of the huts round about. So he went back to bed, fully determined to keep awake and watch for the person who disturbed his rest. But again an uncontrollable drowsiness came over him, and soon he fell fast asleep.

Then there came a gentle rattle at his window, the panel was pushed aside, and the spectral form of a woman entered the hut. Seizing the korowai and kiwi mats which covered the sleeper, this ghostly visitor disappeared with them by the way she had come.

Ornaments awoke with a start, to find himself naked and cold. Sleep was now successfully driven from his eyes: he would watch till morning for the thief who had so impudently entered his hut. But he did not watch long, for the first faint streak of dawn soon appeared above the tall trees which surrounded the pa, and Ornaments thought he would see nothing more of his visitor.

When Maro brought her son his breakfast as usual, she was surprised to see him sitting naked on his bed.

"Where is your korowai?" she asked. "Where is the mat of kiwi feathers which Marino and I made for you?"

"They have been stolen," said Ornaments. "Some thief came, and took them in the night while I slept."

"Who was it?"

"Can I see in the dark? Who gave me eyes to see like a bat? How should I know who the thief is?"

"To-night," said his mother, "put the peg in both window and door, and watch for him. And if he comes again, rush out and throw him down. Then we shall know who the thief is, and what tribe he belongs to."

Ornaments slept during the day, to be wakeful at night; but no sooner had the sun gone down than he was overcome by an unconquerable drowsiness. Do what he would he could not keep his eyes open.

The window and door were both shut tight. Everything was still. The young warrior's hand, which held a keen mere as he fell asleep, dropped limply to his side. Suddenly there was a rustling, and without door or window moving there appeared in the hut the figure of a woman, who kneeling beside the sleeper, shook him by the arm, and said,

"E oho! E oho!" (Wake up!)

Ornaments moved in his heavy sleep, and rolled over on his side.

"Maranga! Maranga!" (Get up!)

The young warrior sat up, and rubbed his eyes. He felt a soft hand laid on him. In a moment he caught the intruder in his strong arms, to find that he held a woman.

"Ko wai koe?" (Who are you?)

"Ko ahau." (I am I.)

"He aha to hiahia?" (What do you want?)

"I haere mai au kia moe taua." (I have come to be your wife.)

"Ae!" (Indeed!)

Thus was Ornaments married.

* * * *

In the morning when the bridegroom's mother came to the hut she found it tightly shut up, with cloaks hung before the window and door to keep out all light, and to prevent people from looking through the crevices.

She knocked on the panel of the door, and shouted to her son, but received no answer.

"He is sleeping more soundly than ever," she said.

However, in the afternoon Ornaments came out of the hut of his own accord, and went straight to his mother.

"Well?" she said.

"Well," said he.

"Did you catch the thief?"

"I did," he answered.

"And who was he?"

"It was a woman."

"A woman!"

"I have her in the hut at the present moment."

"What is her name?"

"I don't know."

"What tribe does she belong to?"

"I don't think she has a tribe."

"Then who is she?"

"I think she is a spirit from heaven. She came into my hut in the middle of the night without opening window or door, and stayed with me, and we are man and wife."

"My son, you have been dreaming."

"Then my dream is very real. Come, and see the woman for yourself."

When Maro entered the hut, she saw sitting there the most beautiful being she had ever beheld, a graceful, gracious creature, who rose and said, "I have come to be your son's wife—he is in great favour with the gods, who have sent me. In three days I shall bear a son, who will be half a man and half a god, and he shall teach your tribe everything about the spirit-world. He shall be above all priests that ever lived, and shall have power over everything in the world. Great is the favour granted to your son and to you, his mother. But remember," she said, turning to her husband, "if you find any fault with our son, or complain of his crying while he is a baby, that very day I will take him away, and you shall see him no more."

* * * *

Everything had happened as the angel-wife had foretold. Her boy had been born miraculously on the third day, and he was growing with a quickness that was unexampled. His father's habit of incontinently sleeping had been conquered, and Ornaments, who devoted all his energies to bringing the choicest food home to his marvellous wife, had returned after a heavy day's whitebait-fishing.

Late in the afternoon he lay on his bed sleeping, when his son set up a wailing such as appears to be common to the sons of men and of spirits, and the father, awakened disagreeably from his well-earned repose, said sharply to the angel-wife, "Why don't you stop the child's noise? Can't you see I want to sleep?"

Immediately the lovely mother rose, and clasping her child to her bosom, looked reproachfully at her angry husband.

Without a word she went out of the hut and, mounting the roof, she sang a song so sweet that all the people of the village came to listen. Then, without effort or noise, she vanished with her child, as a little fleecy cloud evaporates in the blue sky.

THE DEMON OF THE ALBINOS.

THERE can be no doubt about the truth of these things, because my informant is Te Whetu, who—having, as he himself says, "got Ihu Karaiti"—has no dread of the unseen, and can easily discriminate between witchcraft and mere ordinary happenings. He further tells me that the weird misfortunes of Akuhata occurred but a year or two ago, as can be attested by my informant's relatives in Taranaki.

That such things should occur in this new century shows, therefore, that in some places of the earth witchcraft is as powerful as ever, in spite of the Theory of Evolution, the phonograph, Marconigrams, and the Higher Criticism.

Akuhata lived—till his misfortune fell upon him in the year of his bewitchment—at a place inland from Waitara a hundred miles. He was a promising young man with a well-developed appetite for eels, to catch which he exercised much ingenuity in setting his baskets in the river. He was a renowned eel-catcher.

* * * *

The morning was rather cloudy and there were signs of rain. A sudden fresh in the river would certainly sweep his eel-pots away, so Akuhata left the village. In his hand he bore his rakau, a long stick, to the end of which he had firmly fixed a strong hook.

He crossed the ford where the river rippled over a broad bed of gravel, he passed the pile of drift-wood which the last flood had stranded on the boulders, he paused to examine the deep pool which lay a little further up the stream. Here, at first, he saw nothing but what looked like a white stick at the bottom of the river, but presently the stick moved: it had all the motions of an eel, but was white.

"Now, what is that fish?" thought Akuhata. "What kind of a fish would they call that? Not an eel; no one ever saw a white eel. I'll find out. I'll catch him."

He dropped a piece of meat into the water; keeping himself well in the shade, so as to cast no shadow on the surface. The bait sank, till Akuhata was afraid the strange fish was not going to take it, but the white creature made a slow movement with its tail and caught the tempting morsel in its mouth.

"Ah! he likes it," thought Akuhata. "He thinks it good. Now I'll try him with another piece."

He took a long leaf from a flax-bush which grew near, and tore it into strips which he tied together. To one end of this he fastened the leg of a wood-hen, which he dropped into the water.

The bait sank a yard or two, and the white thing rose. The fisherman had his rakau ready; there was a splash, an excited shout, and the glistening fish lay on the bank.

"An eel!" cried Akuhata, "a white eel! How the people will marvel when I take it back to the pa."

There was another shout.

The fisher looked up and, splashing through the water, there appeared a huge man, who came bounding towards him.

"Put that eel back into the water," said the monster, menacingly.

"Not I," retorted Akuhata. "He is my fish—I caught him."

"Put him back."

"That I won't. Why should I?"

"Because he belongs to me. He's my fish!"

Akuhata laughed. But the big man held in his hands a double-edged weapon of tough manuka wood. With this he struck at the young fisher, who avoided the blow and seized a piece of drift-wood with which to defend himself.

But the fight was soon over. Akuhata's weapon was weak and rotten, and broke in his hand. He was at his enemy's mercy, and from a gash in his head the blood flowed over his face.

"Now I've got you," cried his conqueror, "now I will kill you. But no. I will give you another chance. I am Takara, the guardian demon of all albino birds, beasts, and fishes. The white eel you have killed is mine. If you kill another of my creatures, you shall pay for it with your life. Remember that." And taking up the eel, the monster crossed the river, and disappeared in the thick "bush" on the other side.

Akuhata had had enough fishing for that day. Forgetting all about his eel-pots, he went, bleeding and disconsolate, back to the pa.

When he said he had been fighting with a malignant spirit, some laughed, but the wiser ones looked serious and said that their pa was no place for him. They advised him to go away, lest the demon should catch him again, and kill him.

And that afternoon the rain descended in torrents, and in the night the river rose and swept away all Akuhata's eel-pots.

* * * *

Marama was a girl whom any man would love. "She is as gentle and beautiful as a white crane," was what Akuhata said when he first saw her.

He arrived at her village with a great reputation as a fisher; and it is almost a disillusion to tell that he courted his lady-love with eels, as did the hero of another story in this book. But Marama told him that she had no liking for eels: her weakness was for inanga, a delicious kind of white-bait.

One day, when his love-making was at its height and he was bent on catching the delicacy that his sweetheart loved, a white bird suddenly flew out of the "bush" and fluttered against his face. He brushed the bird aside with his hand, but it immediately renewed the attack as though it would peck his eyes out.

Snatching up a stick he knocked the bird to the earth. It was an albino kaka, a bird of the parrot tribe, which should have been reddish-brown.

Almost immediately he heard a voice say, "Ha! killing my creatures again. Didn't I tell you I was the guardian of all the albino birds, beasts, and fishes?"

At a glance Akuhata recognised the demon of the white eel, and in a moment he turned and ran; but he was seized by a great hand, in whose iron grasp he was helpless.

"Now," said Takara, "I will take you to my home, where you shall cook my food and be my slave. I will keep you near me, so that you shall do no more harm to my creatures. Come along with me."

Taking Akuhata by the arm, the demon dragged him through the forest; and Marama watched in vain for her lover's return.

* * * *

The catcher of eels was growing thin. He caught numbers of pigeons, and cooked them with quantities of sweet potatoes, but the demon ate all. So surely as Akuhata stretched out his hand to take the juicy leg of a bird, the morsel was sure to become a piece of stone; if he fancied a tasty eel, it turned into a dry stick as soon as he touched it; a sweet potato became a pebble, and boiled thistles so many twigs. So that the poor fellow was starved in the midst of plenty, and was reduced to skin and bone.

Now, Takara had a wife whose name was Taranui. At one time she had been young and pretty, but her husband's ill-usage had spoilt her beauty and had turned her affection for him into hatred. She looked with pity on the starving slave, and one day when Takara was away and the youth was cooking the dinner against his master's return, she said,

"Are you hungry, Akuhata?"

"Hungry?" he replied. "All I have eaten since I came here are sticks and stones."

"That is because you try to eat cooked food. My

husband has placed that spell on you lest you should eat his dinner when you have prepared it. Now, I will tell you what to do. Avoid everything that may be cooked, for the spell is on whatever your master may desire. But things that may be eaten raw he does not love, such as the edible part of the nikau palm and of the fern-tree, and all sorts of berries. On these he has placed no makutu."

"But they are not very nourishing," remarked Akuhata.

"But they will be better than the poor bewitched stuff you have been trying to eat," said the demon's wife.

Thus was Akuhata saved from starvation.

But when Takara saw his slave grew fat, he was non-plussed, and watched to see if any of his food was stolen. Finding that all was right, he said to himself, "I will put a new spell on him. I will curse him with the kohukohu."

Presently Akuhata fell ill. His skin became dry, his nails grew claw-like. He wondered what was happening to him, but he soon perceived that his body was covered with what looked like bark instead of skin, and knew that he was stricken with a curse which he traced to the malignancy of his master.

"Surely he might kill me outright," said the wretched victim. "I may have outwitted him in regard to food, but I can never hope to cure myself of this disease."

His hands were scaly, and from all parts of his body hung a long fibrous growth, like the lichen that grows on forest-trees. He was in despair.

But Taranui, seeing his distress, said to him secretly, "Akuhata, don't lose hope. I have found out that in a few days Takara is going to a place which is a great way off, in order that he may see a brother-demon. As soon as he starts on his journey, run away."

* * * *

Marama was sitting by the river-side, admiring her

reflection in the water, and wondering why her lover had left her so suddenly, when she saw a strange object approaching her. Its face seemed to be covered with bark like that of the rimu tree, and on its neck and chest grew stuff like the moss that hangs from trees which grow high up the mountains.

"E hika!" it cried. "I have escaped; I have returned. It is indeed great joy!"

But Marama turned with a shriek and fled. She thought the taipo was after her.

As the strange, lichen-covered creature approached the village the people fled for their lives, so that when it stood, dejected, in the middle of the broad expanse of the marae there was no one to witness its sorrow. But it took possession of an empty hut and lay down to rest.

One by one the people returned, and when they found that the strange-looking being was Akuhata they were not quite so frightened; and when they heard the story of his sufferings at the hands of the awful demon who had bewitched him they showed him the greatest kindness.

But nothing they could do had the least effect on the kohukohu. That was, they all thought, quite incurable. Nevertheless all the priests on the river came to exorcise the evil spirit which possessed Akuhata, and did their best to cure his disease, but they availed nothing. And Marama used to sit over against the hut of her bedevilled lover, and cry till she could be heard on the further bank of the river.

But one day a stranger arrived. She was a woman, middle-aged and ponderous. When asked the name of her tribe, she said that she came from Waikato, and that her name was Taranui. Without referring further to her private affairs she asked to see Akuhata, and was shown his hut.

"Ah! Akuhata," she exclaimed, "so you got here safely. Well, when Takara returned and found you gone, he beat me till I was all bruised and bleeding. But that night I determined to leave him; but first I took the precaution of pouring a pot of boiling water over his head while he slept. That will not kill him, for you cannot kill a spirit such as he, but it will make him ill for some time; and as he is likely to be blind he will not be able to find me."

"You are cleverer than I," said Akuhata. "I should have put some of the white man's poison into his food. It would at least have made him too weak to beat you."

"I have come to cure your kohukohu," said Taranui.

First she boiled some water, over which she said an incantation. Into the seething liquid she dropped a piece of earth, a stone, and a bit of bark. Next she undressed her patient, and washed him all over with the bewitched water. Then she left him, and forbade everyone to go near him for three days.

At the end of that time his cure was complete, the kohukohu had peeled off him, and his skin was as smooth and as soft as that of a child.

Imagine Marama's joy at her lover's recovery. Imagine the depth of gratitude felt by the bride and bridegroom towards the old woman. But imagine also the dread of all three lest the demon of the albinos should suddenly come and end their happiness.

But he has not molested them. Till the present he has avoided their village as carefully as the devil avoids a church. Some say that the reason of this is because he is frightened lest the men of the tribe should throw him into the river. But there is no doubt that the true reason is that he dreads his wife. She has taught him a lesson.

THE RIVAL WIZARDS.

RONGOMAI lived on a little island not far from the mainland. With infinite care and excessive patience he had fashioned a greenstone fish-hook, to which, having pronounced the proper incantantion over it, he ceremoniously gave the name of one of his most famous ancestors. Then Rongomai went a-fishing.

He got into his canoe, and paddled along the shore of the mainland till he was opposite a village named Motu, the fishing-grounds of which bore an excellent character for hapuku and kahawai, two species of fish much prized by the Maoris.

He cast his line, and almost immediately he caught a fish some two feet in length.

"That's right," said Rongomai, "my hook is a good hook: the incantation I said over it is strong. My hook surpasses all others, and I am the greatest fisherman there is." As he was reputed to be a terrible turehu, a being who could assume monstrous or human shape at will, nobody in the canoe thought of disputing his dictum.

"I have named my hook Hua-kai, after my grandfather," continued the chief. "The one caught men, the other catches fish. Now again." He re-baited the hook and made another cast. Soon with a jerk the line was pulled taut, and the slack ran quickly through the hands of the fisher, who before long began to pull in the line, with which came the fish, hooked fast by Hua-kai.

"Now my hook is making a reputation for himself, just like my grandfather," said the chief.

He threw the line a third time. The sinker fell

into the water, the line ran out, and Rongomai waited expectantly, while you might count twenty.

"The fish are sitting round my bait, and having a talk," said the wizard-chief. "They can't decide who shall have the first bite." But before the words were out of his mouth the line was jerked suddenly towards the bow of the canoe.

"I've got a big fellow," said Rongomai, as he began to haul. "Hoo! ha! I can't pull him up." The line shot out towards the stern. "I think he is the chief of the fish, the biggest of them all. He has the best of it: I can't move him." Next the line was carried out to sea, and then with a rush the fish shot under the canoe. The chief pulled, the fish pulled; now the chief gained a little, now the fish brought things to a standstill. "I have him, I am getting him bit by bit!" exclaimed Rongomai. "I shall win." And just as he gave a mightier pull than ever the line snapped, and he fell sprawling to the bottom of the craft.

The broken line hung limply in his hands. Picking himself up slowly he peered over the side into the water. "Oh, Hua-kai!" he cried. "Oh, my greenstone hook, where are you? In the belly of some big fish is Hua-kai, whom I made from a piece of greenstone with great toil, from a piece of greenstone belonging to my great ancestor. Over it he had breathed his spell; it was sacred like himself and great in power. It was part of himself. When I made my hook is was indeed the great Hua-kai come back again. Now it is in the belly of a fish: some hapuku has swallowed the sanctity and power of my grandfather: the soul of my ancestor is troubled in hell. He left me all his sacredness and greatness, and I have cast them to the fishes. I am distressed. I am miserable. I am pouri. Take me back to my pa, to the little island of Motiti."

* * * *

Now, watching the whole of these proceedings from the shore was old Te Pou, the chief of Motu. He like Rongomai was a turehu, and it was his habit to take the form of a whale or of a shark when he wished to have a little sea-bathing or a quiet cruise upon the ocean, where he brought terror to everything that swam. At other times he was satisfied to dwell at Motu, and in the person of a chief to lord it over an obsequious tribe.

Te Pou had seen the incident of the fish-hook, but he could make nothing of it. So he went home, and talked the matter over with his wife—for when a turehu wishes to marry, he does so with that part of him which is human, as it has been proved beyond doubt that the human wife exceeds all others in domestic virtues and wifely qualities. Te Pou's wife was sister to Rongomai's, so of course she knew all the gossip of Motiti Island.

"I expect I know what it is," said she. "Rongomai is testing his new fish-hook, which he has been making for the last six months; and it looks very much as if he had lost it." And she told her husband all she had learned from her sister concerning Hua-kai.

"We must try to get that hook," said Te Pou. "I will go and see about it." So after dark he went down to the beach and, stepping into the water, he took the form of a shark and swam about, looking for the hapuku which had swallowed the coveted hook.

* * * *

But Rongomai was not to be outdone. Before dawn he went out with his canoes, and as the day broke the people of Motu could see him dragging his immense net off the mouth of their river.

All the people collected on the beach, expecting to see a huge catch made, as the reputation of Rongomai as a fisher was very great, and they hoped to participate in his luck. Therefore imagine their astonishment when he drew his net full of fish, to find that he would not give them so much as a single rock-cod or even a flounder.

"I want them all," he said, and straightway he and his men began to clean the entire catch.

"There is a big hole in my net," said Rongomai.

"You Motu people may mend that for me, and then I will give you such fish as I don't want."

To this they agreed, and all worked amicably and industriously, while the fishermen examined every fish for the greenstone hook.

The work was half completed when a man appeared walking along the shore. It was Te Pou, who had resumed his human shape, and had come to see the result of the fishing.

"This is a fine haul that you have made," he said to the chief of Motiti.

"Yes," answered Rongomai, "I've caught plenty of fish."

"I see, however, that there is a big hole in your net."

"Yes, that was where a shark broke through, but some day I shall catch him too, and then he will break no more nets."

"Don't be too sure of that. Perhaps he will catch you, my dear brother-in-law, when you are bathing, and then there will be no more fishing—for you at least."

"We shall see," said Rongomai.

Just then one of his men raised a cry, and held up something in his hand. "The hook!" he cried. "I have found the hook Hua-kai in the belly of a big hapuku."

The people crowded round the man to examine the hook that was lost, but Rongomai, pushing them to right and left, thrust himself through the crowd, and seized the precious piece of greenstone.

"Hua-kai!" he exclaimed, "the hook I made from my great ancestor's jade. The next time I lose it will be when I myself am eaten by the fishes."

Te Pou had to turn his back upon the scene to hide his annoyance. He walked back to his whare, which he entered without so much as a word of greeting to his loving wife, who had sat up all night waiting for her lord's return.

"Have you been successful?" she asked timidly.

"No," replied he. "Not only has Rongomai

cheated me out of this hook, which I certainly would have found, but he actually tried to take me in his net. Now, what am I to do with such a fellow?"

* * * *

Rongomai sailed home with his canoes full of fish and his heart full of joy. As the roofs of his kainga came in sight he thought of the triumph of his home-coming. But his expectations were doomed to be sadly blighted.

As he neared the shore he could see a group of disconsolate women wringing their hands and crying.

"Why is all this weeping?" he asked. "Is any-one dead?"

His chief wife, Hinetu, met him with tears. "Come and see your house," she said. "It was through no fault of mine. One of your other wives lighted a fire, and the flames caught the thatch. All is burnt. There is nothing left."

The chief strode quickly towards the village, and there he saw that his house had vanished. Its place was occupied merely by a heap of smoking ruins.

"Who has done this?" he cried. "Bring the culprit to me!"

A wailing girl came forward, ane threw herself at his feet.

"I lighted the fire," she said. The hangi oven, smoking and hot, was beside the blackened embers of the house. "A spark caught the thatch, and all is burnt. Do not hurt me. Oh, spare me! Have mercy!"

* * * *

The sequel of the story as told to Te Pou, was that the girl had been killed and that her body, flung into the fire of her own making, had been burnt to cinders.

"But she was a member of my tribe," said Te Pou. "She was my niece, whom I gave to Rongomai that we might live in peace. This cannot be—he would never be so foolish as thus to provoke me to war."

But he was assured that the thing was not only possible, but true.

"Then there will be another fire," said Te Pou. "We will wait till he has built a new house, bigger and more imposing than the last, and then there will be a bigger fire than ever."

* * * *

Rongomai's new house was certainly better than the old. It had a dado of reeds inside, and its gable and side-posts were carved with skill and care in the true and ancient pattern.

When he moved into his sumptuous new abode, after all the proper ceremonies had been performed to make it sacred to himself and his belongings, Rongomai felt that his loss might be forgotten.

But that same night Te Pou walked down to the sea and turned himself into a fish. He swam to Motiti, where he landed in his true and proper person.

It was very dark, and he could hardly distinguish the huts of his rival's village, but slowly and silently he found his way to the place where the new house stood. He wished to make no mistake, so he felt the carving carefully with his hands. "It is all right," he said to himself. "This is the house. This is new carving—there was none like this in the village. This is Rongomai's new house."

In the middle of the pa smouldered a fire, to which the revengeful wizard crept. Seizing a burning stick he returned to Rongomai's house, into the thatch of which he thrust his firebrand. Then he slunk away noiselessly to the shore.

From the water's edge he watched the flames mount up, till the whole house was ablaze and he heard the roof fall in with a crash which awoke the whole village. Then he plunged into the water and became a fish.

* * * *

Rongomai having been burnt as a man was forced to confine himself to an aquatic existence—this seems to be a rule with a turehu when he "goes out"—so he became a kahawai, big and voracious, and lived a life of seclusion and security in the deep. But he still retained some of his malevolent power, and possessed attributes unexpected in fishes. Thus, though a kahawai, he could command great whales and they obeyed him; he could drive away all the fish from the coast near Motu, and so bring scarcity to his rival.

Yet with all his desire to work wickedness, he could not expect to avenge himself upon Te Pou personally, but that powerful wizard had a little son named Kopara, who was too young to be taught the potent incantations necessary for his protection, and too irrepressible to be safely guarded even by his necromancing father. So against this child all Rongomai's arts were directed.

One day, escaping from the vigilant eye of his doting father, who in the seclusion of his hut was busy manufacturing spells for the discomfiting of some new enemy, the little fellow went to bathe with the boys of the village, and swam out to a canoe in which some men were fishing with but scant success for kahawai.

The fishermen, greatly annoyed at the approach of the boys, who, they thought, would spoil their sport, beckoned them to keep away from the canoe, which direction the swimmers obeyed by making a wide circuit out to sea. But in executing this manœuvre they became scattered, and Kopara, though like all Maori boys a good swimmer, was outdistanced by his companions. Suddenly the men in the canoe heard a cry; little Kopara threw his arm out of the water, and then with a shriek disappeared.

The fishermen paddled with all their might to the spot, to find no sign of the child. The cry of "Sharks!" was raised, and the other boys swam rapidly to the canoe and were pulled in over the stern.

"Who was it?" asked one of the men.

"Kopara," replied the boys, who missed the chief's son from their number. "Did a shark get him?"

"There are no sharks here," said another of the

men. "If there had been, the few kahawai we caught would have fled."

"Certainly you don't catch kahawai when sharks are about," said a third; "but at any rate it must have been a fish as big as any shark."

The trailing lines were now hauled in and wound up, for the fishing was over for the day.

When Te Pou heard the ill news his rage was something phenomenal; but as it was proved that nobody but the boy himself was to blame, his anger gradually gave place to grief, and he wept the scalding tears of a sorely stricken turehu. All day and far into the night he paced the beach, calling for his son, the light of his eyes, the hope of his declining years, the natural successor of his occult power, the recipient of his mystic mantle.

It was then that it suddenly dawned upon his uncanny mind that the author of his woe was none other than his old enemy, Rongomai. What was easier than to prove this surmise by making inquiry of the denizens of the deep, among whom the facts of his little son's death would be current? Nothing was more simple. Changing himself into a kahawai he swam till he met with a shoal of fishes, and joining the piscine crowd he heard his finny companions discussing the details of his son's decease.

"And Rongomai quickly devoured him," said a well-grown kahawai. "He wouldn't give me so much as a mouthful, though I could hardly wriggle for want of food."

"I managed to pick up one of the flippers," said a small rock-cod, "but the crabs had left little more than the bones, at which I was nibbling when up swam Rongomai, who told me that if I didn't take those bones at once and cast them on the beach he would bite my tail off."

"What was that for?" asked a butter-fish, who had strayed far from his feeding-grounds, and was ignorant of the incident under discussion.

"I really can't tell," said the rock-cod. "He came

from the land, they say, and I suppose he likes to give a piece of his catch to the god of the land; but I lost my dinner."

At this point of the conversation an enormous kahawai came swimming rapidly towards the gossiping fish, and said, "Come, we must get away from this shore. The whole shoal of kahawai is under orders for Hawaiki, where Rongomai says the best feeding-grounds in the whole sea are to be found."

Away swam all the fishes, and Te Pou, left alone, turned his nose towards the shore and swam sorrowfully homewards.

Next day, when he had resumed his human shape, he put on all his robes of flax and feathers, called together his whole tribe, and made an oration.

He said that he was about to depart on a journey and might be away for a week, though he did not expect it would be for so long, and during that time they must continue to prepare the ground for next year's crops. "My great desire is to see my tribe increase," said he. "But to secure that end I must get plenty of fish, for when it is known that a tribe has a large supply of food, then all who can possibly do so immediately claim relationship. In this way a large body of people may be got together, and that is the time to make war upon our enemies. Therefore I am going to visit my tuaahu"—it was by that name that he called his sacred place—"and there I will say incantations and perform rites which will cause large shoals of fish to visit our shores. When I have finished I will return, and then you may drag your nets till the pa is full of dried fish and your ovens smoke constantly. In the meantime I advise you to prepare the ground for the crops, and to make nets as fast as you can—big, strong nets which will be able to catch the thousands of fish that I shall bring. All I shall ask in return for this service is to be allowed to pick three fish from each catch before it is divided."

Next day Te Pou was absent. It was supposed that he was at his tuaahu, the position of which was of course a profound secret; but in reality he had gone on a voyage to Hawaiki, where he wished to interview Tangaroa, the supreme ruler of the sea and all that therein is. There, in a coral cave beneath the limpid water, Te Pou was received in audience by the dæmon of the deep.

The formidable monster, moving his mighty fins and curling his stupendous tail, fixed his enormous eyes upon the wriggling supplicant, and said, "Speak!" and the motions of his huge mouth showed how great was his voracity.

Te Pou, in the form of a porpoise, told his tale:—"I had a dear son, great atua, who was the darling of my heart and the hope of my declining years, a boy who would have been a credit to the mighty deep when he had been initiated into its mysteries. But alas! he took to the pleasures of the sea before he had been made a turehu, and was most unfortunately drowned. I intend to hold a great tangi"—which is the Maori for a wake—"at my pa so soon as I return, and I have invited all the tribes from far and near; but I also want a tangi in the sea. I want all the kahawai, over whom you hold absolute sway, to come to Motu, and there at the mouth of the river to weep for my son."

"I am very sorry to hear this," said Tangaroa. "If you had applied to me earlier, I would have had much pleasure in making your boy proof against such an end, but as it is I will order all the kahawai to Motu. They shall start at once."

"There is no immediate hurry," said Te Pou. "I shall not be ready to receive them for at least a fortnight."

"Then they can go leisurely," said the atua. "They can take their time over the journey. I should very much like to be present myself, but I have so many duties to perform in these waters, where I have lately had great trouble with the sharks, who have almost exterminated the hapuku which I had collected here for my own especial use. Consequently, I have had to eat all sorts of little fish and even mussels and cray-fish, a diet which does not agree with my digestion. It may be that when all the kahawai are gathered together at Motu, perhaps I may pay you a visit. A change of water and of food would not only be beneficial to me but very pleasant. You may expect me."

"That would really be a great pleasure," said Te Pou, "but please don't put yourself to any trouble on my account. I fear the water at Motu is hardly deep enough for you; we have such extensive mud-flats, and the river is so shallow, that I fear you would find it a most inconvenient place for a fish of your size. It would be the greatest honour possible, and I should be delighted to receive you, but if you will send the kahawai . . . . ."

"They shall go certainly," said the monster."

"I am more than content," said Te Pou. "I should never forgive myself if anything happened to you in my waters: it would be disastrous to my reputation. It would be said of me, 'How can he protect himself if he lets evil happen to Tangaroa before his eyes?'"

When Te Pou returned to Motu, which he did in a remarkably short space of time, he at once assembled his people. "We are to hold a great tangi for my son," he said, "and are likely to receive visitors from all the surrounding tribes. We must therefore lay in great stores of food, otherwise our guests will scorn us, and we shall become a byword throughout the land."

"But fish are very scarce," said Titipa, the chief next in command and secretly Te Pou's rival.

"Make the nets, and I will bring the fish," said the old wizard.

"How will you do that?" asked Titipa.

"By my spells," replied Te Pou. "Haven't I been to my tuaahu for three days? What do you suppose I have been doing there but saying incantations which shall bring the fish? But if you have no nets when they come, what will be the good of my spells?"

"I also can pronounce spells," said Titipa. "I also have my tuaahu. You will see what I can do. I know an incantation which will not only bring the fish, but will catch them when they come."

However, the people set to work to gather flax and to make innumerable nets.

Every day Te Pou would stand on the shore with his face towards the sea. At length he said to the people, "Everything is ready. The fish are come. Set your nets, and you will catch them by the hundred. I ask one thing only: that before the catch is dried I may pick three fish for my own use."

So the people went to the beach, where to their astonishment they found Titipa pacing up and down and reeling off his spells by the dozen. The canoes were launched, and under the direction of the lesser chief a tremendous haul was made.

The cleaning of the fish was commenced immediately, and hundreds of fish were soon drying in the sun. In the middle of the work Te Pou came down from the village.

"What is all this?" he asked.

"These are the fish I have caught," replied Titipa. "This is the result of my power as a tohunga."

"But didn't I tell you I should expect the pick of the catch?" cried Te Pou.

"If you want fish, catch them yourself," retorted Titipa. "You don't get the pick of my haul."

"Indeed," said Te Pou, and he walked along the beach and inspected the fish that were drying in the sun. "We shall see whose catch this is presently."

Walking to the water's edge and stretching out his arms towards the sea, he repeated mighty spells before the people.

Everyone wondered what would happen, but it was not long before Te Pou came running up the beach.

"Get back!" he cried. "Get back to the high ground, or you will be drowned," and running past his people he climbed the high cliff, where he took his stand, and repeated more spells.

The people, thoroughly terrified, followed helter-skelter, and left Titipa alone upon the beach.

Soon the sea grew dark and troubled and angry, and presently a great wave, which gathered strength as it came, swept towards the shore. It advanced over the sandy beach, sweeping Titipa and all his fish before it till with the noise of thunder it struck the cliff on which the people stood.

"That is one," said Te Pou. "That is for the first fish. There will be two more."

The great wave receded, sucking with in innumerable boulders and the helpless, struggling Titipa.

Then another wave, greater than the previous one, came with tremendous force and, sweeping the shore, struck the cliff with a thunderous roar. This was followed by a third which, when it receded, left the beach scoured and bare. Titipa and all his fish had disappeared.

"I have finished," said Te Pou. "That is all. There will be no more trouble. To-morrow you will catch more fish, hundreds of them, thousands of them. Give me the first pick, and you may have the rest."

The people went to bed that night feeling the deepest respect for their chief, but next day respect was changed to perfect adoration.

Early in the morning two boys were playing at the moari, a sort of giant-stride, which was planted on the bank of the narrow creek beside which the village stood. As the boys swung from bank to bank one of them fell into the water—no unusual thing for a lad playing at the moari—but imagine his astonishment and that of his companion when, instead of sinking, he was borne upon the surface by reason of the multitude of fish which filled the creek.

Scrambling ashore the boy ran to the huts, from which the drowsy people were emerging, and soon the news of the miraculous advent of the fish was in every mouth.

An immense number of nets, laid one upon another, were quickly set at the lower end of the creek, and then the catching of the fish began. Men walked into the water and, taking the kahawai with their hands, threw them on the bank, till their arms were tired. Others armed with long, sharp spears stood in the water, and plied their weapons till they could hardly raise their hands for weariness. As the fish were flung upon the bank, the women carried them in huge baskets to the chief, in order that he might take his pick of them.

* * * *

Te Pou had made his choice. Three big fish, cooked to a turn, lay in flax baskets on the ground before him.

"This," said he, holding up the smallest basket, "is for my son. Let it be thrown into the sea." He took up the next in size. "This is for my wife. Let her eat and be strong. But this"—he held up the largest fish of all—"is mine. This is Rongomai." The steaming fish filled his nostrils with its delightful smell, and his mouth watered. "I will now show you what shall be done with him who ate my son—he himself shall be eaten." He commenced his revengeful meal. "Ah, his flesh is tender. It is nourishing. I snuffed him out of his human body, and when he is a fish I feed upon his flesh. Rongomai is nothing—he is quickly becoming a part of myself. See, I grow in girth, I am forced to let out my girdle, I am increasing in size; but that is not wonderful, for I am consuming the flesh of my enemy. There is not a part of him that I will not devour, except the tail and the fins and the bones and the head, which I will bury carefully at my sacred place, that none may share his greatness with me. Henceforth there is no one like me: I am the greatest chief and the greatest turehu." Suddenly, however, his face bore a look of distress, which fortunately proved but fleeting. "Ha! Rongomai gives me a twinge in my stomach, he is kicking against his fate. But I will digest him. He is becoming part of my flesh, I am absorbing his strength."

When his meal was ended Te Pou leaned back, and said, "Rongomai has ceased to exist. I am Te Pou and Rongomai. Tell the tribe living on Motiti that if they want their chief, he is here," and he patted his distended stomach. "I bear ill-will to no one, but I shall expect my greatness to be recognised. If anyone thinks to thwart me, let him beware lest the fate that has befallen Rongomai should become his. He yawned, and stretched himself. "I have finished eating and talking," he said. "You all may now go about your business, and I will sleep contentedly, for have not I eaten my enemy?"

THE COURTING OF KIRIKA.

TE Pi was a great athlete. He was the fastest runner, the strongest swimmer, the most powerful wrestler in his village, which was situated where the town of Waitara now stands.

It is the fate of the athlete to fall in love. As Samson was bewitched by Delilah, and Hercules by Deianeira, so Te Pi fell under the spell of Kirika, the sweetest and gentlest kotiro of his tribe.

But with that coyness which becomes all women, whether they be brown or white, the Maori girl determined that her lover should give some proof of his devotion. So when Te Pi boasted to her that he was the strongest man in the tribe, she said that to win her he must prove himself the strongest man of all the tribes.

Like the true athlete he was, Te Pi had no wish that his light should be smothered under a bushel; so, getting together a team of young men, he went on tour, challenging all with whom he came in contact.

First he went to Waikato, where he easily won the swimming contest, but was beaten in the flat race by a fleet sprinter named Great South Wind, who, however, when Te Pi challenged him to wrestle, was thrown every time.

The fame of this match reached Kawhia, where there was a celebrated athlete named Hundred Huts. This great man sent a challenge to Te Pi, who delightedly complied, and the meeting was fixed.

In this case, the Waitara heavy-weight came off victorious in every event, swimming, running, and wrestling.

This account of the triumphs of Te Pi may read like a notice in a sporting newspaper, but it shows that the Maori, then as now, had the true sporting instinct.

But things were not always to be rose-coloured with Te Pi. After he had completed his tour and had returned home, loaded with fame and more in love than ever, he was received coldly by Kirika; for during his absence a rival had appeared. This was Manaia, a Hawera chief, who had come from the other side of the mountain* for the express purpose of courting the pretty Waitara girl. And his courting was very captivating. Whereas Te Pi's love-making had been of the boisterous, domineering kind, the "look at me, and resist me if you can" sort of wooing—a method of courtship which, while it may answer in some cases, was not at all to Kirika's liking—Manaia had come with flattery and presents and soft speeches, all of which proved to be sweet as honey to the maiden. So that when, bursting with the glory of his triumphs, Te Pi returned, the indifference that Kirika showed to his successes was like a cold bath after the delights of the steaming hot-spring.

"But I beat all comers," expostulated Te Pi. "No one could stand against me. I am the champion of the Tribe of Mahutu, of the Tribe of the Son, of the Tribe of the River, of all the tribes."

"But not of the Tribe of the Girl"—that was Manaia's tribe—said Kirika.

"The Tribe of the Girl!" exclaimed Te Pi. "Nonsense. I could throw their champion with my left hand. They're a poor lot—let them send their best man, and I will prove my words."

"There is Manaia," retorted Kirika. "He is a splendid wrestler, I'm sure. Besides which he is the most courteous, well-mannered man I have seen. He doesn't bluster or brag, or go vaunting round the country; but you would find your match in him nevertheless."

---

* The conical Taranaki, called by the English Mount Egmont.

"Manaia?" said Te Pi. "I never heard of him. Who is he?"

"He came on a visit while you were away. You may be strong, but he is handsome; you may be a wonderful wrestler, but he is gentle and accomplished. You should hear him sing, or tell a story. Strength of body isn't everything, but I have no doubt that he would beat you at that also, if he had a mind to try."

In a moment Te Pi guessed how the land lay. "Where does this man live?" he asked.

"At Hawera."

"Good. I will go there. I will find this fellow, and I will show you that he is just a child in my hands. If that doesn't satisfy you, I will challenge him to fight to the death, and you may marry the survivor."

"No, no!" cried Kirika. "If there is bloodshed I will marry neither. Now listen, Te Pi. If you quarrel with Manaia I will have no more to do with you."

"I'll break his neck."

"Then I shall hate you."

"But I'll marry you all the same."

Kirika smiled. "Now you are talking like an overgrown boy," she said. "Of course I admire your strength—every woman must—but this boasting is absurd. If you were gentle in manner, if you could sing, or tell amusing stories, then you would be irresistible, and I should be charmed. But first of all you love your athletic triumphs and the praise of the tribes, and then you love me. Now, the man who marries me must love me beyond everything else."

Hereafter picture this Samson in the toils of his dusky Delilah. Imagine him singing love-songs with a full, deep voice, and cudgelling his torpid brains to tell amusing stories, till all the pa was laughing at his uncouth attempts to be entertaining. His rough manners had given place to a demeanonr which was pathetic in its gentleness, his boasting had changed into effusive adoration of his lady-love—so great is the influence of woman—and indifferent to being the champion wrestler he was ambitious of being thought the most accomplished toa in Maoriland. He would sit for hours beside Kirika, as she wove elegant flax cloaks adorned with bright feathers of birds he had caught. Docile and attentive, he would posture his great body in all the attitudes of love, and with soft sentences and tender speeches he would strive to propitiate the goddess of his choice. He long had ceased to talk of his physical triumphs; the memory of his athletic tour was buried in the oblivion of the past; it was as though feats of strength were naught and wrestling a vulgar pastime: his whole being seemed bent upon acquiring the arts and graces admired by his deity. To sing to her was his delight, to dance before her was perfect joy, to tell her the quaint stories he had heard on his travels gave him the greatest pleasure, till from the rough and boisterous wrestler Te Pi had become indeed the polished toa of the kainga. And then the fickle heart of woman changed. With the fruit in her hand, Kirika had desired to have the flower; possessed of the flower, she now desired the fruit. She had admired the physical powers of her lover more than she had cared to own, but now that she had succeeded in weaning him from his rough and boisterous ways, she was alarmed lest he should lose his reputation for feats of strength.

Imagine Te Pi's surprise therefore when one day she suddenly said, "E hoa, we had almost forgotten Manaia. When do you propose to challenge him?"

"There is plenty of time," replied the infatuated athlete. "What is the good of wrestling? I like the dance now, and the story and the song."

"The fact is that you are getting lazy," said the girl.

The huge fellow laughed. "You help to make me feel so, Kirika. I don't want to go to Hawera: I want to stay with you."

Now while such a confession would indicate an unhealthy state of mind in any man who made it, in such a hero as Te Pi it was deplorable. Though Kirika appreciated the compliment he intended to pay her, she felt he must not lose the attributes of youth too soon.

"You must go to Hawera," she said. "You must overthrow Manaia, before I marry you."

The athlete's eyes opened in astonishment. The whims of his deity bemazed him, but the humour of the situation amused him. "That is easy," he laughed, "much easier than composing songs to your beauty, and pleasanter than racking my brains for stories. Manaia shall be properly beaten. Then you will marry me. Is that so?"

"That is so," said the girl. "But if he beats you, then I'll marry him."

The huge fellow laughed again. "I will send him the challenge at once," he said; and rising like a behemoth, he walked off.

* * * *

The match was arranged, and after a short course of training Te Pi, accompanied by his picked team, was about to set out for the great encounter. He was spending the last remaining hour with Kirika in sweet farewell.

"You'll take care not to get hurt, won't you?" said the girl.

Te Pi laughed. "You need have no fear of that."

"And you will . . . . you will, if it's only for my sake . . . you will win the match."

"Have I ever lost one?"

"And you won't stop in Hawera too long? You'll come back soon?"

"As quickly as possible."

"You won't let any of those Hawera girls keep you?—they are so ugly."

The wrestler took Kirika in his arms, and laughed at her apprehensions.

"Tell Manaia, after you have won, that it is no good his coming to Waitara again, for I am your wahine."

"He knows already that you are the prize."

"And I will ask my father to say the proper

incantation that will give you strength and make you win."

"I have beaten all previous opponents without the aid of spells," said Te Pi. "If I have the support of your father's karakia in addition to my own strength, I am bound to be victorious."

When the visiting team reached Hawera there was a great welcome and much speechifying.

Every one in the pa understood that the stake was the belle of Waitara, and the interest in the contest was intense. Quite a dozen Hawera girls were ready to console the worsted wrestler, whichever he might be.

After a day or two's rest, during which the visitors quite recovered from the fatigue of their journey, the match commenced. First, amid the most uproarious merriment, the followers of each chief engaged in friendly bouts. There were foot-races and wrestling, but no swimming, because the Girl's Tribe had no suitable sheet of water near the pa. Then, in the afternoon, the two chiefs stood up to decide the fate of Kirika.

Te Pi threw off his long feather-cloak, and with a flourish of his arm made his challenge.

"I am Te Pi, the great wrestler. I am Te Pi of the River Tribe. I have beaten all Waikato and Kawhia, and every toa I ever met. I am come to challenge Hawera, to challenge Manaia. I will put round his leg a whiri from which he cannot escape, and I will hurl him to the earth. When once I have him in my clutches, he will never get free. A chief named Hundred Huts, of Kawhia, thought he could throw me. He was tall and strong, but I threw him three times. Great South Wind, the Waikato champion, was cunning as well as strong: he wrestled with his head as well as well as with his body, and used all sorts of tricks for overthrowing me; but I was beforehand with him. I threw him five times, and he acknowledged me to be the victor. Now we come to Hawera. This will be the greatest match of all—the prize is the prettiest girl in Taranaki, in the whole country, Kirika, the charming kotiro of my tribe. The champion wrestler shall marry the loveliest girl in the whole world. It will soon be decided. Now, Manaia, come on!" And with awful shouts of defiance he sprang forward.

Motionless and scowling, the Hawera chief had listened to this harangue. But now he dropped his cloak, and stood only in his rustling piupiu, which hung from waist to knee. With a voice deep and gruff with rage he cried, "Come on, Te Pi; come on, Tribe of the River! Manaia is waiting."

Cautiously watching his opponent, Te Pi advanced. With his arms stretched out, his body bent forward, and with feet well apart, he crept slowly towards Manaia, who in a crouching attitude awaited the grip of his adversary with apparent indifference.

Suddenly Te Pi sprang forward. At the same moment Manaia stood erect, and drawing a concealed greenstone axe from beneath his piupiu, buried its blade in the bent head of his antagonist.

* * * *

The summer night was warm and still, the surface of the sea was flecked with the silvery beams of the full moon. Beside the water paced the figure of a girl, dressed in a feather-cloak. Her dainty footsteps marked the track of her walking backwards and forwards along the glistening strand. Tormented with anxiety, unable to sleep for thinking of the trial to which she had put her lover, Kirika had left her couch in the sleeping-house where her girl companions lay wrapped in repose, to wander on the shore till dawn or drowsiness should end her vigil.

"Oh! Te Pi, come back victorious, the conqueror of the smooth-tongued Manaia. Your rugged ways are more lovely to me than the sweet speeches of all other men; there is a charm in your presence, in the poise of your head, in your manner of walking, which is more to me than the honied words of a hundred orators. You have won me in spite of myself. Come back that I may give you all my love."

Her pretty feet were ankle-deep in the rippling wavelets. She stooped to pick up a lovely shell, washed hither and thither in the frothy brine of the incoming tide; and holding in her hand the scintillating gift of the prolific ocean, she apostrophised it as though it were the object of her love:—

"Oh dear lord and master of my being, as I pace draw near; each step of yours tallying with a step of mine. In the morning when the sun rises let the bell-birds sing, for my lover comes back; when mid-day is at hand, I will prepare pigeons and sweet potatoes, I will dig an oven and bury in it the red-hot stones on which I will cook every delicacy that my conqueror loves. Then, when he shall arrive I will hurry to the edge of the forest, where in a thicket I will await his steps, and as he passes along the narrow track I will pounce upon him, like one of his own wrestlers; my soft arms shall encircle his towering form, I shall feel the strong arms about me, but he will not throw me from him—for love is a greater wrestler than strength. Then hand in hand we will walk to the kainga, and I will open my oven and give my hero food after his journey; and when he has eaten I will stand up before all the tribe and say, 'I am the wife of the strong man. Te Pi has overcome all the wrestlers in this country, but a weak girl was proof against him. She scorned his sinewy arms and his huge form, she pitted her wiles against his prowess, and the great wrestler fell prostrate at her feet. She laughed, she was glad, but she hid her joy because she loved to hear the giant's supplications. But when he was absent, she could not sleep for love; she paced the shore, wakeful and yearning for him; she called upon the rivers, she called upon the sky, she called upon the forests and the hills to assist his steps. She was won by the conqueror of men, she was subdued by the great warrior. Te Pi is my lord, and I am become his slave.' Then I will take his great hand in mine, and lead him to my bridal couch."

There was a black object bobbing on the waters.

"It is a piece of sea-weed," said Kirika. "It is a

bit of drift-wood borne on the incoming tide. Oh sea, if my lord chooses your bosom for his way to me, bear him gently, carry him swiftly to my arms. Let not an adverse breath of boisterous wind disturb his coming. What? that floating object is nearer, it is stranded in the shallow water: it looks like the stump of a fallen fern-tree."

She waded a little further into the tide, and lifted the strange piece of flotsam from the sea. With a shriek she dropped it, and it fell with a splash back into the water.

"It is a man's head! The tattooed head of a chief!"

But with quaking limbs and chattering teeth, she again stooped and lifted the awful object, and peered into its glassy eyes."

"Oh how like," she cried. "Oh if this should be."

She held the grinning mazard in the full flood of the moonlight, and scanned its clammy features. Then, sobbing, she wrapped it up in her cloak, and ran towards the village.

Having arrived at the door of her father's hut she called and cried, and hammered on the panel.

The old man, awakened from a sound slumber, told his disturber to go away, but when he recognised his daughter's voice, he opened his door.

"What is the matter, my child? Why do you cry? Has some one disturbed you? Has any one troubled you?"

"Come! Look! I found it on the beach. It came bobbing on the tide to my very feet. Oh, my father, look! Who is it?"

The old man examined the horrible head, and muttered a weird prayer. He held it where the moonlight beat upon it, and with his crooked finger he traced the spiral lines of its tattoo.

"It is the moko—did not I myself trace the pattern?—it is the mouth, this is the nose, these are the eyes of Te Pi."

With a low moaning sob the girl fell limply to the ground, and there lay, weeping.

"But this may be the work of some malignant spirit, of some bad tohunga who wishes to deceive us," said the old chief. "We will wait till daylight. We will wait for news."

He lifted his daughter from the ground, he drew her into his hut, and then, leaving the head to stare with glassy eyes at the moon, he tried to comfort her.

At dawn there there came a voice from the forest, and a boy, running to see who called, found amid the dew and the fern a prostrate, wounded man, who was crawling slowly towards the village. He proved to be the sole survivor of Te Pi's team of wrestlers, and ere the sun was up in the heavens Kirika knew that what she had found by the sea was indeed the head of her lover.

"But how did it get here?" the people asked of their chief. "Did the wind blow it?"

"Oh, no," replied the old man, "it was the mana of the head. When Manaia killed Te Pi he cut off his head, and told one of his men to go to the coast and fling it into the sea. Then my spell was so strong and the mana of Te Pi was so great, that it was borne by the sea round the coast to Waitara."

NOTE TO THE COURTING OF KIRIKA.—When he told me this story, I said to Te Whetu, "Isn't that a fiction invented to surprise your hearers?"

"Oh, no," said he. "That is true talk. The old chief, Tu-iti, was my ancestor; my mother belonged to the Tribe of the River, whose members often tell the story."

"Then, did Kirika marry the Hawera chief?"

Te Whetu looked at me in astonishment. "There was no fear of that," he answered. "She never married him. My tribe fought him to take payment for the men he had killed at the wrestling match, and he fought us to get the girl. That was the beginning of all the wars between our tribe and his. But he never got Kirika. She married my ancestor Te Koko, whose son was Tengi, who married . . . ."

A Maori genealogy is a dreadful thing, so I asked quickly,

"But what became of Manaia?"

"We got him," said Whetu; "that was all right."

For a moment I thought of asking what was done to the treacherous wrestler, but the question would have been superflous as well as in very bad taste. I knew, dear reader, and I imagine that your wisdom is as great as mine.—A.A.G.

THE TALKING TANIWHA.

THE state of things at Kaiapoi was intolerable. No one was sure of obtaining his dinner regularly; no one could say when he himself might not be converted into a dinner for the most dreadful monster that ever existed.

Not far from the pa, in a den of his own special making, lived the Talking Taniwha. Inaccessible, possessing the power of self-metamorphosis, invulnerable, tremendous, voracious, insatiable, this awful beast preyed upon the unfortunate people of Kaiapoi, till their plumpost maidens and well-grown young men, their tender children and well-conditioned women were all devoured, and none but the weeds of the tribe were left.

With things in such a state the miserable remnants sent for help to Kiu, whose fame as a tohunga extended through the length of the three islands. He possessed the power of communicating with departed spirits, and had made his home at Otaki, the headquarters of the Warrior Tribe, where he lived a useful and lucrative life; performing much devilry for the benefit of those who supplied him liberally with this world's goods and tendered him abundant homage.

To this great wizard came the takata hara, the representative of the degenerate people of Kaiapoi, the sinful survivors of a race which spoke the bastard Moriori tongue.

This man, having made obeisance to Kiu, unburdened himself of his message.

"It is true, great priest," said he, "that I am a member of the accursed tribe which has no knowledge of the gods, a people without sanctity. Consequently, my relatives are the prey of a terrible monster, who lives in a deep hole in the low-lying land not far from the seashore. When we go out to fish, this taniwha turns himself into a huge creature of the sea, and filling his hole with water magically, he swims out into the tide, where he upsets the canoes and eats the fishermen."

"Then let your people stay ashore and cultivate sweet potatoes," said Kiu.

"But when the men go to the plantations," said the takata hara, "the taniwha, assuming the form of a man twenty feet high, rushes upon them. The people run, but the monster runs faster, and seizing ten or a dozen of them he takes them to his den, where he eats them at his leisure. We dare not go out to fish, we dare not go into the plantations, for the taniwha gets us either way. My tribe, once numerous, has grown thin in numbers as well as in body; whereas the creature that preys on us grows bigger and stronger every day."

"You should make strong ropes," said Kiu, "and noose this taniwha when he comes out of his hole. Put a hundred men on to each rope, and kill the monster. That's the way."

"We have tried to catch him in that manner half-a-dozen times," said the takata hara, "but each time he has broken the ropes and captured some of the men. We do not know the incantation that will make the ropes hold him: that way is no good. The proper plan is for you to come, and with your spells to kill the taniwha. You are a great priest, and have power over devils and monstrous beasts sent to torment mankind; your fame reaches from north to south; you are a tohunga who can control bad spirits, and cure all the ills that come to men from the supernatural world. We all know that you are the greatest worker of miracles in the country, the greatest tohunga in the world."

To women and priests flattery is sweeter than honey. Kiu's soul melted before the words of the takata hara; he smiled with pleasure; he rubbed his hands together, and beamed on the heathen man.

"I am delighted that you have formed such a high estimate of my powers," he said, "and I will certainly endeavour to substantiate your good opinion by showing you how to catch this taniwha. Go home, and tell your people not to be frightened any more, for Kiu the tohunga who holds evil spirits in the hollow of his hand, is coming to annihilate the monster that torments them. But be most particular to pay attention to one important matter. You must have plenty of food for me when I come."

So the heathen man went his way in a state of ecstatic joy, and Kiu commenced to make preparation for his momentous undertaking. First he ordered his people to cut down a large number of toi trees—known to scientific gentlemen as the cordyline indivisa—from the fibrous leaves of which he directed them to make two great cables. Next he bargained with the skipper of a whaler, who was visiting his kainga, to take him and two-hundred of his men down to Kaiapoi. The price arranged was twenty pigs, a hundred pumkins, and ten sacks of sweet potatoes—passage money to be prepaid.

When the ship reached its destination, the Otaki men were landed with their thick cables, and there was tremendous enthusiasm in Kaiapoi.

After feasting for three days and almost eating their hosts out of house and home, Kiu and his men proposed that the hunting of the man-eating monster should be discussed.

On one side of the marae sat Kaiapoi, on the other Otaki, in long lines between which was an open space, up and down which the speakers might perambulate.

First rose the takata hara who had visited Kiu. He walked up and down three times in silence, in order that everybody might see him; then pausing in the middle of the assemblage, he faced his visitors and said,

"I am the man to make to make a journey; I am the man with the persuasive tongue; I am the man to fetch the great tohunga of the Warrior Tribe to Kaiapoi. He is here, he is in our midst, and we are all delighted. But how did I act? When I returned, I told my people what a great honour was about to be conferred on them. I told them to get food ready for Kiu and his tribe. They got it. They braved the taniwha, they went into the forest and caught pigeons, they went out to sea and caught fish, they went into the plantations and dug sweet potatoes. The taniwha looked out of his den, and said, 'The men are everywhere. I don't know which to catch first. I think I'll eat the fishermen.' So he goes down to the sea. Then he turns back, and says, 'No, I think I'll get the men who are hunting pigeons in the forest.' As he is on the way to carry out his intention, he sees the people in the plantations. He turns aside, but the diggers of potatoes have been quick, they have all the crop in baskets, and off they run to the pa. Then the taniwha goes into the forest, but the men there have got too far in by now, and the monster returns to catch only two women who are too weak to get back from the plantations in time—two skinny old women with no flesh on their bones.

"That's the way. You men of Otaki get the food, you eat the pigeon, the fish, the sweet potato, and you get strong. You are the men to catch the taniwha; your great priest is the man to say charms to make the rope hold fast and render the taniwha weak."

Next, one of the visitors rose to say how pleased he and his people were to come. They had heard all about the awful monster, how big he was, how cruel, how voracious; but they would settle accounts with him. Certainly they would soon accomplish a little thing like that. The men of Kaiapoi were to be much blamed for not having sent to Otaki before; if they would come out to the place where the monster lived, they would see how the trick of catching a taniwha was done. The Warrior Tribe had brought two ropes such as were never made before, ropes strong enough to hold the whale-ship, and able to hold, therefore, two taniwha. He advised his friends not to lose the opportunity of witnessing the sight of their lives.

When he sat down a Kaiapoi man rose. He was old and bent, but still agile on his feet. He hopped about like an oyster-catcher on the sands.

"Men of Otaki," he cried between two hops. "Great men of the Warrior Tribe, I am the man to talk; therefore I have been chosen by my tribe to extol the fame of your great priest, Kiu. The sun is great, the sun is hot, the sun is bright, he sails across the heavens, his strength reaches from coast to coast. He is like Kiu. The mana of Kiu reaches from north to south, from one island to another, from shore to shore. He is the greatest of all priests, he has hold of the spirits with both hands, and can compel them to obey him. He knows their talk, and they know his incantations and quickly do his bidding. Men of Otaki, you are the strongest tribe in your island, your chief is the greatest ruler in all Maoriland."

He gave a last hop, sat down with a jerk, and remained perfectly still except that his head moved like that of a woodhen when she walks.

Kiu rose with all the dignity of the great man that he undoubtedly was. He took a couple of turns on the marae, cleared his throat that all might know he was about to speak, flourished the small taiaha he held in his right hand, and said:—

"Men of Kaiapoi, we have come to show you a thing you have never been able to accomplish. I heard of the manner in which the taniwha was eating you up; I said, 'These men must be breakers of the sacred law of tapu, they can have no proper charms or spells or incantations, so that the taniwha troubles them with impunity. But they possess one thing, they know the fame of Kiu, the tohunga who controls all spirits from the underworld.' Therefore I said, 'I will help these men.' I instructed my tribe to make a taura toi—a rope that never breaks—you have seen it, how thick it is, how strong. Well, I have said incantations to make it stronger still: it will hold the taniwha as easily as a mother holds her child. You shall see what my incantations can do, you shall see . . . ."

To make a long story short, the men from Otaki dragged the hawsers from the shore to the pa; and the great priest went into his hut, and there repeated the wondrous spells for which he was famed.

Next morning everybody sallied forth in the direction of the den of the taniwha. It was simply a hole, dug deep in the earth, over which Kiu's men spread the hawsers, looped into great nooses; the tohunga directing the operation with as little fear as if he were planting potatoes in his own garden.

"The monster knows I am here," said he, in a clear, loud voice, that all might hear. "He is frightened to come out. Now, all of you take hold of one rope, and leave the other for me. I will show you what power I possess."

When his two hundred followers had arranged themselves as they were instructed, old Kiu walked to the edge of the great hole, and called out, "Are you down there, taniwha? Why don't you come? It is I, Kiu the tohunga. I have come all the way from Otaki to talk with you. Do you hear? Come out at once!"

He stepped back from the mouth of the hole, took hold of his rope, and there was a rumbling in the bowels of the earth.

In a minute or two, there appeared in the centre of the two nooses a head like that of a monstrous giant.

"Pull!" shouted Kiu.

But before the ropes were drawn taut, the taniwha, perceiving the trap, made a mighty spring, only to be caught fast round his middle.

He lashed out his enormous arms, took hold of a hawser in either huge hand, and kicked, and pulled and writhed, and groaned in agony; but the ropes held fast and tight, not a man flinched. And Kiu, who held one rope by himself, was as strong as the two hundred who manned the other rope, and stronger than the taniwha.

As the monster struggled in the toils, the priest shouted, "Have you had enough, taniwha? Don't you see that you're caught? Can't you see it is I, Kiu the big tohunga, who have got you in my noose?"

The taniwha ceased his struggles, and lay panting on the ground.

"Let go!" cried Kiu to his men. "I have got him fast. I can hold him by myself."

The men obeyed, and the taniwha, springing from the ground, tried to tear the nooses from his body, and escape. But Kiu put his heels into the soft ground, and held the monster as easily as a man holds a dog.

At last the taniwha stood still, trembling.

"Now," said Kiu, walking boldly up to the awful creature, "tell me what you are. Are you a man?"

"I am," said the taniwha.

"A Maori?"

"Yes, a Maori, before I was made a taniwha."

"What's your name, then?"

"Tuahuriri, that's my name."

'You have no right to such a name! 'The God of War ready for Battle!' I have not met such impertinence in a monster before. Remember that you are now my taniwha, and do what I tell you. Do you hear me?"

"I hear," said the worsted monster sullenly.

"You have been killing my friends here, and have eaten over two hnndred of them."

"I own I have eaten a great number, but how many I don't know, because I never kept count."

"Well, don't you dare to eat any more. If you do I will very quickly make an end of you. You must eat fish and pigs in future. If you eat any more men I will come and kill you without further inquiry. You are my taniwha, and I will now tell you what you must do. You are to make payment to my friends for every member of their tribe you have eaten; you are to catch for them fish and pigs and pigeons, which you shall place during the night outside their pa; you are never to show yourself unnecessarily by day, lest you frighten their women and children with your horrible form; you are to drive off any monsters such as yourself who may wish to molest my friends; you are to protect this tribe as if it were your own. Do you understand?"

"Perfectly," said the taniwha.

"Do all you men of Otaki and of Kaiapoi hear?" asked Kiu.

"We all hear," answered the people, who had now gathered about the hole, and gazed at the conquered monster.

"Very good," said Kiu to the taniwha, "but if you disobey me in the slightest particular, my attendant spirits will inform me, and your doom will be sealed: I will roast you alive, and give your flesh to the pigs and dogs of the pa."

The taniwha looked round in trepidation at the assembled people, his great yellow teeth chattering with fear.

"Now go back into your hole," commanded Kiu, "and stop there till we have gone away."

The monster gave one humble glance at the mighty tohunga, and slunk, broken and dispirited, into his den.

Afterwards the people of Kaiapoi lived sumptuously, for every night, wet or fine, frosty or mild, the taniwha placed a stock of food outside their pa. But in course of time when the debt was paid, Kiu removed his spell and the monster departed without warning. Kaiapoi looked for him in vain, and even sent a special messenger, asking Kiu to send the creature back to them. But the great tohunga replied, "You people are greedy. My taniwha has fed you for ten years; now he shall feed me and my tribe."

THE WIZARD WHO KNEW TOO MUCH.

KOHURU, though young in devilment, was filled with a malignant energy, begotten of a baneful upbringing; for his father had schooled him in sorcery and, upon passing to the spirit-world, had cast his mantle upon the shoulders of his hopeful heir.

To weep over the dead chief came Tawhaki, the arch-priest of Urewera, who brought with him his pretty daughter Titia (i-Te-Rangi), the joy of his heart and the light of his eyes.

Kohuru immediately fell in love with Titia, which was a thing commendable in itself, if it had tended to dissipate his devilments. But, sad to say, it had the directly opposite effect, for when Kohuru broached the subject of his passion to the girl's father, that old sorcerer rebuffed the ardent suitor with the taunt that he was so immature in wickedness as to be unworthy of the daughter of a wizard famed for his diablerie through the length and breadth of the land.

That decided Kohuru's career, and no sooner had Tawhaki departed with his lovely daughter than the young tohunga got to work. It the neighbouring pa lived a priest named Tatuanui, whom the youth had known since he was a child, and who had been a bosom friend of the dead chief. To him, therefore, Kohuru went for wizardly counsel, which was as willingly given as it was eagerly sought.

"The young hawk may fly higher than the parent bird," said Tatuanui, "when he is fully fledged. Now, let us enter into an engagement. For three months we will live in fellowship and communion, and at the end of that time we will go forth to prove whose spells are the stronger." But this he said because he desired to forward his private ends.

At Manukau there lived a tohunga with whom

Tatuanui was at deadly feud, a priest so potent in sorcery that with the breath of his mouth he had slain over a hundred men whom Tatua' had sent to compass his destruction. But since force of arms had failed, the worsted wizard had determined to use witchcraft.

"We will take every precaution that our spells may prove effective," said Tatua', "we will observe all the prescribed rites, but particularly that in regard to the law of tapu. In order to avoid the chance of eating anything which our enemy may have consecrated to his use—an action which would certainly cause our destruction—we will eat nothing by the way. We will enter no pa, we will speak with no one on the journey. Then shall we arrive at Manukau proof against the sorceries of our enemy."

Now, as he was a man of full habit, great in girth and unaccustomed to hard toil, Tatuanui had placed upon himself a heavy handicap, more especially as the journey to Manukau by the beaten track was close upon a hundred miles. But the younger and more daring tohunga had no intention of placing such a restriction upon himself. When the days of priestly preparation were passed, he bade his attendant wahine to go into the woods and cut him a stick which the hands of man had never touched, and to prepare a bundle of fern-root which the eye of man had never seen. The fern-root he tied to the end of the stick, and then he said to his priestly companion: "I am ready; let us set out."

After a full meal, and without telling their friends whither they were bound, the two wizards departed upon their diabolical mission. They travelled by unfrequented ways, and because of Tatua's fatness and the sultriness of the weather they made but slow progress. The first night they rested in the glade of a thick forest, but before going to sleep Kohuru ate a little of his fern-root; taking care to plant his stick upright in the ground, so that the small store of food should touch nothing. Tatua', however, refused to share this meagre meal, but, after a night's sleep, arose considerably refreshed.

The second day's journey lay through hilly country covered with thick forest, and the older wizard soon began to show signs of fatigue, and this more especially as he could not be persuaded to drink from any of the rivulets that were crossed. Towards mid-day his strength almost gave out, but after a prolonged rest he struggled on till nightfall, when the travellers camped in a thick clump of manuka scrub. Here Kohuru partook of a scanty repast of fern-root, and again failed to persuade his companion to eat.

On the third day Tatua's powers gave out, and when the heat of the sun was at its greatest he collapsed. Still he could be persuaded neither to eat nor drink, but towards evening he managed to walk a mile or two further.

Next morning, when Kohuru arose and tried to awake his companion, he found the fat old man dead and stiff.

Covering the body with boughs plucked from the neighbouring bushes the young chief went on his way, determined to effect his mission unaided, and on the fifth day he reached the country overlooking the back of the fell Matuku's pa, and there, hiding himself in the fern, he rested till daylight.

Now, it was the custom of the wizard of Manukau to repair to a small knoll behind his fortress soon after sunrise, that he might watch any strange canoes voyaging across the broad waters of the harbour, and to cast his spells upon them if they should prove inimical. It was thus that he had discomfited the war-party of the departed Tatua', and it was thus that he hoped to protect himself from all his foes. This habit of the Manukau chief was well known to Kohuru, who, therefore, had taken up a post from which he could overlook the uncanny deliberations of his enemy.

The sun cast its first beams of light upon the dark and tranquil tide, and the birds of the forest roused Kohuru with their matin songs. The day broke brightly over land and sea, and from the gates of the pa there issued the solitary figure of a man, dressed in a long korowai cloak. He ascended the ridge upon which the covert wizard lay amid the fern, and approached the knoll of witchcraft. Long and intently the guardian priest gazed upon the sea: he had raised his hand, preparatory to making his accustomed orison, when Kohuru stood up and hurled at him his ruthless malediction. Down fell the upstretched arm, and as though struck by lightning the priest of Manukau dropped to the earth. Approaching the motionless form, Kohuru gazed at the glassy eyes and the rigid limbs. From the dead chief's neck he took the greenstone hei tiki, from the deaf ear he plucked the treasured shark's tooth, from the stiffened hand he snatched the honoured taiaha, and taking a last look at the sleeping pa, he stole into the forest and retraced his ruthless steps.

* * * *

Kohuru now justly considered that he had proved himself a past-master in devilment and a wizard worthy of being allied to Tawhaki, the arch-priest of Urewera. So, after duly performing the obsequies of the swag-bellied Tatuanui, he set out to claim his bride.

With a retinue befitting a great chief, and an armed force sufficient to afford protection by the way, he started with magnificence. Having reached their destination, after a long and tedious journey, the travellers were greeted with proper ceremony, and when they had been feasted for three or four days, and speeches of welcome had been received and acknowledged, Kohuru recommenced his courtship. Titia he found as beautiful as ever and by no means unwilling to be won, but her father gave no sign of encouragement to the suitor, who therefore determined to make sure of the girl's affection, and then with her aid to seek the consent of the arch-priest.

All went well so far as the first part of the programme was concerned, for Kohuru was as handsome as he was dauntless, and Titia was as feminine as she was beautiful. In a hundred little ways, which could only be invented by a woman, she showed him her affection in the pa, and in the cover of the forest where she subsequently met him by arrangement she undisguisedly gave him her whole heart.

"I will now approach your father," said the young tohunga. "In my own country I have gained a greater mana than even my father possessed. I am worthy to be the son-in-law of the greatest chief in Urewera."

He proceeded to the winning of the father with as much address as he had employed in wooing the daughter. He would sit and korero with the ancient sorcerer all the morning and far into the night—the afternoon, however, he usually reserved for a tete-a-tete with the charming Titia. But in his interviews with Tawhaki he was careful to let the ancient wizard do most of the talking, for he knew that the best way to gain an old man's regard is to be a good listener.

Day after day the two necromancers sat in Tawhaki's whare in close conversation and, beginning with the deeds of his youth, the white-haired priest recounted all the devilments of his long life. When at length he had finished, he said: "But what are my karakia and priestcraft to me now that I an old? I am like a warrior whose strength has failed; his skill remains, but his power to display it is gone. So it is with me. I possess the strongest spells of any tohunga in the land, but age ties me to my whare. I seldom have the chance to show what I can do."

"But your mana is the envy of all who deal in sorcery," said Kohuru. "There is not a chief who does not respect your name; from end to end of the land you are regarded as the greatest of all wizards."

I am glad to hear you say so. It is a great pleasure for me to know that my powers are not forgotten in places I can no longer hope to visit."

"But your witchcraft reaches from north to south, from sea to sea; your makutu is dreaded from Taranaki to Tauranga, and from Whanganui to Hokianga."

"Yes, yes; but tied as I am by age to my pa, I cannot go on those great progresses through the country which were once such a pleasure, and receive the homage which the tribes invariably extended to my mana. Soon I shall die and be forgotten, and who will then remember my fame?"

"Your descendants."

"I have no son to whom I may teach my karakia and makutu; I have but one daughter—beautiful beyond measure—who, however, cannot be expected to perpetuate my witchcrafts."

"But she might perpetuate your family—if you can find a man worthy of being your son-in-law."

The old wizard smiled.

"But where shall I find him?" he asked.

Kohuru felt that the time had come for him to plead his cause.

"Some time ago when I spoke to you of the marriage of your daughter, you declared that your difficulty was that you could not find a man of sufficient mana in witchcraft and sorcery to whom you might unite her."

"That is so; and I have not found him since."

"But I think I can help you in the search," said Kohuru, nothing daunted. "I know of a tohunga who possesses almost as much power over the unseen world as you do yourself. Perhaps you have heard of Matuku of Manukau?"

"Ah! he, now, is worthy to be a son-in-law of mine—but he is too old."

"Worse than that—he is dead."

"Dead? I never heard the news. When did he die?"

"Just before I left home. But what I wish to tell you is the manner of his death. He was killed by another wizard, a man better versed in devilments than he was himself. As the old man stood outside his pa, at Manukau, launching his spells at any enemies who might be bent on harming him, there rose from the earth behind him another priest, who with one single curse struck old Matuku to the ground. That is the man for your daughter."

"Excellent, excellent; I would accept him. What is his name? Where am I to find him?"

Kohuru rose to his feet.

"He stands before you. It was I myself who slew Matuku."

But Tawhaki laughed.

"This taiaha that I hold in my hand," continued the young man, "I took from the grasp of the tohunga I had killed with my witchcraft. This hei tiki, at my throat I took from his neck, and this shark's tooth that I am wearing I took from his ear." One by one he placed the articles in Tawhaki's hands, and the old man's eyes gleamed with interest. "You told me that when I had proved myself to be well versed in witchcraft, I might entertain hopes of your daughter. I come to you as a tohunga second only to yourself. I have the mana of my father, of Matuku, and of myself, and nowhere outside this pa can you find my equal."

"Possibly that is so," said old Tawhaki, dubiously, "but I should require other evidence than your own statement; for, you see, we tohunga-men are given overmuch to exaggeration when describing our deeds."

"That may be so, but the men whom I have brought with me will corroborate every word I have said."

"Very likely, yet we need not trouble them. It is near the time when the women return from the plantations. Go out, and put your spell on the first woman that comes up the track, and then if she dies I shall know that what you say is true, and you shall marry my daughter. What is the life of one slave-woman in comparison with the settling of this important question?"

The two wizards sallied forth through the gate of the pa, and stood silently watching till the figure of a woman appeared walking slowly up the steep path that led to the fortress from the fertile valley below.

"Now is your time," said Tawhaki.

"It has come," said Kohuru. He stretched out his hands, and from his mouth poured the potent spell which had slain Matuku of Manukau, and before the last word had left his lips the woman was seen to tumble to the ground.

"Well done!" exclaimed old Tawhaki. "You have done splendidly."

"Am I now a tohunga worthy of your daughter?"

"You are, indeed you are. You shall be married to her as soon as you please."

"Then it will not be long before I am the happiest man alive," cried Kohuru. "Come, let us see that the woman is really dead, and that my witchcraft does not do its work by halves."

They hurried down the path with all the speed the aged priest could command. The woman had fallen on her breast, with a tangle of hair lying in the dust, so that as the wizards approached they could not see her face.

"She is dead enough," said Tawhaki, lifting a hand, which fell limply to the ground. "Turn her over, and let us see who she is."

Kohuru took hold of the dead body and lifted it up; and, as the wicked old Tawhaki caught sight of the upturned face, he gave a weird and fearful shriek, for it was the face of his daughter!

TE IHONGA AND THE TANIWHA.

EVERY one who has read these tales knows that a taniwha is a fearsome beast, which carries out the behests of a tohunga, and settles scores for him with his troublesome rivals, but it is not commonly known that a most malignant taniwha may be created out of a fish of but ordinary voracity.

Such a taniwha was Tutae-poroporo, the monstrous retainer of Te Ahuru. That great wizard had caught a little shark, which he took home to his pa at Rangitikei, to be a plaything for his small son, and for a while the fish was kept in a wooden tank beside the river, but as it grew in size and intelligence its captor designed for it a vast and interesting future. By his incantations he turned it into a taniwha, with jaws twelve feet in the gape and armed with innumerable rows of horrible teeth, and bade it protect him through good and evil.

Now, Ahuru had good cause to put this injunction upon his attendant monster, for, like all chiefs of importance, he possessed a deadly enemy. The revengeful person's name was Whare-tuturu. He lived at Whanganui, a warlike man, who was bent on the destruction of the Rangitikei chief, and such was his craftiness that he took Ahuru unawares, and slaughtered him and all his people. Only the taniwha escaped.

Whare-tuturu returned to the banks of the Whanganui in triumph, and settled down to enjoy the reputation he had won and a surcease from care, now that his enemies were annihilated. But he made his reckoning without considering the taniwha.

That awful beast had been endowed with such power by his dead master, that he surmised with perfect certainty the identity and habitation of the murderer, and straightway swam along the coast, and took up his abode in a deep hole in the Whanganui River, some five or six miles below the pa where Whare-tuturu dwelt in false security.

But soon strange developments occurred, which proved that a normal state of affairs had ceased to exist on the river. A canoe, loaded with people who went to fish in the estuary, never returned; the catastrophe, however, was attributed to accident. But when three canoes, which voyaged in company, were overturned in the smooth waters of the pool where the taniwha lived, and the terrible monster swallowed all the crews, then the murderous chief became alarmed.

As has been said, he was of a superlatively crafty nature, so it is not surprising that while investigating the cause of the unaccountable disappearance of his people, he took every precaution for effecting his own protection. Calling all his dependents about him, he addressed them thus:—" No doubt you have all guessed that the fate which has overtaken those of our tribe who have lately gone out to fish, shows clearly that all our enemies are not yet dead. Doubtless some of the relatives of the Rangitikei people have determined to take utu for Ahuru and his hapu, but our numbers are so great and our pa is so strong, that we have little to fear. I do not propose to await the attack of our foes, but will go down the river to meet them. Arm yourselves, therefore, and we will avenge our kindred."

But when the canoes were manned, he took care that his own craft was the last in the procession which dropped down the stream, and that he followed at a safe distance the more daring occupants of the ten canoes which thus formed the vanguard. All went well till the pool of the taniwha was reached, and then Tutae-poroporo's presence immediatley asserted itself. With a ram from his great snout and a lash of his long tail, the monster upset the leading canoes one after the other, and gobbled up the struggling crews by six or a dozen at a mouthful before they could swim ashore, but Ahuru kept aloof, and seeing the fate of his companions, turned his canoe up stream, and fled home in fear and trembling.

He had thus lost nearly all his warriors, and it was evident that he was physically helpless to rid himself of the monster that had come to scourge him, and as he was a warrior and not a tohunga versed in incantations, he determined to call in the aid of his friend Te Ihonga, of Waitotara, a chief of wide fame and a most notorious wizard.

As the messenger to Waitotara had to journey overland on account of the presence of the taniwha in the river, Te Ihonga and his accompanying taua were long in coming, by which time, as no canoes had passed down the river since the presence of the taniwha had been detected, that voracious monster was ravenous.

So soon as the Waitotara chief learned the facts of the case, he shut himself up in a hut, and for three days did nothing but repeat incantations and cast spells. At the end of that time he emerged, and after eating heartily, he shut himself up in a wooden box, seven feet long, three feet wide and three feet deep, which he had commanded his men to fashion out of a solid piece of white pine. For twelve hours he remained a prisoner, his life sustained by the air which found its way through the holes, made for the purpose of lashing on the lid. At the conclusion of that period he tapped the side of the box, and Whare-tuturu liberated him.

"That is very good," said Te Ihonga, as he stepped among the wondering people. "You will now see something which you will never forget. I am the sworn enemy of these taniwha and such-like monsters. They come to eat up my friends, they fill their bellies with my relations; but now they have to deal with Te Ihonga, and they will find him more than they can digest. To-morrow go to the cliff which overlooks the place where the taniwha lives, and about midday you will see something which will cause you much wonderment."

With the dawn the people set out through the tangled forest to the top of the cliff, which towered above the deep pool where the taniwha disported himself; and, as has been said, Tutae-poroporo was famished with hunger. They saw him swim now up stream, now down; they watched him lash the water with his tail, so that the river foamed again, and they thought of the awful fate that awaited anyone who was foolhardy enough to voyage down the river.

In the village Te Ihonga tarried with six chosen friends: he was engaged all the morning in making an enormous meal, "For," as he said, "I do not know when I may make another." Then, armed with a sharp mira, or knife edged with shark's teeth, he entered his box and, fastening him down securely, his companions carried the coffin-like kumete to the water's edge and, towing it into midstream, let it float down the river.

On the cliff overlooking the pool of the taniwha all was hushed and still, though hundreds of eyes peered through the scrub at the face of the water; for it was now noon, the time when Te Ihonga had predicted that strange things would happen. Presently, far up the river, the people saw something white bobbing on the surface of the water, and a long way behind a solitary canoe, paddled by a few men. As the white object drew nearer the watchers recognised it, and whispered to one another, "The kumete of Te Ihonga—it is floating down the river." But the taniwha had seen it too, and as has been said, he was mad with hunger.

The box was now approaching the rapids, and for a few moments was whirled about, now this way, now that, now on the surface, now under water, but presently it reached the smooth pool, and the taniwha, making a dart at so conspicuous an object, swallowed Te Ihonga and his box at a gulp.

The people on the cliff could not restrain a cry of horror, and hearing it, Tutae-poroporo said to himself, "That last mouthful was not so good as I thought it would be; but evidently there are people on the river-bank who will be more tasty. I see how the matter stands. They have given up using the river as a highway, and walk about on foot; but I will waylay them in the forest, and catch them as easily as I did in the water."

He swam slowly to a pebbly beach not far from the cliff, and walked ashore.

"Dear me," he said, "that last thing I swallowed does not seem to be settling down comfortably; it makes me feel very queer. It is quite plain that it is not safe to eat everything that comes floating down the river. I will be more careful in future."

But that was the last resolution he ever made, for at that moment Te Ihonga, perceiving by his motions that the monster was walking on dry land, commenced to cut his way out of the taniwha. For a moment or two Tutae-poroporo stood still, first in wonderment and then bellowing with pain, but the operation was soon over, and out dropped Te Ihonga, and with him all the greenstone axes and ornaments of the people whom the taniwha had eaten, and that great beast fell on his side and expired without another groan.

THE BEDEVILLED EELER.*

EVERYBODY should be warned against the patupaiarehe, for not only has that extraordinary demon been falsely described, but few Pakeha people know anything of his evil proclivities and malignant nature. By some writers he has been pictured as a Puck-like fairy, a diminutive denizen of the forest, more bent on mischief than on evil-doing. But this story will show that he is a devil whose wickedness was undoubtedly acquired in the depths of the underworld, whence he came and whither he indubitably will return. When on earth, he makes his headquarters at Pirongia, a mountain of Hauraki, from whence, however, he finds his way to every part of Maoriland ; for he travels with incredible swiftness, working wickedness wherever he goes. In size and shape he resembles a human being, except that his legs are thin like sticks and end in hoof-like feet ; his body and limbs are covered with with lichen-like kohukohu ; in complexion he is white, with red hair. Indeed, he is uncommonly like a Pakeha—especially one of the Celtic race—though it is not for a moment inferred that a ruddy McTavish or a red-haired O'Connor is more like this devil than is a Saxon Smith or Johnson.

The patupaiarehe seems to seek this world for no serious purpose, but spends his time here in the pursuit of mere devilment. He appears to owe allegiance to the great wairua tribe, which is composed of the departed spirits of the greatest 'tohungas' who ever lived. Into his hands have been committed, doubtless for his sustenance when on earth, all albino creatures, such as white parson-birds, white rats, white eels, and white

* It appears to me that this is the origina! patupaiarehe story, from which such tales as "The Demon of the Albinos" have their origin.—A.A.G.

fish; and though he is always evilly disposed towards men, his most implacable hatred is reserved for those who interfere with the creatures committed to his care.

This, however, does not seem to have been the opinion of Ruru, as the story will show. In company with a man named Kareawa he went to fish for eels. Each armed himself with a kind of sword, made of hard akeake wood, a weapon better suited than hook and line for catching eels in the upper reaches of the river which flowed into the sea not far from the kainga.

They started in the forenoon, purposing to fish in the afternoon and to return in the cool of the evening. The river, flowing through the thick forest, rippled over a bed of stones, except where the swollen waters had scoured holes in time of flood. It was in these holes that Ruru and Kareawa expected to catch their eels.

They reached their destination in good time, and after rest and refreshment they began to fish. Casting off his garment, each man took his wooden weapon, and waded up stream. Before long they came to a deep hole, where they saw lazily swimming to and fro four large eels, and immediately the sport began. Wading up to his neck, Ruru drove the black, snake-like fish down stream towards his companion, where they one by one fell beneath Kareawa's blows.

Placing the four eels on the bank where they could easily find them, the fishers waded up stream to the next hole, which, to their surprise, they found to be occupied, like the first, by four eels.

"This is strange," said Kareawa. "We find four eels in the first hole, and we find exactly the same number in the second. I don't like the look of things. I think we have discovered the preserve of a patupaiarehe who has stocked this river with eels; and if we touch them misfortune will certainly overtake us."

"Nonsense," said Ruru, "nothing is more natural than to find eels in such pools as these, and that each of them should contain four is a mere coincidence. I see nothing remarkable in the fact."

"I see a great deal in it," replied Kareawa. "I will do no more fishing in this river."

"As you please," said his companion, "but for myself, as the stream is evidently full of tuna, I mean to have a good day's sport. I am going further up the stream."

"Very well," said Kareawa, "you must go alone. I will return to the place where we left our clothes, and there wait for you."

So the two men parted.

Pursuing his way up stream, Ruru presently came to another hole, in which to his surprise he saw four white eels swimming idly. All his sporting instinct was aroused, and it was not long before he had captured one of these strange tuna ma, the like of which he had never seen before. Hastening with his prize, he rejoined his friend.

"Look, Kareawa, at what I have caught! What is it?"

"It is a white eel."

"There were four of them in one pool."

"Then I am certain that we have found the river of the patupaiarehe, to whom all white animals, birds, and fish are tapu. I beg you to put it back in the river."

"I will do nothing of the kind," said Ruru. "I am going to eat it."

So saying he made a fire and cooked the white eel.

"It's good," he said, after he had tasted it. "Have a piece, Kareawa. It is sweeter and more delicate than an ordinary eel."

"No white tuna for me," said his companion. "It is the food of the patupaiarehe!"

"Who gave the patupaiarehe all the eels in the country? I like white eels better than black." Ruru had finished his meal. "Good-bye," he said, "I'm going to catch the three others I left in the pool, and take them to the pa for the people to see."

He quickly reached the pool of the tuna ma, and set to work to catch them. Being white they were clearly visible in the water, and before long Ruru had caught two of them, but the third, which was bigger than the others, put him to so much trouble that when he had killed it he sat down on the bank to rest.

He looked up the river and down. "I think I'll leave these white tuna here," he said to himself, "and see if I can't catch more like them in the pools above." So with his trusty ake rautangi he waded up stream. But in the next pool there were no eels.

"That proves what I thought," said Ruru. "If a patupaiarehe owned this river he would put eels into this hole as well as into the others." He pushed further up the stream, but in the next pool he came to there were no eels.

He waded on, examining pool after pool, yet in none of them was there a single eel. "It is strange," said Ruru, "that there should be plenty of tuna in the pools below and none up here." But his eye caught sight of a tributary which fell into the river amid a bower of foliage, and he said to himself, "I'll go up that side-stream, and see what luck I have there."

The day was now drawing to a close, and the long shadows of the trees stretched across the river, but Ruru took no notice of time, and forgot his friend Kareawa in the keenness of his desire to catch eels. He explored the tributary stream, but there the holes were as strangely empty of eels as had been the higher reaches of the bigger river. And then, before he was fully aware of it, night was upon him.

He was a long way from the camp where he had cooked his eel; he knew that Kareawa would be anxiously expecting him; so, instead of wading down the now somewhat difficult river-courses, he determined to strike across country. With the idea of reaching his friend more quickly, he plunged into the trackless forest, and accustomed as he was to the bush, he had no apprehension of losing himself. At first he found the way fairly flat and easy, but before long the forest became exceedingly dense and the ground extremely broken; he found his path barred by crops of stinging-nettles and entanglements of supplejacks and lawyer creepers. More than once he thought of retracing his steps to the creek, for what with the impentrableness of the forest and the roughness of the ground, he made but small progress, and began to think he had lost his way. Push on as he best might, he failed to reach the river long after both by distance and time he should have heard the ripple of its laughing waters. At length, convinced that he was lost, he called desperately to his mate.

An answer faint and far was borne upon the gentle wind of night, but it came from behind him. Again he called, and again the answer came from behind him. There was no doubt now that he had mistaken his way. Altering his course, he pressed on in the new direction, calling as he went, the answering cries growing louder and at length so loud that Ruru expected to reach the river at every step.

"Kareawa!"

"O-o-o-e-e!"

"Where are you?"

"O-o-o-e-e!"

"Are you over there?"

"O-o-o-e-e!"

"Did you think I was never coming back?"

"O-o-o-e-e!"

He thought to catch sight of his friend's fire at any moment, and had ceased to call, so sure was he that he was at the end of his troubles, when there suddenly appeared from all sides a dozen or more white creatures, who, stretching out their long, naked arms, seized him violently, and with a shriek Ruru perceived that he had fallen into the hands of the patupaiarehe.

* * * *

Kareawa waited for his companion to return. Through the long black night he called and called, and piled dry wood on the fire, so that its flames might guide the benighted fisherman. But when the grey dawn penetrated the trees, Ruru had not appeared. After a hasty meal, Kareawa began to search the river, examining the deep holes and the wooded banks. He came upon the three white eels which Ruru had hung over the bough of a tree beside the water. He pressed on till he came to the tributary which his deluded companion had explored, but he found no trace of the man who had laughed at the patupaiarehe. Then he reluctantly returned home, with nothing but Ruru's feathered cloak and the skin of the white tuna that had been eaten, as mementoes of the disastrous eeling expe dition.

* * * *

"The river belongs to the patupaiarehe," Kareawa told the people. "All the eels in it belong to the demons of the underworld. In one pool we found nothing but black eels, in the next nothing but white. One of these tuna ma Ruru persisted in eating, though I warned him that it was tapu to the patupaiarehe. Here is its skin."

Everybody was lost in wonderment.

"When I discovered the nature of the river, I refused to have anything more to do with it," continued Kareawa; "but Ruru went wading on, killing all the eels he could find, and when night fell he did not return. Till morning I called and called to him, but he did not answer. Without doubt he will return no more, for the patupaiarehe have got him."

Tangiroa, Ruru's young wife, stood by, listening and weeping, and when she heard of her husband's horrible fate she bewailed him as one dead, and gashed her breast till the blood flowed in streams, so disconsolate was she in her widowhood.

* * * *

Though thus mourned for, Ruru was not dead. The patupaiarehe had dragged him into their den, where he was kept a close prisoner. Day and night he was watched by gibing, gibbering attendant demons, who treated him most infernally. First of all, they bedazed him by sitting in a ring round him and staring at him with big, unearthly eyes; then they slobbered over him, and all his hair dropped out; they next rubbed him all over with the palms of their hands and the soles of their feet, a process which caused a kind of moss or lichen to grow over his body and limbs; and after that they slowly awakened him from his stupor.

When he came to his senses, Ruru could not recognise himself, for, save that his skin was still brown and his face tattooed, in other respects he seemed to be like the patupaiarehe with whom he lived. But, considering the offence he had committed, his captors treated him with marked consideration. They brought him pigeons, parson-birds, and eels, but, as the patupaiarehe use no fire, Ruru was forced to eat his food raw. He was allowed to wander through the forest, and gather berries and the white grubs which live in dead red pines, and this liberty he never attempted to abuse, for he had not the slightest idea how far the demons had carried him, though he fully realised that their den was in the middle of a vast and trackless forest. The days came and went, the moon, which was visible from the clearing in front of the devils' den, waxed and waned, summer was succeeded by winter, but of time Ruru took do account. He was as one dead to the world. The demons might gibe and gibber at him, they might dance demoniac dances round him, screech demoniac songs, but Ruru remained stolid and indifferent, so deeply was he bedevilled.

* * * *

But things went on as usual in Ruru's kainga. There the lost eeler was soon forgotten. His pretty wife's grief, at first so poignant, gradually gave way to resignation, and finally, after many months, to consolation. This last Tangi' received from Kareawa, who, unable to do anything for his vanished friend, directed his attention to the bereaved wife.

Tangi' resisted her new suitor so long as she had any hope of Ruru's return, but when eventually she began to give way, another suitor declared himself. This was Maringirangi, a somewhat aged chief.

Kareawa, indeed, was young, but as against that Maringi' was a tohunga of no small reputation. Tangi' felt flattered at being courted by a priest, and for a while she listened to his solicitations. This tendency in her made Kareawa redouble his efforts. He paid her every attention; bringing her fish from the sea, pigeons from the forest, and eels—but not from the river of the patupaiarehe. Sometimes, when the weather was fine and the sea smooth, he would even persuade her to trust herself with him in his canoe, and for a whole morning he would thus be free to press his suit without interruption. But the tohunga, though he was too old and dignified to use such a method of courtship, would turn the tables on his rival when he brought the girl back; for Maringi' was a famous man to korero, and far into the night he would hold Tangiroa and a large audience spell-bound in the big wharepuni with tales of his ancestors, till the girl felt that if she wanted reputation and station, Maringi' was the husband for her.

It was true that the tohunga was a man of mana, and that Karewa was a nobody in the tribe; but on the other hand the young man was handsome, and the old man ugly. Tangi' did not know what to do. She was afraid to offend the priest by refusing him; and she felt a natural inclination towards the younger man. She had spent a year of mourning, and now she spent a year of indecision, when something occurred which ended her irresolution. Another girl fell in love with Kareawa, a girl named Urunga, as beautiful as Tangi' and younger, who made no attempt to disguise her passion.

All Tangi's womanliness was immediately aroused. Heedless of the old tohunga, forgetful of Kareawa's lack of birth and prestige, consumed with a determination not to be supplanted by an interloping maiden, she proclaimed her approaching marriage with her departed husband's friend.

At first Maringi' was thunderstruck at this decision,

then he became enraged with Kareawa, and finally he gave way to veiled threats.

"All the tribe knows," said he, "how great my grief was for the loss of Ruru, and how I sympathised with his young wife. I even went so far as to console her by offering to marry her myself—I, the most renowned tohunga in these parts. But I am set on one side for a nobody, a man who has done nothing more remarkable than to lose his friend in the forest and then court the widowed wahine. The thing is a scandal, but I will see what can be done. It would be a strange thing if a tohunga of my reputation were to stand idly by and do nothing. Rest assured something will happen. There are three persons concerned in this business. There is the wahine Tangiroa, there is the tutua Kareawa, there is the tohunga Maringirangi; and there is a fourth person concerned—Ruru, whom the patupaiarehe carried off. Tangi' is nothing, Kareawa is nobody—neither can do anything. Ruru—who can say where Ruru is? But there remain Maringirangi and the patupaiarehe. The issue is between those two, and you will see what you will see."

With much dark talk of this sort the tohunga created a feeling of such apprehension in the minds of the people that the heads of the tribe postponed the marriage, and Tangi' and Kareawa were left in suspense.

The tohunga continued to wear an air of mystery, to talk obscurely and to act strangely. Everyday, with a regularity equal to the rising of the sun, he perambulated the beach which stretched along the coast northward of the pa, and could be seen gesticulating wildly as he repeated his incantations. This he did each day for a month, and in expectation of something terrible the people watched him apprehensively.

* * * *

In the den of the patupaiarehe everything continued as usual. The coterie of devils pursued their evil ways; amusing themselves in their spare time with plaguing the wretched Ruru. But, perhaps because the supply of food in the vicinity of their den gradually decreased, or it may have been because they were recalled to the nether regions, they at length decided to depart. Then in demoniacal debate they discussed what should be done with their miserable captive. One demon declared that the presumptuous mortal should be left to starve, another proposed that he should be carried off to Pirongia for the amusement of the devils there, but the majority were of the opinion that as they had caught him they should have the pleasure of tormenting him to death. The chief of the patupaiarehe, however, suggested that the most exquisite punishment would be to return the bedevilled man to his pa, where he would be an object of continual scorn and derision to those whom he had held nearest and dearest; and with an appreciation which was fiendishly unanimous, the demoniacal crew acclaimed their leader's proposal.

* * * *

The morning was clear and bright. Maringirangi, watched by a wondering crowd of people, walked, according to his daily custom, from the pa to the beach.

"He has gone to cast more spells," said one.

"His spells seem to have very little effect," said another.

"If Kareawa marries Tangiroa," said a third, "he will be overtaken by a fate similar to Ruru's."

"What was Ruru's fate?" asked a fourth.

"Who can tell?"

"Ah! who can tell?" said everybody.

They saw the tohunga walk along the shore towards a headland half a mile away.

"Be sure he will work something," said an old woman. "I have known him these many years, and he has done marvellous things in his time. Something will certainly come of his incantations."

"Kareawa is foolish," said another woman; "Tangi' is not worth such a risk as he is taking. Are there no other women in the pa whom a man may marry? My girl, Urunga, would marry him tomorrow."

But the people smiled, and watched the tohunga till he disappeared behind the headland.

When well out of sight of the pa, Maringi' sat down, and threw pebbles into the tide. He didn't seem bent on any particular business, and at length, the warmth of the sun producing drowsiness, he stretched himself on the sand and fell fast asleep.

How long he remained thus he did not know, but eventually he was awakened by a noise uncommonly like a cough, and turning suddenly, he saw, sitting on the sand close behind him, the most remarkable creature. In form he was much like a man, but in place of clothes his body was covered with what looked very much like moss, and the crown of his head was as bald as a boulder.

"Tena koe," said the tohunga.

There was no reply.

"Where have you come from?"

The extraordinary being refrained from answering.

The tohunga arose, and examined the stranger. He fingered the kohukohu, and passed his hand over the bald head.

"What tribe do you belong to?"

There was no response.

"He must be a porangi," said the tohunga. "Now, tell me who you are. What is your name? See if you can remember."

The creature replied by speaking gibberish which had no meaning.

The tohunga examined the tattoo on the stranger's cheeks.

"You must be a Maori," he said, "for you have the moko."

"I am a Maori," softly said the stranger.

"Then what is your name?"

"Ruru."

"Ruru!" exclaimed the tohunga. "Wonderful! marvellous! Where have you been this long while?"

"In the den of the patupaiarehe."

"In the den of the of the patupaiarehe? Then you have to thank me that you are not there still."

But Ruru made no sign of appreciation.

"Do you feel as if you could walk?"

Ruru rose slowly to his feet.

"Take a step or two," said the tohunga.

Ruru walked about ten yards.

"Very good," said the tohunga. "If we go slowly you will be able to reach the pa." And so they set out, the priest walking in front, and the man with the kohukohu behind.

The people were sitting around the ovens inside the pa, eating their mid-day meal. Through the gate walked the tohunga, and everybody looked up as he approached. Behind him came the bedevilled man, walking like one in a dream. In a moment, all the people were crowding round the tohunga and his strange companion.

"I want you all to look well at this man," said Maringi', so that everybody could hear. "What do you think of him?"

"A porangi! a porangi!" cried the people, commencing to run away. "A madman! a madman!"

"Come back! come back!" shouted the tohunga. "He's not a porangi. He'll not hurt you. See, he is quite harmless." And he took the stranger by the hand.

The people returned, reassured.

"Now, you remember that a man of our tribe was lost in the forest," said the tohunga.

"We remember it quite well," said the people "He was the husband of Tangiroa."

"Very good. Ask Tangi' to come here and tell us if this is her husband."

The pretty young woman was pushed through the crowd, and stood facing the priest and the man with the kohukohu.

"You lost your husband, did you not?" asked the tohunga.

"I did."

"Well, here he is. I have restored him to you."

Tangi' uttered an exclamation of horror. "This is a porangi!" she cried.

"No, no, he is not a porangi; he is your husband. Do you remember his name?"

"Of course I do: he was Ruru."

"Yes, that is so: he was Ruru. Now," said the tohunga, turning to the weird object beside him, "what is your name?"

"Ruru," said the man with the kohukohu.

"You see," said the tohunga, "he knows his name. He is your husband. Take him."

Then poor Tangiroa burst out crying. She stood looking at the bedevilled Ruru, and Ruru looked at her.

But the tohunga was a humane man, and he was truly fond of the afflicted young woman. He told the people to bring him some warm water, and while it was being fetched he said, "I think that every one will now see that my word has come true. I have brought back this man by my karakia, and by the same means I will cure him of his kohukohu."

With warm water he washed Ruru all over, and then he said a long and impressive incantation; again he washed him, and then with his hand he rubbed the bedevilled man's body and limbs, and the kohukohu fell off as if it had been nothing but lichen; and Ruru's senses returned, and he spoke and acted like other men.

But nothing that the tohunga ever did for him could cure his baldness.

THE TALE OF THE IMMORAL NGARARA.

URUHAPE was a chief who possessed such powers over the unseen world that everybody thought he would have respected such personal property as he had made tapu, or sacred, to himself. But Tonga was a woman who lacked foresight, a creature of impulse and carelessness, who could not realise the awful responsibility of living in close contact with a wizard, the hair of whose head she was not worthy to comb. And, strangely enough, it was a comb which caused all her trouble.

Uruhape went on a journey to the Urewera Country, where lived relations of his whom he had not seen since he was a child. He left all his belongings in his hut, knowing full well that nobody in Hauraki would be so foolhardy as to rob him in his absence. His mats of ceremony and his weapons he took with him; but such things as his fish-hooks, his mata-tuhua, used for tonsorial purposes, and the combs with which he was wont to deal with the kutu which took refuge in his locks, he left in a carved kumete in his wife's keeping. Everything in the box was sacred to himself, and of that fact Tonga was fully cognisant. However, in the mind of a foolish woman familiarity breeds contempt. Uruhape had treated his wife with such consideration and affection that she had forgotten the gulf fixed eternally between her mediocrity and his sanctity. So that he had been gone hardly a week when, being much troubled with the kutu in her own hair, Tonga lightly seized one of her husband's combs to rid herself of the pest.

She finished the operation without realising the enormity of her offence against her spouse's tapu; she returned the sacred comb to its box; and full of satisfaction she went down to the sea-shore to eat mussels. There retribution overtook her. While she bent over the succulent bivalves and drank the juice out of their nacreous shells, there hovered on the horizon a dark and ominous object, which flying swiftly over the surface of the sea, rapidly swept down on the misguided woman. Too late she heard the flapping of the great membranous wings, too late she saw the black abhorrent form. She had barely time to cry, "The Ngarara! the Ngarara!" when she was seized, and borne captive over the desolate sea.

That, you will think, was the end of the unhappy Tonga, that was the last ever heard of the woman who failed to respect her husband's tapu. But it was not so. All day the Ngarara flew over the sea with his prey, and as night fell he reached a solitary island, where he had made his home in a dark, unwholesome cave; and there he deposited his living burden.

Of course the terrified woman imagined that she was to be eaten alive; but the Ngarara had preserved her for a fate even more terrible. "You are to be my wife," said the monster in a language which Tonga could not as yet understand, but which she was to speak with fluency ere she had lived out half her days. "I have not the least intention of hurting you; I have brought you here simply to love you," said the Ngarara, and he took her on his knee, and wrapped her in his dreadful pinions.

Now, it so happened that Tonga had been married to the Ngarara only a couple of months—and such was her womanly ability of adapting herself to circumstances that she had become almost resigned to her new manner of living—when she gave birth to a dear little brown girl.

"This," said the Ngarara, "is no daughter of mine—she has no wings, no webbed feet."

"No," replied Tonga; "she is the daughter of Uruhape, my former husband."

"Then I will eat her," said the Ngarara.

"Don't do that," exclaimed his wife. "She will

grow up to be more beautiful than I am, and then you will be able to have two wives."

"I never thought of that," said the Ngarara. "That is a very good idea." And such was his immoral nature that he determined to carry out the plan.

There was one advantage, however, in being married to the Ngarara—he caught plenty of fish, and these Tonga cooked for herself and her child, to whom she had given the name of Kura. And this little girl throve and grew, but without knowing the fate that was in store for her; for when Kura had grown up, the Ngarara turned the faded mother out of his cave and took her daughter to be his wife.

The aged Tonga wandered over the island till she came to a sheltered cove at the end furthest from the den of the horrible monster, and there she made herself a hut out of flax leaves and manuka boughs, in which she lived a comparatively happy, if lonely, existence.

* * * *

Watch, now, how retribution overtakes the evildoer. In the pa where the story opened was a tohunga, named Raukura, who possessed a hook celebrated far and wide for its magical power of catching fish. This hook was just as tapu as had been Uruhape's comb, and yet an infatuated young man named Kirikiri stole the consecrated implement and took it with him on a fishing-expedition.

In his canoe were twenty other men, his accomplices, and when they were well out to sea, the priest whom they had robbed discovered the theft and cursed the thieves. Then the wind began to blow and the sea to rise; and driven by an awful storm, which lasted seven days, Kirikiri and his companions were shipwrecked on a desolate island, upon whose rocky shore they were cast by the ruthless waves. Kirikiri, the prime cause of the catastrophe, was drowned, and of his twenty comrades but six escaped with their lives.

The shipwrecked mariners took refuge in a cave till the storm was past, after which they set out to explore the island. As they walked along the beach looking for some place where they might scale the precipitous cliffs which encircled the island, they caught sight of an old woman walking towards them along the sand. When she saw them, she hastened her faltering steps, and clinging to them wept tears of joy, and rubbed noses with them all, one after another.

"You have come at last," she cried.

"Very much against our will," said the man who was the leader of the band now that Kirikiri was dead.

"I know you," said the old woman to the man who had spoken. "You are Kauhata, and you are Tuara, and you are Ririwaka, but the rest of you are strangers to me."

"We come from Hauraki," said Kauhata.

"And I come from Hauraki too," said the old woman; "but the three of you whom I do not know have grown into men since I was brought a captive here. I am Tonga, the wife of Uruhape."

"Oh! we remember hearing of you long ago. We thought you were dead."

"Twenty years ago I was brought by the Ngarara to this island, where I have remained ever since."

"What? The Ngarara!" All the men were struck with horror.

"Yes, he took me in his claws, and flew over the sea till he brought me to his den, which is at the other end of the island, and there I lived with him until my daughter grew up."

"Your daughter? Was she carried off too?"

"She was born soon after I arrived here. She is young and pretty, and I am old and feeble; so the Ngarara has cast me off and married my daughter."

The men muttered the deepest curse, and vowed vengeance on the infamous reptile.

"We will make short work of him," said Kauhata. "We will free your daughter, and she shall marry which of us she chooses."

"Be not so sure," said the old woman, tremblingly. "But do this. Make fire, and set a light to this dry brushwood growing along the beach, so that the smoke may be carried into the nostrils of the Ngarara and prevent him from smelling you. For if he were to discover your presence he would quickly make an end of you all."

So they made fire by rubbing two pieces of dry wood together, and soon set the scrub in a blaze.

"Now," said Tonga, "I will take you to my hut, where I have plenty of food, for you must be well-nigh dead with hunger."

Once inside the old woman's hut they were safe, for the Ngarara never went there, so great was his dislike for his former wife; and they had oysters and cockles and fish and fern-root and pigeons, and sweet potatoes which Tonga had found growing wild and had cultivated till they were large and delicate.

When the men were rested and refreshed, the old woman unfolded her plan for compassing the death of the Ngarara.

"You must understand that he is a great glutton," she said, "and that if he can get food enough he will eat till he can hardly move. After such a debauch he will be stupid and sleepy for days. Now, I propose that you set to work to catch all the fish you can, and when you have taken enough to satisfy the hunger of two or three hundred people, I will ask you to carry them to within a safe distance of the monster's den, and I and my daughter will see that he gets them. When the Ngarara has gorged himself and fallen into a heavy sleep, I will get you to build a taiepa-whare of strong beams, placed close together and roofed with toe-toe, round which you must pile quantities of dry brushwood; and it will be for my daughter and me to decoy him into the trap. But when we have done so it will be for you to accomplish his end."

When the old woman had finished the men with one accord approved of her sagacity and determination, and taking care to keep the scrub constantly burning, so that volumes of smoke were blown towards the Ngarara's den, they began to fish. As luck would have it, they found their canoe lying upon the beach, and in it they found the magic hook, which had been the cause of all their trouble, tied to one of the thwarts. With it they quickly made a great haul, and before nightfall they had caught more fish than even the gluttonous Ngarara could eat at a sitting. In the meanwhile Tonga had been busy making flax baskets, and into these—one hundred and twenty all told—they put the fish, and began to carry their bundles. In this task the night helped them, and before dawn they had placed all the food within easy distance of the monster's cave. Then Tonga sent them back to her hut to sleep, and as the sun shot its first beam of light above the far horizon she approached the mouth of the Ngarara's den.

* * * *

"Good morning, Te Ngarara!" A growl of disapproval came from the recesses of the cave.

"Call him 'Te Wai Rangi'"—the water of Heaven—"he loves that name, and hates the other," whispered a girlish voice.

"Good morning, Te Wai Rangi!"

"Come in, come in," cried the Ngarara.

"I've come to make you a present," said Tonga, for it was she who had awakened the reptile from his slumbers. "I have been fortunate in catching a great number of fish—kahawai, hapuku, snapper, rock cod, and all the best sorts—and I have come to ask you to accept them."

"How many have you caught?"

"About five hundred."

"I cannot count so far as that. Are there enough to make me a breakfast?"

"There are enough for your breakfast, dinner, and supper."

"Very good, then you may bring the food in. I will eat it."

"You are very kind," said Tonga, "but as there is more than I can carry, I must ask Kura to help me."

"Go!" cried the Ngarara gruffly to his young

wife. "Why are you dawdling here when you might be bringing in my breakfast? Go!" and he raised a threatening claw to give emphasis to his injunction.

The women began to carry in the baskets of fish, one in each hand, four at a journey, as quickly as they could. As the baskets were opened before his greedy eyes, the Ngarara began to snap his horrible jaws in expectation of the feast. As the food was placed in a huge heap before him he became so excited that he rose up and stretched himself to see that his gastric apparatus was in working order, and then he went outside his den and rolled in the dust, which is a regular practice with all Ngararas.

"Now I am ready to begin," he exclaimed; but the women said, "Don't be in such a hurry, for as yet we have only brought half."

The Ngarara was delighted. He rolled on his back, he kicked up his heels, and threw the dust, which lay inches thick before the door of his cave, in clouds over his body, but when the women had at last carried up all the food, the Ngarara began to feast. As quickly as they could untie the thongs of the baskets, first Tonga and then Kura emptied the contents into the capacious mouth of the beast, who swallowed with ease a basketful at a time. At length, when the meal was half done, Tonga said, "Dear Te Wai Rangi, hadn't you better finish your meal inside your cave?"

"I'm very comfortable where I am," replied the Ngarara, "I'm getting on famously. Another basket, please—that one there which seems to be full of moki."

"It is very nice here in the sun," said the old woman, "but I was thinking that perhaps you might wish to retire to your cave after you had finished eating."

"Well, why not?" asked the Ngarara.

"It is a pleasure to see you enjoy the food so much, but the more you eat the greater you grow in size. Unfortunately the door of the cave is narrow, and perhaps there might be some difficulty later on."

"Nonsense," laughed the Ngarara. Rising

clumsily, he jocularly waddled towards the mouth of his den, but he found that, as the old woman had surmised, he was already a tight fit.

"Very well," he said, squeezing himself through, "bring all the food into the cave, and I shall be able to finish the meal without fear."

Such, then, was the feast of the Ngarara, and when it was finished the monster was a prisoner in his cave.

* * * *

For three days the Ngarara slept. Seizing the opportunity of enjoying a little freedom, Kura went to see the strange beings, of whose arrival her mother had hastily told her. With interest she gazed at Kauhata and his companions. First she dallied with one and then with another, charmed with their presence, till she came to Kauhata, with whom she dallied the longest.

"And to think that I am married to the Ngarara!" she exclaimed. "It will be dreadfully hard to go back to him."

"It will only be till we have killed him," said Kauhata, "and that will be to-day, if you are as clever as you look."

The girl laughed. "What have I got to do?" she asked.

"Everything," replied Kauhata. "We have made the trap, but you must decoy him into it."

They took her to see the taiepa-whare, which they had built in the middle of the island. It was constructed of the trunks of manuka trees, and was thatched with dry toe-toe, and in the middle of the doorway they had dug a hole, beside which lay a strong and heavy post.

"I want you to make a bed of dry fern in that corner," said Kura, "and you must fetch at least fifty baskets of fish and some big gourds filled with water."

"That shall be done," said Kauhata, "and see, there is the hole in the roof through which you are to escape."

Every preparation being made, and the time approaching when the Ngarara should awake from his heavy sleep, Kura regretfully bade good-bye to her new-found friends, and returned to the den of her dreadful spouse.

"Wake up, Te Wai Rangi, wake up!" she cried, giving the monster's tail a sharp twist. "It's time you had something more to eat."

The Ngarara slowly rose, stretched himself, and opened his eyes.

"Have you had a good sleep?" asked the girl.

"Beautiful, beautiful," replied the monster. "I've had the most lovely dreams. I dreamt that I was in a country where the fish came up out of the sea and walked straight into my mouth as I lay on the beach."

"That was splendid," said Kura, "but I don't expect you feel much the better for it. Now, if you will come with me, I will show you the loveliest feast ever prepared for a Ngarara."

"Who by?" asked the monster suspiciously.

"By my mother," answered the girl. "She loves you so much that she has built a house for you, where she has placed a soft bed of dry fern and fifty or sixty baskets of the choicest fish."

"Does she hope to make herself my wife again?"

"She is wonderfully fond of you—she does nothing but talk about you every time I see her. I believe she has hopes."

"Let her hope," said the Ngarara. "So long as she supplies me with food I hope she will go on hoping," and he laughed as only a Ngarara can laugh.

Just then there was a noise near the entrance of the cave, and a shrill voice cried, "Good morning, Te Wai Rangi! Good morning, good morning!"

"Come in, come in," shouted the Ngarara. "I know the old woman when she calls."

Tonga entered.

"I hope you are well after the little feast I provided."

"Very well," said the Ngarara, "but thirsty."

"I have some bowls of the coolest water and some delicious fish, besides tender pigeons and tui."

"Bring them in," said the Ngarara, "the mention of them makes my mouth water."

"I want you to do me the honor of living in a new house which I have made for you."

"Is it far?"

"Only about half-way to my hut."

"I wish you would accept my mother's offer," said the girl, "for then we could clean out this dirty den while you were away."

"The cave is clean enough for me," said the Ngarara, "and should be clean enough for you."

"I want to clear out all the fish-bones, and get in fresh bedding for you to lie on," said his young wife; "and in order that you shall be put to no inconvenience, I hope you will accept my mother's invitation."

"I promise to provide you with plenty of food while you are my guest," said Tonga.

"Are you sure you have plenty?" asked the Ngarara.

"Quite sure," answered the old woman, "and equally sure that I can get plenty more."

"Very good," said the Ngarara, "I'll come. But I am afraid that my appetite will not be what I could wish after having its edge taken off by the fish I have already eaten."

"Whatever it is I promise to satisfy it," said the old woman.

So the Ngarara arose and squeezed himself through the door of his cave, and the women conducted him to the taiepa-whare.

Around the trap was piled a quantity of dry brushwood and toe-toe and fern.

"Isn't it rather small," said the Ngarara, looking through the doorway.

"When you get inside you will find it large enough and warm and snug."

"Go in first," said the monster to his young wife, "and see if it is big enough for me to turn in, and if the food is there."

Kura entered. "Everything is ready," she said;

"the food is here, and water for you to drink, and the softest of beds for you to lie on."

"I can smell the fish!" cried the Ngarara, and thrusting his head through the doorway he crept slowly inside.

"Are you all right?" asked the old woman.

"Quite right," replied the Ngarara. "Everything is as you said; but it is a little cold," and straightway he began to eat and drink.

"I will close the door," said the old woman, "and so shut out the wind. Soon you will be warm enough."

She placed the door-post upright in its hole, and secured it safely by means of stout crossbars, and then heaped brushwood and toe-toe against the closed entrance, and the Ngarara was trapped.

The old woman went quickly to the place where Kauhata and his companions were hiding, and bade them come to the taiepa-whare.

Armed with heavy spears, six of them stationed themselves about the trap, while Kauhata stood to leeward with a burning brand in his hand.

They could hear the monster grunting with satisfaction over his food, and the voice of Kura soothing him in the Ngarara language. But at length the meal was over; all the birds and all the fish had disappeared into his capacious maw, and with repletion sleep fell upon the greedy reptile.

For a while all was still; then there was a rustling in the thatch, and presently, clambering through the hole in the roof, came the beautiful and resourceful Kura.

"He's fast asleep," she whispered. "Now is the time to begin."

Kauhata thrust his brand into the dry brushwood, and the smoke of the fire began to ascend in a thick cloud. When the flames had caught good hold of the structure there was an ominous movement inside the trap, and soon the Ngarara began to bellow and lash out with all his might, till the entire structure rocked; but the men straightway drove their spears between the beams of the house, and transfixed the monster as he roasted. Gradually the struggles of the Ngarara ceased, and the flames, feeding on the joists and beams, cremated him where he lay. Thus was Kura freed from her dreadful husband and gained the pleasures of liberty.

Soon after this just and happy consummation, the weather setting fair, Kauhata and his companions placed their canoe in order, and putting the old woman and her daughter on board set out for the mainland. The voyage was long but uneventful, and when they arrived at the pa of their tribe they were welcomed as though they had returned from the grave.

Tonga found that her husband, Uruhape, had long been married to another wife, named Iringa, who, however, was so touched by the tribulations which the old woman had suffered, that she welcomed her as her companion in matrimony, and lived with her harmoniously till death parted them. With regard to Kura, her father declared that she could best show her gratitude to her deliverers by marrying one of them; so she chose Kauhata, who restored the magic hook to its rightful owner and lived happily ever afterwards.

There is, however, a thing I had almost forgotten. The children that Kura bore were half human and half Ngarara, which was a monstrous thing not to be endured. So they called in the aid of old Raukura the sorcerer, who out of gratitude to Kauhata for restoring the magic hook which Kirikiri had stolen, consented to pronounce a karakia over the afflicted wife, and afterwards her children were like those of any other woman.

But what perhaps is stranger than this miracle is the fact that when Kauhata went on a voyage of curiosity to see once more the Island of the Ngarara where his wife had lived so long, he found it did not in reality exist, but had been the work of magic, which had brought it into existence and, when it had served its purpose, had caused it to disappear.

POTTED PIGEONS.

MATANGI was a clever man in his way, but he had no true insight into the female character.

In Hineuru he owned a wife who possessed those qualities that seem most desirable in a woman. She was a good cook, comely and good-tempered and the mother of two small boys; and yet her husband was not satisfied.

He left his kainga on the Pelorus river, determined to traverse the South Island on a matrimonial expedition. At Waikawa he saw plenty of young women, but none of them pleased him. At Port Underwood he fell in love with a girl named Pokaka, but he could not persuade her to take him seriously; at the Wairau, where he was well known, all the girls asked him where his wife was; but as he proceeded down the East Coast he found that the further he went from home the more he was esteemed. At the Awatere he was somebody, at Kekerangu he was a considerable person, at Kaikoura he was a rangatira with a famous ancestry.

In a place where he found greatness thus thrust upon him he decided to stay, especially as he had caught sight of a wahine, named Inuwai—the Water Drinker—who exactly suited his fancy. She was not too old and not too young, she was of a comfortable presence without being too fat, and she was a woman of importance who had waited long for a man of statiou with whom she might suitably ally herself. Such a man she thought she had met in Matangi.

"Your tribe, you say, is a strong one?"

"Very strong," said Matangi. "I can put three hundred men in the field."

"Have you large plantations and plenty of food?"

"I expect we shall have thousands of baskets of

kumara and taro this year, besides dried shark and fish in plenty."

"But what about pigeons?—I am particularly fond of pigeons preserved in their own fat."

"Our woods are full of pigeons."

"I should like to live in your pa."

"But our women are not very skilled in potting the birds."

"Then I could let my slaves take along some of my own—I have about fifty pots put away for my own use—and I would soon teach your people how to pot pigeons."

Such was the manner of Matangi's courtship, and it was both short and successful.

Inuwai never asked any questions about her husband's domestic affairs; they did not interest her. He had volunteered the information that he had a slave-wife who was the mother of twin boys, Te Iro (The Maggot) and Te Haruru (The Evil-Smelling One), but Inuwai gave no further thought to the matter, because such a woman would merely be her servant, an additional slave, in fact.

Matangi had left his home alone, and he returned with a company. First came the bridegroom and his new wife, then his new wife's personal attendants—girls who thought it an honour to wait on the great lady—and then a long string of slaves bearing gourds as big as pumpkins, which contained the preserved pigeons so much loved by the bride.

Everybody in the kainga wondered at Matangi's suddenly-acquired greatness, but there could be no doubt of its reality, for there was the imposing retinue. The men were puzzled to know how the fellow had managed to outstrip them all, and the women marvelled at the exalted rank of his new wife, and immediately became obsequious. Hineuru watched the home-coming with a strange choking in the throat and a dimness of the eyes, but there was no bitterness in her heart towards the great woman who had superseded her. Iro and Haruru had eyes for neither their father nor his newly-acquired wife; their whole attention was riveted on the seemingly countless papahuahua which they knew to contain food, the very thought of which made their mouths water.

What his Stilton and port are to an old gentleman, such were her potted pigeons to Inuwai. Of course they were strictly tapu to herself, and so soon as the ceremony of greeting was over, they were placed in a whata, or storehouse, elevated on polished posts, inaccessible to rats—but not to little boys.

Now, the Maori small boy is grossly material. He may be made to understand that a cloak, or a mere, or a piece of land is tapu—he has no interest in such things—but it is impossible for him to appreciate the meaning of tapu in connection with potted pigeons.

Once when a papahuahua had been opened—it seemed years before—Iro and Haruru had been allowed a taste of the contents, as a great treat, and they had never forgotten it. They had often dreamed of the bellying gourd with the round hole at the top, but they had never seen another until their father had come back with this fat wife who brought a hundred papahuahua. They watched with almost painful interest the big pots as they were put one by one into the storehouse, and they went away, smacking their lips and hatching mischief in their hearts.

Behind the whare-puni they tarried to take whispered counsel.

"Papahuahua!"

"Dozens!"

"There's going to be a feast!"

The imps rubbed their little stomachs in expectation.

"When will it be?"

"To-morrow."

"That will be ka pai!"

"Ka nui te pai!"

Inuwai counted her precious pots as they were placed in the storehouse. To be exact, there were fifty-three. But next day she took out one, and ate the contents. She offered none to her co-wife, much less to the greedily expectant boys. There was no feast, not even the mention of such a thing, and Iro and Haruru were plunged into the depths of disappointment. But not for long.

Now that their father had another wife, they were turned out of the family whare, and slept in an old unused hut, which the great Inuwai said was quite good enough for boys.

"No potted pigeons for us," mourned Iro dolefully, as he lay by his brother in the dark.

"They're all for the new woman," said Haruru.

"The glutton's going to eat them all herself."

"Every one."

There was a pause, and each boy lay buried in thought.

"If we took one pot, she wouldn't miss it from among so many."

"Not if we put the empty pot back."

"That's a good idea. Let's get a pot."

"And eat it here."

"To-night?"

"Yes, to-night."

Every one in the kainga was fast asleep. The moon shone palely through the trees. Into the summer night stole two naked little boys, who approached the whata where the potted pigeons were kept. One small boy climbed on the shoulders of the other small boy; the panel was gently pushed aside, and a small figure disappeared inside the storehouse. Presently a round thing was pushed noiselessly from within, and before long the imps were carrying with their united strength a heavy pot of concentrated joy.

The hut was reached in safety.

"When we've emptied it we'll put it at the back of the other pots in the whata."

"At the very back."

"It'll be easy to carry."

There was a suppressed chuckle, followed by the sound of munching.

"How many can you eat?"

"About three. How many can you?"

"About four."

"How many are there in the pot?"

"Four in the top layer."

"How many layers?"

"Wait till I get my hand down to the bottom. Two."

"How many pigeons altogether?"

"About six."

"And the two we've taken out, eight. Ka pai!"

"Ka nui te pai."

The greedy boys' scheme worked admirably; the empty gourd was returned to the whata, where with its lid on it looked just like a full one. But it was difficult for the gorged imps to eat with their accustomed appetite at breakfast next morning, but they did manfully and deceived their fond mother, whose kind offices were on this occasion almost torture to her sons.

For three or four weeks the pilfering went on, and then Inuwai discovered the empty gourds, and the murder was out.

She went to her husband in a towering rage.

"Who's been stealing my potted pigeons? Half of the gourds are empty! It's a fine tribe you've brought me to live with—a tribe of thieves! When you married me you said you were a great man—and your people rob your wife! You said you were a tohunga—then why don't you tell me who's been stealing my pigeons? A chief of marvellous mana! A tohunga of wonderful power! It's a pretty figure you make me cut before your people!"

Matangi had enough sense to know when to hold his tongue. He walked quietly to the whata, and pulled out all the empty gourds, placed them in a row, and counted them. There were twenty-two.

He looked at the array of pots, then at the crowd which had collected, then at his angry wife, and felt that he was on his mettle. And on the skirts of the crowd dodged Iro and Haruru.

"This theft is the grossest outrage that has ever been committed," he began. "Not one or two people have done this thing; it is the work of a large company. It is disgraceful to think that the kainga contains such scoundrels. I bring from afar a wife of the highest rank and mana, and she deigns to live among my low-born people, and give their kainga an air of respectability and superiority which is the envy of Wairau and Waikawa. And my taurekareka people rob her of her kai tapu. It is abominable! low-bred! disgraceful! But there shall be retribution. I will not have thieves in my tribe. They shall be blighted! They shall vanish away! I go to repeat my incantations." And gathering his cloak about him he strode back to his whare with as much dignity as if he were a true chief and tohunga.

Full of shame the people put the empty pots back in the storehouse, and when Matangi and his indignant wife had disappeared, broke into a Babel of recrimination, invective, and vituperation. This one had done it, that one had done it, this was the guilty family, that was the guilty family, nobody had done it, everybody had done it. The true culprits stood by, and listened to the hubbub with satisfaction and glee.

Inuwai was determined to prevent further theft. One by one she took what remained of her precious pots, and hid them iu the "bush." Then when her soul yearned for potted pigeons, she would slip away from the kainga and gorge in peace.

But this scheme of things proved distressful to Iro and Haruru, whose taste for pigeons preserved in their own fat was now thoroughly established. Their nights were spent in dreams of bulging papahuahua, and their days in vain endeavours to find the coveted cache. They watched the movements of their father's chief wife with more interest than they did their mother; they often left the kainga before the people were awake, they were frequently absent at meal times, they sometimes did not return till dark. But no one paid any attention to them: they were the sons of an inferior woman whose time was fully occupied in attending on her mistress, the wahine nui, and they were lost in the host of small boys that filled the kainga.

But diligence is always rewarded. One fine day the greedy woman left the kainga in the middle of the forenoon. "I am going down to the river to drink," she said to her husband, but he knew she was only making her usual excuse.

The boys watched her enter the "bush," and followed, one on either side outflanking her, so that whether she turned to the right or to the left they were able to keep her in view. At length she halted beside a hollow rata tree, from which she pulled out a papahuahua, sat down, and began to eat. From behind thick cover the boys watched her with covetous eyes. It seemed as if she would never stop eating, as if she would leave nothing for them, so great was her gastronomical capacity; but at length she could eat no more, and returned slowly to the kainga.

Then came the boys' innings. They found there were twelve pots in the hollow tree. Fearful lest the gluttonous woman should return unexpectedly they carried a pot to a sheltered spot beside the river, and there ate in comfort and security. When they had finished their delicious meal they broke the empty pot into little pieces, which they cast into the river. Thus they hoped to destroy all traces of their crime.

But though their stomachs were full, their consciences were uncomfortable; for they could not banish thoughts of their father's imprecations, and their youthful souls were stricken with fear.

They hesitated to return home, but loitered by the water's side till they heard voices of people on the river, who might have been near or might have been far, and they scuttled away into the forest. Once more in a place of safety they sat down to rest.

"Do you think the wahine nui will count her pots?"

"I expect she will."

"Will she tell our father?"

"Yes; but she won't know it's us."

"But the karakia?"

"Aye, the karakia. But it only reaches bad people."

"We're very bad; first we break the tapu of the wahine nui, and then we eat her pigeons."

"Does the karakia hurt?"

"It turns people into dogs; it drowns people when they are in canoes, and it gives people to the taipo."

"Which will it do to us?"

"I don't know, but I think it will be the taipo?"

"Let's run to where the taipo can't find us!"

"Let's run!"

They bolted through the "bush" till they were out of breath, and when again they were forced to rest, their sportive fancy was attracted by the flutterings of what appeared to be a tame kaka. Naturally enough they tried to catch the bird. It would fly a few yards away, and then perch on a low branch, but though a dozen times it seemed to be within their grasp, it always managed to elude the naughty little boys. On and on they were led, deeper and deeper into the forest, till at last, even if they had thought of doing so, it was impossible for them to have returned home. The parrot did not move faster than they could conveniently travel, and with a halt every few yards it kept the little thieves at the height of expectation. But though they thought a hundred times that they had caught it, they always found that it had escaped. At length they reached a place where beneath some tall totara trees there was no underscrub. The bird whirled round and round at no great distance from the ground.

"Iro, stand over there. Wait till it comes round. I'll stop here. As it passes we'll grab it."

The kaka set up the wildest screeching, but continued to circle, and the boys tried vainly again and again to catch it as it passed. The circles of the bird's flight grew narrower, and the boys closed in.

"He's porangi! He's gone mad!"

"We shall catch him in a minute."

The circles were growing smaller and smaller; it seemed that soon the bird would fall to the ground; indeed, Iro had actually got it by the wing, when there was a loud crashing of branches, and into the clearing rushed a terrific monster with arms, outstretched quite twelve feet, and claws six feet long.

With shrieks of "The taipo! the taipo! the maero! the maero!" the boys turned to run. But the parrot had decoyed them so close together that with one clutch the avenging monster had caught Iro and Haruru in his awful claws.

After that nobody stole Inuwai's tapu pigeons, and that great personage was left to empty her precious pots in peace.

THE BLIND FISHERMAN.

STOREHOUSES was sitting in the sun, and performing his toilet. With the aid of a couple of cockle-shells, which he used as tweezers, he was pulling out the scanty hairs of his grizzled beard.

"Well, how does that look?" he asked of his wife, who stood by, watching.

"You're getting on," said she, "but there are still some on the left side."

"I can't manage," said Storehouses. "You try, Rua."

His wife took the cockle-shells, and pulled out half-a-dozen hairs at once.

"Ho!" cried Storehouses. "I say, that was awful. That was too much. Come, come, I can't stand that sort of thing, though I wish to appear at my best. Take care. And, Rua, mind what you do with the hairs. Do not drop them. It would never do for my hairs to be left lying about—they are so sacred that any one, excepting yourself of course, who handles them dies at once."

When the plucking process was finished he said, "Now for the head:"—he ran his fingers through his hair—"it's too long; it needs cutting." So Rua took a sharp piece of volcanic glass, and commenced to saw at her husband's locks—a painful process, which brought the tears to the old man's eyes and caused him to cry, "Oh! ah! be careful."

"I'm getting on beautifully," said his wife.

"Oh! But that was a good bit. Take care of it, Rua. Take care of every sacred hair; don't leave one on the ground, lest it should bewitch the whole village, and people should die. All you cut off must be taken to the sacred place where I repeat my incantations."

"I've not lost a hair. I have them all in a little box. Never fear; they shall be taken to your tuaahu as soon as I have finished."

"I'll look well. I shall be quite a catch for the young girls. Have you done, Rua?"

"Almost. There is but one more lock. There, I have finished."

All of which was a piece of comedy, acted for pure love of the thing and the delectation of a group of people who had gathered about the door of the hut. For old Storehouses was the wit of the village. When a man came to him and said, "I've caught a fine big fish," Storehouses would ask, "How big?" "Oh, as long as my arm." "That's nothing. I caught one this morning as long as my body." If a man came in from the plantations and said, "Storehouses, I've got an enormous sweet potato," the old man would take the tuber in his hand, feel it all over, and then he would say, "I don't call that big. I call it small. Why, in my plantation I have got sweet potatoes as big as your head." The humour of the thing lay in the fact that Storehouses was quite blind, and could not see whether one fish was larger than another, or one potato more to be desired than another. But the result of his good-humoured way of taking his affliction was that his friends invariably brought him the pick of their catch and the choicest samples of their crops.

One day when the time for planting had come, his old wife said to him, "What are we going to do about putting in the seed?"

"You plant it," said Storehouses.

"I'm too old," said his wife. "Plant it yourself."

"I'm too blind."

There was a pause in the conversation, during which husband and wife were buried deep in thought. At length the blind man said, "I know how I can get over the difficulty. I will dig the ground—that is easy—then I will put in the seed, and beside each sweet potato I will put in a stick. By and by, when the plants must be separated and transplanted, I shall easily find them because of the sticks. Wait and see—we shall have a fine crop. Every one will come to see it."

So the blind man dug his ground and carried out the planting according to his plan, but when the young plants should have sprouted Rua said she could not see a single leaf. The sticks were there, but there was nothing in the earth beside them. The rats had eaten the seed.

"Never mind," said Storehouses. "I will catch the rats."

Approaching his friend Piki, he said, "I want you to lend me your dog to kill the rats that eat my potato seed."

Anxious to help the blind man Piki lent the dog.

"Will he catch them quickly?" asked Storehouses.

"Oh yes, he'll catch all of them in one night. He's a good dog."

"Very good then; as soon as the rats are dead I will plant some more seed."

So in triumph Storehouses took home the dog, which proved to be all that its master had said. During the first night he caught eight rats, and the next ten, and the next four, including a big buck rat, the chief of all the others.

"That's very good," said the blind man. "We'll eat that big fellow, and the dog shall have the rest."

But the dog's appetite could not keep pace with the liberal supply of rats, and as Storehouses was digging a hole in which to bury the rodents that were over, Rua said, "Why not use them for bait? The rats ate our seed: at least make them catch fish."

"Certainly," said her husband. "It's a capital idea, and I will carry it out."

So he got out his fishing-line, cut up the dead rats, and went off to the beach.

Now the dog, seeing the last of the rats being carried away, followed the old man, and Storehouses soon heard the dog panting behind him.

"Hullo! What are you doing here?" cried he. "You are a good dog for catching rats, but no good for catching fish. Go back, do you hear? Go home."

The dog paused, cocked up its ears, put its head on one side, watched the old man walking away, and then ran after him.

Soon Storehouses again heard the dog panting.

"Now what did I tell you? Go home! Quick!" and raising his stick the blind man made mighty and ineffectual blows at the dog, which ran back as fast as its four legs would carry it.

"That's all right," said Storehouses. "He's gone. Now I shall catch fish." But above the tussock grass which fringed the dry white sand appeared a head with two prick cars, inquisitively turned on one side.

The blind man carefully baited his hook, and rose to make a cast. Thrice he swung the heavy sinker round his head, but just as he threw the line his foot caught on a stone, and he fell sprawling on the sand. Picking himself up, he drew in the line carefully and prepared to make another cast. This time his foot caught against a piece of drift-wood, and again he fell. By now, what with tumbling about and excitement, he had lost his bearings, and when he made the third cast he was facing the land instead of the sea.

But it was a famous cast: the line fell far beyond the edge of the sand, amid the tussock grass. And the dog no sooner saw the sinker fall to earth than, with loud barks, he ran towards the bait.

"Ha! there's that dog again," cried old Storehouses, and picking up a stone he threw it into the sea. "I'll teach him to go home when he is told." He had flung the stone with his full force, and immediately there was a howling such as only a stricken dog can make.

"Ah!" said the blind man. "I hit him that time. Listen to his howls. I'll teach him to follow me when I go fishing. Why, he might get caught by my hook as I cast the line, and he's a good dog . . . . Catches rats well."

The dog's howling continued, but grew fainter and fainter, and the line ran through the blind fisher's hands.

"Hullo!" he cried, "I've got a bite. Now then, steady, steady," and he paid out the line. "I think I've hooked a big hapuku, by the feel of him. Hullo! the line's run out," and he held the piece of wood to which the line was attached.

The dog's howling now sounded far away, and the fish dragged the blind man about the sand. "Ha!" he cried, as he panted with his exertions, "listen to that dog. He's going home as quickly as he can." But after the fisher had played his catch skilfully for quarter of an hour, the line became still, and Storehouses began to haul in his fish.

"My word! he's a big fellow. He's hard to pull in. He must be enormous. Perhaps he's a young shark."

The dog's howling had ceased, and as Storehouses drew his catch to him he broke its head with a heavy stone.

"There, he's dead," and the blind fisherman grunted with satisfaction. "My word! he's fine. He's not a shark, or hapuku, or a kahawai. Ha! what a fish to catch."

He wound up his line, placed his catch in his basket, felt on the ground for his stick, which he could not find, swung his burden upon his back—and walked into the sea.

"Hullo! I'm going the wrong way. That's a very foolish thing to do—to forget the way home." But as his feet were bare, of course the mistake was of no consequence.

When he reached home he found Piki waiting for him.

"Tena koe," said Piki.

"Tena koe," said Storehouses.

"I have come for my dog. There are numbers of rats at my place now. I want the dog to catch them."

"The dog's about here somewhere. He followed

me to the beach, but I sent him back. I've been fishing."

"Did you catch anything?"

"Did I catch anything! When ever did I go fishing and catch nothing? But this time I caught a bigger fish than ever."

Piki smiled. He knew the story that was coming.

"Now what do you think I caught?" asked the blind fisherman.

"Oh, a few rock-cod."

"Better than that. Feel the weight of my basket."

"A stingaree."

"What should I bring home a stingaree for?"

"The oil. They're good to eat, too."

"No, no. Guess again—I don't like stingaree."

"A young ground-shark."

"That's better. That's nearer. But that's not it."

"Well, what is it?"

"Am I the most skilful fisherman of this tribe?"

"Yes, you're a good fisherman."

"Am I the best of all?"

"Yes, the best of all."

"You know that?"

"I know it."

"All right. This will prove it. Look at that!" and he turned the contents of his basket out upon the ground.

Piki laughed. "Come here everybody, and see this fish!"

The people came crowding round, and Piki continued, "Storehouses went out to fish, this morning, and this is what he caught. Isn't it fine?"

The people roared with laughter, so that they drowned the blind man's expostulations.

At last, when they perceived he was trying to speak, they restrained their merriment, and the old man said, "You well may laugh. He's a fine fellow." Upon which the laughter redoubled.

"Now be quiet, all of you," said Storehouses—"he will be enough food for half the village."

Some of the people were now laughing so much that they could hardly stand.

"What are you all laughing at?" asked the blind man. "I see nothing to laugh at. Piki, look again closely. What do you say I have caught?"

"Storehouses, you always were comic!" exclaimed Piki, who could hardly get the words out, he was so filled with laughter. "But this beats all. It's a dog!"

"A dog!" cried the blind fisherman. "Pooh! Your're blinder than I am. Take another look at him. That's not a dog."

"Oh dear, he says it's not a dog!" exclaimed Piki, appealing to the crowd. "I shall be ill with laughing. Here, Storehouses, feel his fur." Taking hold of the blind man's hand he placed it upon the catch.

"That's not a dog!" cried Storehouses. "That's a seal!"

At this the shout of laughter was so loud that people came running from the furthest end of the village.

"Did you ever know anything like it?" Piki appealed to his growing audience. "It's too funny! You're the man to make us laugh," he said, slapping Storehouses on the back. "You're the man for a joke. A seal! The story will be told in every village. Oh dear, I must go and lie down, or I shall die with laughing."

"Wait a minute," said the blind man. "Don't be in such a hurry. If it's a dog, Piki, tell me whose dog it is."

Piki took up the dead creature by the tail. "This is Storehouse's seal," he said; "observe its black-and-white markings." But suddenly his features grew long, and a serious expression came over his face.

"Continue," said the blind man. "Tell me whose dog it is."

Piki turned the animal over, and examined first one side of it and then the other. "Why it looks like . . . ." He looked at its head and at its tail. "I believe, really, it is . . . ."

"Well, tell me," said Storehouses. "I'm waiting."

"You rascal, I'll teach you to joke!" suddenly cried Piki, raising his hand to strike the fisherman. "It's my dog!"

The laughter which greeted this confession was such that it could have been heard at the edge of the forest. The enraged Piki was held back by a dozen hands, and the blind man said,

"Don't get angry. If it's your dog it's not mine—though I caught it. I don't want it: you can have it. I don't eat dogs. Take your dog." And amid renewed shouts of laughter, Storehouses shuffled towards his hut.

THE STRANGE ELOPEMENT OF TINIRAU.

TINIRAU* was a maiden whom all the pa loved. Her beauty, good humour, and laughter made her the life of the tribe. But Manoa, her father, was an austere man who greatly loved decorum, valued dignity highly, and thoroughly disapproved of his daughter's levity. He said it was time she was married and settled in life. But her mother, Te Ira, had something to say on that subject.

"If you are in too great a hurry to get the girl married," said she to her husband, "you will make a very great mistake. Let her choose a husband for herself when she is a little older."

"But I have him ready at hand," replied Manoa. "A very good man he is too, a chief of much reputation and authority."

"Indeed. Who is he, pray? I should like to see him."

"The chief of the neighbouring pa. Kapu—that is the man."

"Kapu!" exclaimed the mother. "He has a broken nose; he is as ugly as the figure-head of a canoe. I am surprised."

"He is a man whose fame reaches far and near, and his tribe is most powerful. He will make a good son-in-law."

"I don't think so—Tinirau hates him."

"Allow me to know," said Manoa, conclusively. "I am the best judge of such matters. The girl shall marry Kapu."

So Tinirau was informed that the time had come when she must give up her liberty—it is the Maori

*Pronounced Tin-ee-rou, and meaning "a hundred hosts," or "a hundred myriads."

spinster, not the matron, who can do as she likes—and she was told that her husband would shortly appear.

Now Kapu had found it hard to get a wife, that is to say a wife who was anybody to speak about, for all the girls laughed at his broken nose, and yet not so much at it as at its history. Formerly he had been married, but he had quarrelled with his wife and thought to tutor her with blows; however, her prowess had proved the greater, for she retaliated with a tomahawk and spoilt Kapu's beauty for life. Then, adding defiance to injury, she had run away to her own tribe, whose members sympathised with her warmly and awarded her a more amiable husband.

So when her friends heard it was intended that Tinirau should be given to the broken-nosed wife-beater, they advised her to go delicately and to carry a full-sized stone axe under her cloak.

But the paths of match-makers are not always smooth. Though Kapu was altogether transported with joy when he was informed that Manoa considered him a most eligible son-in-law, there was a snake in the grass whose name was Tawhiri. He was a young brave who lived not very far from Tinirau, and who for many months had marked her budding beauty.

Better is a young warrior of the handsome sort than a blue-blooded chief with a broken nose. So at least thought Tinirau. And therefore it happened that when Kapu arrived on a visit of state as the guest of Manoa, Tawhiri arrived as the guest of his equals, the fighting-men of the tribe. Both visitors promptly became suitors for the hand of Tinirau, the one being supported by his prospective father-in-law, and the other by nothing but his good looks.

Now Kapu was a great fisherman and, as there was a magnificent river near the pa, he determined to combine love-making with sport. With a line and a basket of bait carried by Tinirau, who had been detailed by her relentless parent for the duty, he set out for the river.

When he had selected a spot which seemed favourable to his pleasant sport, Kapu halted.

"Here I will fish," he said. "You, Tinirau, shall stand-by, and watch while I display my skill."

He baited his hook carefully and made a cast.

The baited hook disappeared beneath the surface of the water, and Kapu waited for a bite.

Fishing is a contemplative occupation and does not tend much to conversation—anglers do not talk till after the event, when, as is well known, their display of words and imagination is marvellous. Therefore it is not surprising that Kapu had but little to say, and the girl quickly became bored.

From the fisherman her attention wandered to the further bank, where presently there appeared a figure which quickly absorbed all her interest. It was that of a young man whom she knew well, and whose personal attractions she fully appreciated. His conduct, however, was as strange as it was laughable.

Whenever Kapu's attention was fixed on his line, the man half-hidden behind a flax-bush on the further bank seized the opportunity to signal wildly to Tinirau. At first she was at a loss to know what he meant, but subsequently she perceived that she was directed to go down stream to a point where the river turned suddenly above a shallow ford.

"You have a bite, you have a bite!" exclaimed the girl.

"Hush," said Kapu. "You will frighten the fish."

But she did not, for presently he pulled up a big eel.

Quickly he unhooked it, and placed it in a shady spot behind a flax-bush; and as he was stooping, forgetful of all else but his catch, the waving on the opposite bank became frantic.

Tinirau responded surreptitiously, and Kapu continued fishing.

When the number of the eels behind the flax-bush had increased, Tinirau remarked that she would take a turn along the river-bank, to see if she could find some water-cress below the ford.

Kapu, intent upon his sport, in which he was favoured with excellent luck, never noticed the prolonged absence of his fiancee. She, journeying to the ford, was followed along the further bank by the man who had been beckoning to her, but before she went she was careful to take with her all Kapu's fish from behind the flax-bush.

Without fear of detection she crossed the river at the ford, and quickly joined Tawhiri on the further bank.

Taking her burden of fish he led her through the thick forest which grew down to the water's edge, and soon the two lovers were lost in the mazes of the leafy wilderness which covered the country for miles.

When Kapu had caught another eel, he arose to place it in the shade of the flax-bush with the rest of his fish. For a while he stood looking in stupid astonishment at the place where they had been; then he glanced up and down the river, and called, "Tinirau! Tinirau! what have you done with my eels?" But answer there was none.

* * * *

The totara tree is tall and straight, with bushy branches high up the bole, and above that, sometimes, dead wood. Indeed, you may know an ancient totara by the fact that its top is dead and grey.

The great forest which spread round the pa where Tinirau lived was noted for the immense size of its totara trees. Far in the depth of the matted jungle, it was at the foot of one of these giants that Tawhiri stopped. Glancing up, Tinirau could see that the tree was broken off just above a thick, bushy clump of branches, which threw out their leaves some forty feet above the ground. Against the top of the trunk a neighbouring tree, dead and barkless, was resting, and thus formed an easy means of communication between the ground and the top of the totara.

Shaking loose a long creeper which was attached to the summit of the stricken giant, Tawhiri walked nimbly up the slanting tree, and soon Tinirau followed.

Upon reaching the top she found a safe retreat provided for her. The tree-trunk was hollow to a depth of some five feet, and over this Tawhiri had built a roof of bark, while the inside of the nest was lined with dry leaves covered over with flax mats, and in one corner were quantities of dried eels, sweet potatoes and Maori yams. By standing up and looking over the edge of her strange abode Tinirau could plainly see the ground through the bushy branches which grew about her, though from below she had been unable to distinguish anything unusual at the top of the tree.

"Here," said Tawhiri, "is the house I have made for you. Here we are safe from the broken-nosed Te Kapu and all his tribe."

Drawing up the trailing creeper by which he and his bride had pulled themselves up to their peculiar house he coiled it loosely on a bough; then with difficulty he levered the dead tree from the bole of the totara, and it fell to the earth with a resounding crash. The lovers were safe from pursuit.

Such was the wedding of Tinirau, romantic, novel, and containing that element of adventure which rendered it doubly sweet to the bold young warrior and his pretty bride.

* * * *

When Kapu found his fish stolen and his kotiro gone he wound up his line and went to speak to Tinirau's papa. That old man was seized with such a paroxysm of rage that the whole pa trembled, but when the cataclysm of wrath was past the people commenced to search diligently for the erring girl.

First they examined the river, up and down; then they scoured the forest—an endless business—for some trace of the lovers. The people hunted in couples, and old Manoa and the broken-nosed suitor always kept together. They searched the beds of dry water-courses, bowers of tree-ferns, hollow rata trees, caves in the limestone cliffs, but they found nothing to show them where Tinirau and her lover lay hid. However, after many days' search, an old, grey-haired man brought home a brace of pigeons which he had found dead at the foot of a tall totara tree, where there were footmarks and other signs of human beings.

* * * *

"How cleverly you have made the roof," said Tinirau. "Not a drop of water came through in the night, though it rained in torrents. But I should very much like to stretch my limbs."

Tawhiri looked over the edge of the nest, and touched the coiled-up creeper. Then he turned to his bride, and asked, "If I were to let you down, do you think you could climb up again?"

Tinirau placed her head beside his and peeped through the screening boughs. It seemed a great distance to the ground.

"I could get down," she said, "but it would be difficult to climb back again. Shall we have to stay here all our life?"

"When the cold weather comes we will go to my kainga—your father's anger will have died out then."

"I don't think so," said Tinirau. "I'm afraid you don't know my father. If he could catch us he would certainly marry me to the broken-nosed man, and most likely he would kill you."

"You can hardly tell," remarked Tawhiri. "Perhaps I might kill him.

"Hush! Listen! Did you hear voices?"

"No. It must have been a parrot screaming."

"Hsssh! There! Did you hear?"

It was as the girl said: the sound of voices drew nearer and nearer. Underneath the tree appeared a party of five or six men, among whom Tinirau quickly recognised her father and the man he had intended should be her husband.

"Look! The earth is trampled," said Manoa. "There have been people here."

"The pigeons lay under this tree," said the old man who had guided the party to the spot.

They looked down; they looked up.

"What is that aka doing up there in a coil?" asked Kapu. "I never saw a creeper coil itself up like that before."

A young chief, filled perhaps with sympathy for the runaway girl, pointed to the dead tree which had fallen against the totara.

"You see that?"

"Yes. What of it?" replied Manoa.

"As it fell, the dead tree broke the aka which the wind has tangled on the boughs up there."

The lovers, who had heard every word that was said, crouched inside their bark house and clasped each other with trembling arms.

His disappointed love filled Kapu with energy. He ran here, he ran there. At last he fastened on a neighbouring tree, tall, straight, and overtopping the hollow totara. With the help of his friends he clambered to the lowest bough, whence his ascent was quick and easy, and before long he had reached a height from which he overlooked the lovers' nest.

"They are there!" he cried. "There is a hut built on the top!"

"It did not take him long to climb down from his perch, and soon the base of the totara was attacked with fire and stone axes.

The fate of the lovers looked very black; but though they heard the sound of the chopping and the crackling of the flames Tinirau and Tawhiri showed not the slightest sign of their presence, but clung the closer to each other, ready to die together. Their agony was the greater in that the process of felling was so slow, but at last the tree began to rock ominously, and then with a crash it fell. Fortunately for Tawhiri and Tinirau their tree lodged in the fork of a huge black birch, and there stuck; thus their fall was broken, though they were thrown with considerable force to the soft and spongy earth.

Gathering themselves up they ran, expecting every moment to be overtaken. But the attention of their pursuers was for the moment drawn to the old man who had been their guide. In his enthusiasm to fell the tree he had tarried over long beside the tottering trunk, and the butt, in slipping off its severed base, had crushed him like an egg-shell. By the time his lifeless body was extricated the lovers were a mile or more away.

* * * *

"Do you think, beloved one, that they will find us? Do you think, heart of my heart,* that we shall be left to love in peace?"

"Quiet, little frightened pigeon. We have escaped so far. Let us forget our troubles till to-morrow."

Such is the infatuation of love.

Tinirau and Tawhiri had taken refuge in a piece of rocky country beside the river, upon which they gazed from a high limestone cliff. Their eyrie was inaccessible save by a single path, which Tawhiri had rendered as difficult as possible by such poor means as were in his power. But all Manoa's tribe was on their track, and it was evident to all but their love-deluded minds that sooner or later the lovers must be discovered.

That day was nearer than they thought.

"Let us flee to your pa, beloved one, and there stand and fight my cruel father."

"If I were a great chief that plan might prove successful, but as I am nothing more than a common warrior I fear my people would deliver you up rather than incur a war with your father."

"Then what will become of us? Are we to wander in the forest all our days?"

"For the present I'm afraid we must; but by and by we will go to some distant pa where none know us, and where Manoa will never think of looking for us."

And just then the sound of voices reached their ears, and crowding the overhanging cliffs above them they saw a number of fierce fighting-men.

* * * *

* This may seem to some a strangely un-Maori expression, but it is a free rendering of "Te tau o taku ate," which was the phrase used by Te Whetu.

A.A.G.

"Mataki, I am full of grief. My life is one long rainy day. My lover is dead and my future is with the man I hate."

"He isn't so bad," said the girl who had been told off to watch Tinirau and keep her company. "True, he is disfigured by a broken nose, but then he is very fond of you. You'll be happy enough after a while. Forget the mad toa who asked you to live like an owl in a tree."

"Tell me, Mataki: When is Kapu coming?"

"To-morrow. You will be given to him before the tribe, and after a few days he will take you to his pa, where he is a man of much authority. You will be a great lady."

"To-morrow? Then we have time. I want you to take me to the place in the rocks where I last saw Tawhiri, and then they can give me to Kapu as soon as they like."

The day was young when the two girls started, and before mid-day they had climbed the intricate path which led to the place where the lovers had been captured.

The view from the cliff recalled to Tinirau all her former joy, with which she contrasted mentally the doleful future which lay before her.

But Mataki had no such memories. She was a happy low-born girl, whom no one sought to restrain in matters of love. To herself she sang:—

"The white cloud rises up like a bird,
Like a bird,
From the leaves of the forest-trees,
In the breeze,
And with its snow-white wings outspread,
Overhead,
Flies over the cliff to the valley below,
Where the fern-trees grow,
To the tribe of the holy dead."

Tinirau listened to the song, and when Mataki had finished it, said, "Sing it again: I like that song—it seems to suit my frame of mind. Let me learn it."

Mataki sang it again.

"No," said Tinirau, "I have not yet got it off by heart." So her companion repeated it, till Tinirau said, "I know it now. I will sing it."

Seemingly regarding the landscape below, she walked up and down. Then she sang:—

"The white cloud rises up like a bird,
Like a bird,
From the leaves of the forest-trees,
In the breeze"—

Her voice sounded like the sobbing of a child, and then with a wail which carried with it signs of a fierce impulse, she continued,

"And with its snow-white wings outspread,
Overhead,
Flies over the cliff to the valley below,
Whither I go, whither I go,
To the tribe of the happy dead!"

Her voice rose in a shrill crescendo, till with the last word it terminated in a shriek. Then with a desperate leap she sprang over the precipice, and vanished from the sight of her horror-stricken companion.

THE MOON GIRL.

THEY were mere lads, and had been left orphans by the death of both their parents in one day. The elder was named Two Heavens, and the younger The Shell-fish; and beside them there was no one living in the "clearing," deep in the forest.

"Now, look here," said The Shell-fish to his brother, "we have been lonely in this hut since our father and mother died. You, who are the elder and a good-looking fellow as well, must get a wife who can cook for us and make us comfortable."

So Two Heavens, quite agreeable, went into the nearest village, and brought back a wife, who was named The Moon Girl.

Everything went well till The Moon Girl fell ill.

"You must take me back to my father and mother," said she to her husband, "in order that they may give me their medicine,"—by which she meant, of course, spells and incantations.

"Of what use would that be?" said Two Heavens. "You would die on the road, and what good would the medicine be then? No, we have medicine here, given us by our father, Pakira, which is just as good."

But, nevertheless, The Moon Girl died, in spite of all the mystic rites which the brothers performed. Therefore you would imagine that the story of Two Heavens and The Moon Girl ends here, but in reality it has only just begun.

The brothers were now as lonely as ever, and after the tangi, when all the girl's relatives came to weep with them, Two Heavens was like a man who had lost all interest in life.

"Now, this won't do," said The Shell-fish. "You must cheer up. You are still a good-looking fellow: take another wife, stronger than the last and needing no medicine."

But Two Heavens said that he had married The Moon Girl, and he would marry no other.

"Well," remarked his brother, "if you want The Moon Girl still, you must go down into Hell to fetch her."

"And down into Hell I will go," said Two Heavens.

"If you go, I will go too," said The Shell-fish.

So the brothers set out, each bearing three baskets of sweet potatoes, and journeyed along the sea-shore. By the time that they had emptied two of the baskets, they had reached the hau mapu, where the spirits of the departed descend to the nether regions. The opening, which was at the foot of a tall cliff, was covered with drift-wood which the receding tide had left high and dry. This debris the brothers pulled aside, and there was the mouth of Hell before them.

"I am frightened," said The Shell-fish. "I cannot go down."

"Then you don't wish to see your father and mother again," said Two Heavens.

"Oh, but I do."

"And I want to see The Moon Girl. Now, I will go down first; I will call when I reach the bottom, and you can follow me."

So Two Heavens scrambled down the hau mapu; sometimes he slid, carrying rocks and earth with him; sometimes he jumped from crag to crag, till at last he stood on flat ground at the bottom. Then he called.

Soon his brother came scrambling after him, and reached the bottom safely.

"What sort of a place is it?" asked the Shell-fish.

"I don't know," replied his brother, "but I think it looks very much like the country we have left behind. Come on; let us see."

So they took up their baskets of food and went on.

Soon the prospect broadened, and they found themselves in the underworld, full of trees and grass and fern, just like Maoriland itself.

"Why, this is as good a place as that we have left behind," said The Shell-fish.

"It is better," said Two Heavens, "for here we shall find The Moon Girl and our father and mother."

They went on slowly, peering about them, scanning everything they saw, till at length there appeared in view an old woman, who was bent and walked feebly.

"I'm not afraid of an old woman," said The Shell-fish.

"Certainly not," said his brother. "We will ask her the way."

When the old woman caught sight of them, she shaded her eyes with her hand, and called out, "Haere mai! haere mai te manuhiri!" thinking they were spirits bound for the underworld.

"Well, who are you?" asked Two Heavens.

"I am here to show new-comers the way. What tribe did you belong to?"

"Ngapuhi."

"Ngapuhi?" said the old woman. "Why, only a few days ago a girl belonging to that tribe arrived here. Her name was The Moon Girl."

"She was my wife," said Two Heavens.

"Then you will be glad to join her," said the old woman—"Your pa will be the second one on the other side of the river—the first belongs to Te Arawa."

"Very good," said Two Heavens, "but how are we to cross the river?"

"Oh, that will be easy enough," replied the old woman. "The Nettle is there. He is the ferryman, and will take you across in his canoe."

"Well, good-bye, we must be getting along."

"Good-bye," said the old woman, "but I shall see you again. If any of your relatives arrive, I will tell them that you have gone on. Plenty of people come this way every day, plenty of people, plenty of people."

So the two brothers continued on their way. The

old woman was so blind that she had not perceived that they were not spirits, but material flesh and blood.

When they reached the river, which was broad and deep, they saw a pa on the other side, just as the old woman had said.

"That must be the Arawa pa," said The Shell-fish, pointing to a large collection of huts on the opposite bank.

"We will go further down, till we see another," said Two Heavens, "and then we will call for The Nettle, this man who ferries us across."

So they journeyed on till another pa appeared in sight.

"That belongs to Ngapuhi," said Two Heavens. "We shall quickly be with our relations now."

The brothers stood on the edge of the river-bank and called together with all their might.

Soon a canoe shot out from the opposite bank, and swiftly made its way towards them. It was propelled by a most forbidding-looking man, who drew his little craft to the bank without a word of greeting.

"Get in," he said roughly. "Be quick. I have plenty besides you to ferry across."

"No, no," said The Shell-fish, "your canoe is too small to hold us both."

"It will hold you easily: it has carried over twenty people at a time," said the ferryman.

"Yes," said The Shell-fish, "but spirits are light. Hasn't your river any fords?"

"There is a ford lower down," said the ferryman. "I am The Nettle. I carry every one across. Why should the spirits wet their feet?"

"Two Heavens," said his brother, "I will go with this fellow. Do you go lower down the river till you come to the ford, and cross over there."

Two Heavens understood: The Nettle was a malignant person, and might discover that they were human; therefore, while The Shell-fish kept him engaged, he, Two Heavens, could slip into the pa, and if the worst came to the worst the ferryman would get but one of them, and that the unmarried one. He thought the better of his brother for suggesting this plan.

But The Nettle gave no thought to the matter; his object was to get The Shell-fish over the river as quickly as possible, and before long the two brothers were standing outside the pa.

As soon as the people caught sight of the strangers, they cried out, "Haere mai! haere mai! haere mai te manuhiri!" thinking that two lost souls had come over the river. But there the brothers saw, standing, Pakira, their father, and Toretu, their mother, and with them The Moon Girl, as beautiful as she was before she died.

They ran forward, and soon were rubbing noses with their relatives, just as they used to do on earth.

When the greeting was over and The Moon Girl could speak, she said to her husband, "Oh! I am so glad you have come. I was afraid I should have to wait years and years for you, and lo! in a few days you are here. But tell me, how did you die? Did you suffer as I did, or did you die quickly?"

"I am not dead," replied Two Heavens, "neither is my brother."

"Not dead!" exclaimed The Moon Girl.

"No. We came of our own accord, to fetch you back."

"To fetch me back! How did you get here?"

"We came the same way as you did—the hau mapu is always open; any one can come who likes."

"But no one can go away," said his father.

"We shall see about that," said Two Heavens. "At present, we are very hungry. What have you got to eat?"

They took the two brothers into a hut, and their mother said, "We don't want very much to eat down here—spirits do not have great appetites. That is the only food they give us," and she placed before them something which looked for all the underworld like a piece of fossilized wood.

"It's very hard," said The Shell-fish.

"Wouldn't it be very indigestible for a real live Maori?" asked Two Heavens.

"It's all we eat," said their mother, "and we seem to get along all right."

"I have had no appetite since I came here," said The Moon Girl, "but now that you are come, if you eat I will eat.

"Stop!" cried Pakira. "If you eat that food, my sons, you will certainly die. This is the spirits' food, and you are mortals. If you eat this food you will never return to earth."

"Very good," said Two Heavens, "we have some food of our own. These four baskets are full of sweet potatoes."

"That is very good indeed!" said his father. "You and your brother can eat that food, and it will be well for The Moon Girl to eat it also. She is but half a spirit—she has not eaten the food of the underworld—she is half human, half spirit."

So The Moon Girl cooked some of the sweet potatoes, and the brothers and she had a meal.

When it was finished they went out to see all their friends who had died, and there was the happiest reunion.

However, so many were the friends and relations they wished to see, and so much was there to be told of what was going on in the world above, and so interesting were the experiences of those who had come below, that before the brothers were aware of the fact their stock of human food was nearly exhausted.

"We must be going back soon," said Two Heavens.

"We must start in the morning," said his brother.

"I have not noticed that there is any morning here," said The Moon Girl.

"Then we must have one more meal, and then go," said The Shell-fish.

So they collected all their friends and relations, and amid much weeping bade them good-bye.

"Farewell. It has been pleasant to see you," said The Moon Girl to the spirit-people.

"We shall be sure to tell the tribes on earth that you all are well," said The Shell-fish.

"Be comforted by one thing," said Two Heavens: "we are bound to return."

"It is well, my children," said the father, "but you should be going."

So they went towards the river.

The Shell-fish crossed by way of the ford, and his brother and The Moon Girl got into the ferryman's canoe.

"Where do you want to go to?" asked The Nettle.

"To the other side," replied Two Heavens.

"What for?" asked The Nettle. "Why don't you stay with the rest of your tribe?"

"We wish to pay a visit to another pa."

"There are no spirits living on the other side, you will find no one there. I am the man who ferries people across. I bring people to this side, by the hundred every week; but I have never taken any one back."

"Then this will be the first time you will do it," said Two Heavens.

"This is the side for the spirits of men," said the ferryman. "I take no spirits to the other bank."

"Spirits!" exclaimed Two Heavens. "You are quite right, we are Maoris. We are not dead men."

The ferryman approached him, felt him all over, and said, "No, you are not a spirit. You must be a man. Why didn't you say so at first? You have no business here at all."

"Very good, then take us over to the other side. We will go away as quickly as possible."

When they reached the further bank the ferryman said, "Get out."

Two Heavens rose to go, and was helping The Moon Girl out of the canoe, when the ferryman said, "No, no, I intend to take the girl back. She is a spirit."

"Oh no," said her husband, "she is the same as I. We are both human."

"You may not have died, but your wife did."

"My wife has not eaten of your kai o te Reinga;* she has eaten only the food of mortals. She must come with me."

"I will take her back," said the ferryman.

"She shall go with me," said her husband.

The Nettle seized The Moon Girl by the ankle, and Two Heavens took hold of her by the arms. The ferryman pulled, the husband pulled, and the girl cried out. Just then The Shell-fish, who had crossed the river, ran to assist his brother. They two were on the bank, the ferryman was in the canoe, and the girl was half on land and half on the water, when Two Heavens gave the canoe a mighty kick which sent it and the ferryman out into the stream; and the brothers and The Moon Girl stood upon the land.

They wasted no more words upon the ferryman, but hastened towards the hau mapu.

When they got there they again saw the old woman, who greeted them, and said, "That's all right: going for some more. Bring them down; there's plenty of room." So they passed by, as if they were malignant spirits of the underworld bent on capturing the souls of men.

When they reached the exit of the hau mapu, everything was as they had left it: the world was the same good world that they had loved so well, and before long they were in the hut where formerly they had lived happily together.

"You must heat some water," said The Moon Girl.

So Two Heavens lighted a fire, and heated water by placing hot stones in a big calabash which he had previously filled at a spring.

"Now," said The Moon Girl, "you must go to the place where I was buried, and dig up my body."

In obedience to her wish, Two Heavens went to the burial-place, and dug up the body of his wife.

---

* Food of Hell.

When he returned, The Moon Girl said, "Did you dig it up?"

"Yes," replied her husband.

"Then, get the hot water, and let me wash," said The Moon Girl.

When she had washed herself from head to foot, she said, "Now, let us go to the place where I was buried."

But when they got there, the grave was empty and every sign of death had vanished away.

"Feel me," said The Moon Girl, turning to her husband joyfully, "embrace me, love me, for I am your own Moon Girl, come back in the flesh."

THE END.